To my Mom and Dad who are no longer with me; but are forever present in my soul; I am eternally grateful for your foundational love, caring, kindness, and truth. You will never be forgotten and as time goes on, my appreciation deepens for your sacrifice, selflessness, and never-ending support.

Acknowledgements

So many people have helped me in my life and specifically on this book. The process of writing it has been the realization of a dream; your assistance has truly made me aware of how much I need others. I am eternally grateful to everyone!

A special thank you to my primary editor, Sarah G. Schwartz, whose talent, attention to detail, and support were beyond compare.

Thank you also to Paul Pond, Michael Bradford, and Susan Grace who helped me with the editing of the book and, in particular, the material related to Gopi Krishna and the evolutionary energy of Kundalini.

I want to thank the following "Angels", whose consistent help, offered without question, went so beyond the call and moved me deeply:

Jerry and Dorothy Hiegel, Lezlee Westine, Lynn Westine, Marc and Astrid Vaccaro, Laszlo Kaveggia, Teresa Croxton, and Mark Gullickson.

I also want to thank these special people who assisted me at critical times and in critical ways. I was touched by each one of you:

Nancy Aldrich, Diane M. Allen, JoAnne Hiegel Anderson, Stuart Baker, Felicity Belford Boyer, Duncan Carroll, George Davis, James Doyle, Patti Drake, Mary Fowler, Jolene Hemeon, Mark Hiegel, Sandy Hiegel, Jim Hofmeister, Peggy Huff, Gene Kieffer, Tony Lautmann, Christy Lewis, Thomas Madsen, Judee and Michael Martin, Gail Hiegel McAdams, Jane M. McKean, John Miclot, Dave Moen, Bob Molloy, JFW Ndikum, Marny Pierce, Dale Pond, Kathleen

Quinn, Elizabeth Rinker, Debbie Shore, Theresa Corbley Siller, Jimmy Skerston, Susan Stoneking, Jack and Patty Stutz, Patrick Sweeney, and Kit Turen

Contents

Foreword
by Sarah G. Schwartz

Which of us hasn't longed for an experience of Heaven on Earth? Is such a thing even possible and how do we get there? These are questions I have asked myself over the years. The journey to Self-discovery it is said, begins with a single step and the burning question: Who am I?

Through a mutual acquaintance, I had the privilege of meeting Scott Hiegel and reading this manuscript of his life journey to find the pearl of great price. Known by many names across cultures, this gem may be revealed through the living of our lives if we are willing to take the time to open the door, to look within and to learn and grow. When a Kundalini experience arrives, if we are not prepared it can be a frightening experience that we have no frame of reference for and find difficult to integrate into our understanding. Yet it can be a jewel beyond compare, bathing us in its living light of love, wonder and grace! How can we invite this experience into our lives safely so that we each may discover this great pearl? For me it involved an ongoing process of seeking and searching, self-examination, meditation, prayer and the study of my dreams.

Through a series of unexpected transformational events in his life, a rigorous practice of spiritual and personal disciplines, as well as making an effort to live a more simple, noble, less materialistic life, Scott came to have ongoing experiences of this wondrous and glorious new state of consciousness. Perhaps many of us have "glimpses" into an awareness beyond ordinary reality. But in our culture, we have little understanding of how to anchor, integrate and grow from them.

Is humanity really graced with an opportunity to evolve into more mature human beings, truly wise men and women "homo sapiens," where we can work together to create peace, compassion, and greater joy and love, not only in our personal lives but for the sake of Mother Earth and all Her kin? There was a man who lived in India who thought so named Gopi Krishna. Mr. Krishna believed that experiencing Kundalini is a common biological potential in every human being and that by conducting experiments on the brain, this hypothesis could be proven. It was his life mission that has deeply moved Scott Hiegel. And a worthy mission it is!

Not only will this story and its implications extend the opportunity to the reader to be inspired to grow in new ways of being, but also to usher in a kingdom of wonder on Earth, where all may evolve and be restored. I am reminded of Beethoven's finale to his 9th Symphony, Ode to Joy and the lyrics of the poem written by the German poet Friedrich von Schiller...

...Joy!
Joy, bright spark of divinity,
Daughter of Elysium,
Fire-inspired we tread
Within thy sanctuary.
Thy magic power re-unites
All that custom has divided,
All men become brothers,
Under the sway of thy gentle wings....

Sarah G. Schwartz is a Music Educator, Cellist and Certified Therapeutic Harpist

Foreword
by Marc Vaccaro

It was December 17, 2004, the day that our company was to do an Initial Public Offering (IPO) of stock. I was 41 years old, cofounder of the business, and at the top of my business career. Everything went according to plan, in fact better than plan. My partners and I rang the bell opening Nasdaq as the headline IPO that day. We had our 10 seconds of fame. The images of us opening the exchange flashed across the screens of CNBC and CNN, with relatives calling to share in the excitement of witnessing our exalted victory.

My wife and I literally stood in the median strip of New York's Times Square, watching the electronic ticker tape dance along until finally our stock revealed its first trade. It was UP 50% in its first trade! My first thought was "Oh my God, I'm rich" (at least on paper). My second thought without even a second of hesitation was "I am still just as miserable inside."

There was a hole in me I thought money, status and all the freedoms that come with it would provide. But I instinctively and immediately knew that was not to be the case. It was almost as if I had climbed K2 and God said, "You have climbed the wrong mountain; Mount Everest is over here". And so, it has been ever since.

Since that time, almost 18 years now, I have been on a profound spiritual journey. I am a member of a Twelve-Step program. My heroes used to be the likes of Warren Buffett and Bill Gates. Now they include Krishnamurti, Ramana Maharshi, Gopi Krishna, Bill W., and others who have seen beyond the human intellect to a reality sublime.

Through all of my hard work and purification, I have had moments of this sort of peace and majesty. The kind of peace and majesty that passeth all understanding. But just momentary.

Scott and I have known each other for some 30 years. In fact, we grew up in the same idyllic village of Maple Bluff, less than two miles apart. Our age difference of eight years meant that we ran with different groups and lived worlds apart. His best friend was my best friend's older brother. But eight years apart is an eternity when you are a kid.

I really came to know Scott as an adult when we were both treading our paths toward "certain" success and stardom in our respective fields in business. In my few business-related interactions with him I sensed a kindred spirit. He was always very kind, soft spoken and humble; qualities which attracted me.

It was really in the last 18 plus years that we have become very close, as we realized we had common histories and were on similar paths. In my journey, I was on a search for people who had achieved authentic spiritual awakenings, even traveling to India to further that pursuit and my own growth. When Scott shared what had happened to him and what he was now experiencing, I just couldn't believe it.

What I was searching for had taken place within him and was fully formed. I can tell you from meeting hundreds of people from different cultures, and reading at least as many books, that a genuine spiritual awakening of Scott's magnitude is probably pretty rare; maybe like winning the Powerball, when the purse has grown to ridiculous proportions. From all the time I spent with him, I knew his was authentic. I would be less than truthful if I didn't also admit that I was envious of what he had achieved knowing that, in fact, his awakening sought him, not the other way around. I wanted what he had and was willing to make it my life pursuit.

Like many of us, I am watching a world that feels like it is on the brink of a colossal disaster. Countries and institutions feel as broken and far apart in working together as I have witnessed in my lifetime. Within most countries one senses the same deep division, with maybe a harder edge than ever before. With almost eight billion of us on this earth, the stakes are much higher and costs to our precious planetary environment much starker.

What every great yogi, prophet, mystic and saint has always stated is the same: that positive change must start "within" each of us, before positive change can happen "outside" of us. They also often talked about how they had experienced a new and much more exalted state of awareness, using terms such as heaven, nirvana, cosmic consciousness, paradise, bliss, and samadhi to describe such a state.

Scott is one of a small group of people bringing forward Gopi Krishna's transformative theory that the human brain is evolving, that there is a mechanism in the body responsible for this evolution, and that human beings are hard wired biologically for a much more glorious and exalted state of consciousness. Maybe the most exciting news is that we may be at the technological point to test this theory with our modern instruments, and possibly prove that what Scott shares in his book is real. If so, this could bring much hope and excitement to people and eventually be a unifying force for humankind. Frankly, it could change the direction of humankind's thinking almost immediately to a more positive direction. God knows we could use such hope and positive change at this time. I firmly believe Scott's book will provide much hope and inspiration to you.

Author's Note

Now that I have finished writing, I've had the time to reread my story and poetic verses. I realize they have profoundly good news to share. They are a summary of my lifelong journey from a normal state of mind to a new state of consciousness. I believe this new consciousness is the preordained next goal for human beings. It is a journey that has been filled with great challenges and many struggles, but also overwhelming joy, peace and love.

In the book I describe the pinnacle of this new state of mind, Cosmic Consciousness, and some of the ways we will need to live to attain this treasure that is within. I also describe the engine behind our evolutionary ascent to this new state of consciousness and heaven on earth. This engine is the Intelligent force and biological mechanism of Kundalini.

I believe my life experiences show evidence of a more powerful, peaceful, happy, and sublime state of mind. They also demonstrate the gifts of new knowledge, talents, healing, and love that can result from the Kundalini process and our spiritual unfoldment.

I'm hoping that sharing my story will help you realize you are not alone on this journey of life; that you come to understand that no matter what happens to you in life, and no matter how hopeless and difficult things may seem at times, there is a Guiding Light within each of us. This Guiding Light, a kind of Divine GPS system, can direct us through the turmoil and challenges of our lives and lead us to a life of greater promise and fulfillment. I will share how I came to find and strengthen my connection to this Inner Guidance.

I hope you will enjoy coming along on my journey. I am a regular person, who was suddenly catapulted into a new world by a series of unexpected events, into a mystery that defies imagination, but eventually brings greater meaning, deeper love, and a happy ending. May you have a sense of hope and wonder for what lies ahead. The future is bright, despite the many challenges now facing us.

Preface Part I – Hope and Inspiration

This is a book about hope and possibility with profoundly good news for people at a critical time in history. I will share what I believe is one of the most important discoveries ever made, a groundbreaking new theory of human evolution about the continuing biological evolution of the human brain and the glorious future ordained for humankind.

I'm also going to share some selected stanzas throughout the book, as well as 11 complete verses, from a collection of 48 poetic verses I composed over an 18-year time period ending in February of 2009*. The verses speak to the objective reality of our souls and the existence of a Higher Intelligence. They include breathtaking descriptions of the majestic and glorious states of higher awareness that await humanity through the further evolution of the human mind and brain. Finally, they speak of hidden wonders existing in the brain and the eternal nature of the soul.

This new theory remains mostly unknown to humanity and desperately awaits recognition and acceptance. This discovery provides further insight as to who we truly are as human beings and what our future potential can become. It also provides deeper insight into the origin and nature of the universe, how the brain functions, and whether God as a Higher Intelligence exists. It answers the question of whether the brain is still in a state of organic evolution. Finally, during this time of the COVID-19 pandemic, the theory touches upon why we are facing such problems and enduring such great suffering now, despite our relatively high historic level of economic prosperity. I believe knowledge of this theory and its implications will bring great hope to the world. Verification and acceptance of this theory will eventually change our individual and collective lives in a profoundly positive way.

Let me also say this discovery is not the fundamental elementary particle or "God particle" that science recently discovered exists in matter. In fact, the greatest news about this discovery is that you don't have to be an esteemed scientist, mathematician, or physicist, own a particle accelerator, have millions of dollars, or be a member of a particular race, ethnicity, religion, or social class to discover it. This wonder is available to us all. It is about a "God particle" of sorts, but this God particle is of divine origin. Phrased more in the language of modern science, it is composed of a subtle form of Intelligent Energy and substance that exists inside each of us, whether we are aware of it or not. Verifying this discovery is not the work of one individual, group, nation, science, religion, or generation. Instead, it is going to take a united effort by us all - the entire world - today and in generations to come to experience and harvest the fruits of this discovery for humanity.

This is an uncertain time in the world with many good things happening, yet also some very frightening things. So many people are unsure of what the future holds. The world and its events are changing at breakneck speed. No one knows for sure what will happen next. Many people are unsettled, anticipating greater disasters; while others are hopeful, seeing a bright future beyond our current challenges and sufferings.

If you will slowly read and reflect on the content and meaning in this story, it may serve as an oasis of peace, floating within the current turbulent waters of the world. It may bring you hope, a more positive outlook on the future, as well as a new way of seeing yourself and your potential. It may also impart to you new ideas on how you may better realize your life purpose. It contains the blueprint of how I improved myself and my life circumstances and discovered this God particle within me. I firmly believe this book speaks a deep truth.

I wrote this book because I believe it can be truly helpful for people. And I needed to bring it forth to express the depths of my own soul and being. As I've searched for my truth and purpose during the journey of my individual life, I have discovered what I feel are some pretty amazing things about life and its purpose. I sense some of these discoveries may not be known to most people. They are hopeful things, and I believe knowledge of them can bring hope to many. At the Albert Einstein Memorial in Washington, D.C., a large bronze figure shows Einstein seated on a three-step bench of white granite. The following quotation from Einstein is engraved into the granite:

> "The right to search for truth implies also a duty; one must not conceal any part of what one has recognized to be true."

This quote resonated with me and called me into action.

I also felt "God", or a "Higher Intelligence" was directing me to write this book. I watched as this amazing power, welling up from within, seemed to direct me, step by step. In fact, I felt this Inner Intelligence, through the vehicle of the book, wrote itself through me.

This Inner Intelligence showed me over many years, one step at a time, how I could live a simpler, nobler, less materialistic, and slower-paced life. While I have fallen short at times, I have tried my best to embody this. This Inner Intelligence exists in everyone, and is working to bring us - you, me, and the whole of the human race - to a happier and more profound way of living and being. For the most part, many of us are unaware of this truth and are unconsciously placing in our paths various obstructions to our glorious, ordained future, by the unhealthy ways we live. This in turn, forces Nature to respond in unpleasant ways to clear away the blockages and set us back on the path of balance to a healthy evolution.

I am not a writer by vocation, so this has been a new experience. Given how painful and difficult the process has been, this may be a one-time event (written with a smile on my face). I did feel it was important to write this book and share my experience in my own simple, imperfect, vulnerable, and hopefully somewhat humorous way. My hope is that you will be able to better relate to my experience and the content of this story, because I have written it in my own words. It may not be a perfect literary work of art, but it expresses who I am and what I experienced. And it is real.

The book has three main sections. The first section is *My Personal Story,* the story of my rise, fall, and rise again from the ashes. I thought I would be living one type of lifestyle but ended up living a completely different life. This unexpected change was a good thing, but for many years I wasn't sure. I went from a fairly normal life to where my whole world turned upside down. I experienced a period of terrible financial upheaval and difficult personal challenges, yet at the same time I also experienced rapid personal growth and life-changing spiritual development. Slowly my world was righted again. I am not the same person I was, and life now looks very different. Finally, I found myself where I am today: a changed human being living a happier and more fulfilled life: writing this book, sharing my poetic verses, experiencing a profound state of consciousness and life's deeper purpose, and advancing a new theory of human evolution.

The second section of the book contains the *Poetic Verses*. It includes a selection of 11 verses that summarize key milestones of my journey to this new state of consciousness as well as describe, in sometimes metaphorical language, different facets of my voyage and this new dimension of mind.

The journey of the verses began for me in a place of great fear and uncertainty and ended in a place of joy, inner peace, beauty, happiness, and love. The verses in their chronological progression tell the story of the metamorphosis of my consciousness and deepening journey to God. And they show how my concept of God slowly evolved from faith in a Christian God to an experience of a Universal Intelligence or Consciousness that underlies and sustains all of creation.

The third and final section, entitled *Inspired Prose - Creation, Life, Love and Our Future Path,* is an inspired composition that I wrote in 2018, nine years after I had written my last poetic verse. It occurred at the culmination of a pinnacle phase in my spiritual journey. It describes the important pillars underlying the journey to the Cosmic Conscious state of mind (described in Part II of the Preface below), the ongoing evolution of our mind and brain, the purpose of our existence, and our relationship to God and the never-ending journey toward the Infinite. It also depicts the meaning of creation, the infinite number of creations that exist, and how they all eventually unite in one titanic jigsaw puzzle of Love. It is a truly hopeful and inspiring summary of what has been communicated to me through the living of my life.

As you read this book, please do as they suggest in the 12-step programs: keep an open mind. Take what is meaningful and leave the rest. I'm not trying to convince the reader of anything or persuade others to my point of view. I'm simply sharing my life experience, some amazingly hopeful things and, some of my heart. I hope you may learn something new, and this may help you to live a more fulfilled life. I'm also hoping my story will help people see the wonder of life in a more positive and expansive way. I am always learning new things and am open to sharing ideas. Thank you and please enjoy!

* **The complete collection of 48 verses may be found in a soon to be published book entitled <u>A Soul's Revelation of Heaven on Earth</u>.**

Preface Part II – Gopi Krishna's Theory of Kundalini and Its Revolutionary Implications for Humanity

This is a concise summary of some of the main premises and implications of the ground-breaking theory of human evolution advanced by late Indian sage Gopi Krishna (1903-1984). This theory relates the ancient Eastern concept of Kundalini to the evolution of human consciousness and the human brain. I believe his theory has far reaching implications for the future happiness and survival of humanity. It also includes my thoughts on the possible ramifications of his theory which has had a strong impact upon my life. **While it is not necessary for the reader to read Part II of the Preface to understand and enjoy my story and poetic verses, it would be helpful.**

The theory posits that human evolution is planned and that individuals and the whole human race are evolving to a much more expanded and profound state of consciousness. This evolution is happening through the actions of a biological mechanism and Intelligent Energy in the human body called Kundalini.

Kundalini means "coiled energy" and it is sometimes referred to as a "serpent" because this power reservoir of energy is said to be coiled up like a snake at the base of the spine, waiting to be activated to a more powerful functioning. This more powerful functioning can be present from birth or it can be activated during one's life through an applied practice of spiritual, physical, and mental disciplines, or as a result of spontaneous occurrence. This can result in the birth of a new man or woman with an expanded consciousness. The functioning of

7

the Kundalini mechanism and Intelligent Energy impacts the whole human body, and its most powerful activity involves the organs, nerves, brain, nervous as well as reproductive systems.

Evolutionary changes in consciousness generally occur slowly in human beings. However, when Kundalini is "awakened" it's as if a booster rocket has been ignited to speed up our evolution, and a person's experience of a more expanded and profound state of consciousness can occur quickly. The zenith of this expanded state of consciousness was termed "Cosmic Consciousness", by Dr. Richard Maurice Bucke in his 1901 landmark book, Cosmic Consciousness - A Study in the Evolution of the Human Mind.

In speaking of Bucke's book, author Robert May wrote in his 1991 book Cosmic Consciousness Revisited:

> "Psychology and its sister, psychiatry, have hardly begun to assimilate the archetypal psychology of Carl Gustav Jung, let alone the spiritual psychology of Richard Maurice Bucke. Bucke's psychology is a whole domain of consciousness deeper than Jung's..., and leaves Freud far behind... Dr. Bucke was a century ahead of his time."

I believe Gopi Krishna's concept of Kundalini is the next step beyond Bucke's and May's thought as it relates to Cosmic Consciousness. It is supremely important because it identifies the biological mechanism and Intelligent Force behind this further advancement of our consciousness and the further evolution of the human brain. This in turn leaves the concept of Kundalini as the evolutionary energy and mechanism in humankind open to being proven by science, as well as the preordained goal of Cosmic Consciousness, by individuals in the laboratory of their own experiences.

At the center of Gopi Krishna's theory resides the idea that there is an independent existence to mind or consciousness, and that consciousness, not physical matter, is the underlying reality of the universe.

What this essentially means is that the world, which we see as something separate and outside of ourselves, is in reality not outside and separate, but is projected out from our minds. Our consciousness acts like a movie projector, projecting out from within us a picture of the physical world. One could say we don't live in the world, rather the world lives in us! Furthermore, it is our consciousness or awareness that is permanent and lasting, and the world we see is temporary, subject to change as our brains evolve and we attain another dimension of consciousness. This is the heart of Gopi Krishna's new theory. The implications of this are astounding and will reverberate out into the world in many positive ways and have a profound impact on so many different facets of human life!

This theory explains that this process of evolution in the human body and brain is responsible for upgrading the brain! It is often said that human beings use only a small percentage of the capacity of our brain. How do we use a greater percentage? The unfoldment of the Kundalini evolutionary process leads to changes that allow us to use a greater capacity! It is also what makes it possible for us to attain the "Cosmic Conscious" state of mind. The implications of this are also astounding and not yet understood by humankind!

Kundalini researcher Michael Bradford, who wrote the book Consciousness: The New Paradigm, stated the following.

> "Evolution has proceeded since life began from simple to more complex life forms, with more evolved brains and nervous systems. The intellect is the most recent development in mental faculties. Cosmic Consciousness is the natural progression to the next faculty of mind that will allow us to perceive reality in a new way, i.e., directly as consciousness.
>
> Even though humans currently have the same 5 physical senses and brain structure as other higher order primates, such as chimpanzees, our highly evolved intellect gives us access to areas of creation that they cannot access. This includes art, music, language, poetry, aesthetics, logic, mathematics, and countless discoveries of science, such as the scale of the universe on both the microscopic and macroscopic level. In the same way, the development of this new sense will reveal more levels and aspects of creation currently hidden from us."

What do I mean by the Cosmic Conscious mind ("Cosmic Consciousness") or a more expanded and profound state of consciousness? Let me describe it and the evolutionary process of Kundalini this way: the next goal of human evolution, working through biological evolutionary processes occurring in the body and brain, is to expand our awareness beyond the limitations of our five physical senses and intellect. The world of consciousness opens up, a new view of creation appears, and a new source of knowledge becomes directly accessible. The world looks and feels different to the transformed mind - more expansive, light, radiant, beautiful, and joyous.

This ongoing process of evolution to the Cosmic Conscious mind may expand the intellectual capacity of our minds, foster the development of new talents and genius-like abilities, and result in psychic and paranormal gifts. It also provides access to new intellectual and spiritual knowledge.

Finally, this process has the potential to result in a profound ongoing inner experience of love, light, beauty, melodious sound, joy, peace and happiness, as well as the loss of fear of death, an enhanced moral elevation and the realization of our eternal nature. In its highest transformation, the human mind may be able to perceive the unity underlying creation as well as the living, loving, conscious, and titanic intelligent presence behind life.

What amazingly hopeful news, to realize that the potential of Kundalini and the Cosmic Conscious mind already resides in each of us.

Some or all of the elements of the Cosmic Conscious mind, to varying degrees, were most likely evidenced by the founders of our major religions, our most venerable saints, masters, mystics, sages, yogis, etc., as well as some of our most outstanding secular geniuses. The Cosmic Conscious mind might represent what has been referred to metaphorically in the spiritual, religious, and secular literature of the world as Paradise, Bliss, Samadhi, Nirvana, the Holy Grail, the Fountain of Youth, and finally the Treasure Within.

Gene Kieffer, former President of the Kundalini Research Foundation, said:

> "Buddhists, Taoists, Christians, Protestants, Muslims, everyone is destined to evolve to that same status... Cosmic Consciousness. No one religion will be seen as 'the only true one', and all religions will be seen as being on the same track."

In addition, many gifted people such as composers, literary giants, inventors, poets, artists, discoverers, philosophers, etc., have also demonstrated "Genius" or higher faculties of the mind, making significant contributions to the positive advancement of the human race. Luminaries such as Thoreau, Emerson, Einstein, Edison, Tesla, Newton, Whitman, Beethoven, Michelangelo, Plato, Victor Hugo, Socrates and Mozart fall in this category.

Both "Cosmic Conscious" individuals and "Geniuses" might be seen as specimens of the evolved men and women of the future. I believe these people will collectively be the leaders who help to build a "New World". This New World will represent what metaphorically has been referred to in the spiritual, religious, and secular literature as the new Heaven on Earth, the new City on the Hill, the new Jerusalem, the new Eden, the Land of Milk and Honey, the Promised Land, Utopia and Shangri-La.

Gopi Krishna said that despite the current wayward direction of our present civilization, this New World, or Heaven on Earth, is predestined to happen.

This quote from Einstein was also engraved in the Einstein Memorial:

"Joy and amazement at the beauty and grandeur of this
world of which man can just form a faint notion..."

The accelerated evolutionary processes of Kundalini have the potential
to bring this notion of a more beautiful world quickly and clearly into
view.

Gopi Krishna talked about how Kundalini is a physiological
phenomenon in the body with a regular rhythm and process. It is the
creative power that is responsible for both pregnancy and spiritual
transformation. As compared to the physiological process of
pregnancy, the biological process of spiritual transformation is more
subtle, and therefore more difficult to measure and observe. The
physiological processes of spiritual transformation are more easily
detectable when a person is undergoing a full-blown Kundalini
awakening, which is rare.

I believe this new state of consciousness represents the evolutionary
potential available to us all. As such, it speaks to the intrinsic equality
and value of every human being and to evolution as the great equalizer.

I feel this theory will serve as a unifying force for humanity. It will
become clear that the destination and goal are the same for everyone
and that we all need to unite and learn to work together to achieve this
goal.

I believe most people would agree this is an exciting possibility. Some
or all aspects of this transformation may indeed be proven in varying
degrees in the laboratory of our own experience. As this theory and its
implications become better known, it will become reality for more and
more people.

In fact, I personally believe that a mass experiment is already underway, albeit in an attenuated form, in the 12-step programs of recovery (which I will discuss further below and in chapters 15 and 25). Although this is not the goal or stated intention of the 12-step programs, some of the results happening to individuals in these programs are indeed validating some attributes of this more expanded and profound state of consciousness.

I also believe the biological changes and processes that occur in the human body and brain will in the immediate future, be subject to confirmation by physical science. I have confirmed the validity of this transformation through my own physical, psychological and psychic experiences and that these changes came about through a regular biological process in the body.

Furthermore, I believe this process of evolution is already underway in all human beings, but for most people, it is working in a very gradual fashion. However, the potential for an accelerated evolutionary process as a result of Kundalini exists for everyone. In most people this accelerated process either lies in a dormant form, or it is occurring in a less powerful and/or more subtle way, and the person may not be consciously aware of it, particularly its biological aspects.

I believe more people will step forward and confirm some of the things Gopi Krishna wrote about regarding this discovery, as well as some of the things I am sharing in my story. Frankly, I believe this could quickly create a "caravan" of people, united in trumpeting this exciting news to the scientific, medical, spiritual, and religious communities of the world, as well as all of humanity. The eventual building of a groundswell of support for this theory will help humankind scale the mountain of ignorance and resistance around this momentous secret lying hidden in the human frame. This will lead to a massive expansion in scientific research and general public awareness on our human potential that will benefit people and the world greatly.

The characteristics of the Genius and Cosmic Conscious states of mind represent examples of the changes in consciousness that can manifest as our bodies and brains continue to evolve in a healthy fashion. It is imperative that we recognize our evolving brains and bodies require effective spiritual, mental, and physical disciplines for their ongoing healthy development. It is equally imperative that we create a healthy environment to live in, and practice healthy ways of thinking and behaving, so these inner evolutionary processes can proceed in an optimal fashion.

Gopi Krishna said that in addition to physical laws, there are spiritual laws or laws of consciousness, as well as a cosmic law or "Law of Evolution", that rule the life of humankind. These laws collectively govern the direction of human evolution, as well as the physical, spiritual, mental, moral, and emotional development of humankind.

To stay in harmony with the requirements of evolutionary laws, Gopi Krishna felt it was necessary that individuals and societies, as they become more materially advanced and mentally evolved, develop a more natural, simple, slower paced, cooperative, spiritual, moral and less materialistic way of life.

It is important that science and religion/spirituality work together to bring this way of life about if we are to avoid a modern-day Armageddon. The urgent need for this to happen cannot be overstated as Gopi Krishna had an ominous warning for the human race if evolutionary laws are not complied with. He wrote in his book <u>The Awakening of Kundalini</u>:

> "This state of surpassing trans-human rapture [i.e., Cosmic Consciousness], intended by nature to be a permanent feature of the future human consciousness, in the present state of our knowledge about this biological mechanism, can trail off into depression and fear or lead to neurosis and even insanity, because of our woeful ignorance about this vital aspect of human growth".

Most importantly, the negative consequences that arise from violating evolutionary laws apply to not only individuals, but also to the condition of the collective human race. I feel some of the serious troubles we are facing in society are related to our excessive striving for material success, power, and prestige. This in turn has helped fuel the development of a society that is overly fast paced, technologically and materially/consumeristic driven, self-seeking and competitive, as well as excessively glamorous, entertainment focused, and leisure seeking. Our ethical and moral behavior has not kept pace with our material progress. We've lost our balance as a people and society. This has had negative consequences for our healthy evolution, as well as the ongoing health of our evolving brains and minds.

Gopi Krishna said in the early 1980's that despite all the incredible progress in the world in the last few centuries, our civilization is poised for a fall, like all other civilizations that have come before us. He said this is due to humankind's ignorance of the evolutionary requirements of the human brain - placing the needs of the body ahead of the needs of our evolving minds and souls. I think this is just as true today, if not more so, if one looks at the scope and severity of the current problems confronting society.

Michael Bradford made the following comment about the Law of Evolution in relation to the Law of Gravitation and the negative consequences of violating evolutionary laws:

"In the same way that jumping off a tall building will have serious consequences for one's well-being due to the Law of Gravitation, persisting in modes of behavior that deviate too far from the requirements of the evolutionary process will have drastic consequences for the future mental health of humanity.

Looked at in another way, if we force a rapidly growing child to wear shoes that are too small, the growth of the foot is not halted. Instead, a deformed and crippled foot is the result. Similarly, if the evolutionary process is thwarted, the result will be widespread mental aberration and ill health.

The activity of this law can be seen quite clearly in the rise and fall of civilizations throughout history. The vast empires that were built through skill, discipline, hard work and the rule of law came crashing down one by one as the succeeding generations degenerated due to over-abundance and excessive behavior.

It is the evolutionary forces which result from this Law, working at a deep subliminal level in the populations of these empires, which brought many of them to their knees through rebellion, revolution, anarchy, and extremism.

In our present-day civilization, it is these same subliminal forces that are behind the rise of terrorist and anarchist groups around the world. There is no other explanation for why so many young people, with a minimum of persuasion, give up lives of abundance and plenty to join these groups and commit horrific acts of violence against our society."

Modern life today is filled with many serious problems, including threats and acts of terrorism; risk of a nuclear, biological, or chemical holocaust; fears of World War III; an exploding world population; environmental, climate, and pollution issues; epidemic of workplace, school, places of worship, and other shootings; high rates of mental disorders and brain diseases; high attention deficit disorder and autism rates in our children; significant rates of addictive behaviors (drugs, alcohol, food, gambling, sex, etc.); a widening gulf between the haves and have nots; and most recently, the worldwide pandemic resulting from COVID-19. All these problems combined point to the fact that something has gone wrong in our mental and physical environments and the way we currently live our lives.

I'm in agreement with Gopi Krishna's and Michael Bradford's belief that many of the increased troubles we are experiencing today, both as individuals and as a collective race, have a common or root cause, and reflect our violations of this Law of Evolution and the spiritual and physical laws governing the human race. These digressions have resulted in a malfunctioning evolutionary mechanism. For the most part, we are unaware of the evolutionary laws governing humankind and the target of the next step of human evolution. As a result, humanity does not realize that it has diverged from Nature's intended path and the path of healthy evolution due to its unhealthy behaviors and discordant ways of living.

The good news is that Gopi Krishna's theory of intelligent evolution provides great hope for lessening and eventually solving these seemingly intractable problems.

Gopi Krishna shared that the propensity of most human beings to practice some form of religion or to be engaged in spiritual practices is actually due to a natural human impulse planted deep in the human body, stemming from this biological evolutionary mechanism.

He also said that the goals and ideals of all healthy forms of religion and spiritual practices actually serve an evolutionary function and are structured in the human brain. They are some of the guideposts we need to follow to allow the evolutionary processes within to function in a healthy fashion.

This in turn points to the immense importance and necessity of the practice of all healthy forms of religion and spirituality as well as the immense importance of human development practices (all spiritual, mental, ethical, and physical disciplines), which promote healthy physical, mental, psychological, emotional, moral and spiritual development. These practices are necessary to facilitate not only our overall healthy development and evolution as human beings, but also the healthy development and evolution of our brains!

I think it will become increasingly understood that such practices are not a luxury to be practiced by a few in their spare time but are actually a necessity to be practiced daily by almost all people.

I also talk in the book about how the 12-step programs of recovery have become universal healing and spiritual recovery programs. I further discuss how I believe that the confirmation and acceptance of this momentous theory of Kundalini and continuing brain evolution will eventually lead to a further expansion and acceleration into the mainstream of societies, particularly in the West, of the 12-step programs of recovery.

I view the 12-step programs as universally important and necessary at this time in history because of their ability to help individuals heal from the widespread negative effects that excessive materialism and consumerism are having on humanity's physical and mental health and continuing evolution. I also see the programs as critically important due to their ability to help us stay in harmony with the requirements of the evolutionary processes occurring within and to live life in a healthy way.

I hope more people will realize that they can benefit from participation in the 12-step programs, and that they are not just for people dealing with addictions and their effects. I believe new 12-step programs will blossom and grow which will focus on spiritual growth and personal unfoldment and will help people develop higher consciousness more safely.

In summary, I hope I've been able to shed some light on the essential elements and profound implications of Gopi Krishna's theory of Kundalini and human evolution. I would imagine that this may be a new concept for most people, and it will take some time and deeper study for the idea to take root and greater understanding to germinate in one's mind. I think it is well worth the effort. By sharing my story, I hope to make Kundalini more concrete and understandable by showing the effect it has had on my life. I will also discuss the overall profound positive impact it has had on my understanding of the purpose of life and how it has led to my living a life of adventure, joy, wonder, peace and love beyond my wildest dreams.

For information on Kundalini theory, source books and other materials by Gopi Krishna, please visit the Institute for Consciousness Research (ICR) at <u>www.icrcanada.org</u>.

Section I - My Personal Story
Introduction

In the summer of 2008, I shared my personal story at a conference on spirituality and consciousness on a farm just north of Toronto. It was a small, intimate gathering. I felt at home. I began my story with the following:

> "My life has not turned out anything like I thought it would. My vision when I was younger, was that at this time - age 50 - I would be happily married, have four or five kids, be a CEO for a large company, or an investment tycoon, live in a big house on a lake, have a country club membership, play golf on the weekends, go on incredible vacations, help the less fortunate, etc.
>
> Instead, I became one of the less fortunate - or as I mistakenly thought them to be. I'm divorced, own very little materially, share an apartment, do not live on a lake, play minimal golf, and found out the hard way that God, not myself, is CEO and in charge. And yet today I do work that I love, and I've never been happier and more at peace."

When I was a young boy growing up in Madison, Wisconsin, I dreamed of becoming a professional golfer or basketball player. Somewhat disappointingly, these dreams didn't materialize, and, instead, I became an accountant, an investment professional, and entrepreneur. I eventually discovered these professions were not the end of the road, but rather were stepping-stones to new dreams and my life purpose.

It is now 2021 and if somebody had told me thirty years ago when I was feverishly trying to climb the ladder in the financial industry, that one day this shy Catholic boy would be writing a book containing my personal story, inspired poetic verses, thoughts on a new theory of evolution, as well as sharing experiences of a new state of consciousness, I would have laughed and thought they were absolutely crazy. In fact, it wasn't even in the realm of possibility that something like this could ever happen because it just wasn't who I was or who I thought I'd ever be. Yet here I am today doing just that!

I have found that life will always have surprises. If you want to give the universe a good laugh, just tell it what the plan for your life is! One thing I believe you can ask the universe for guidance on, is how to fulfill your passion and dreams. I know this is one area that the universe has not let me down.

This is my story of personal and spiritual growth, which happened through a long healing, growing, and recovery process. This process eventually led to my entrance into a wholly new and unexpected world, a fascinating inner world of great majesty and glory; a world that I never knew existed; a world that I know one day awaits us all. It also led me to where I find myself today: a changed person, living a different, yet more happy, peaceful, and fulfilled life.

I'm also going to share some selected stanzas throughout the book, as well as 11 complete verses, from a collection of 48 poetic verses I composed over an 18-year time period ending in February of 2009*. The verses speak to the objective reality of our souls and the existence of a Higher Intelligence. They include breathtaking descriptions of the majestic and glorious states of higher awareness that await humanity through the further evolution of the human mind and brain. The verses also speak of hidden wonders existing in the brain and the eternal nature of the soul. Finally, they share spiritual knowledge and insight and reveal answers to some of the big questions in life including:

- Why are we here?
- Is there a God or intelligence behind life?
- What happens when we die?
- Is humanity evolving toward a divine like state of awareness?
- What is the evolutionary agent responsible for humanity's ascent?
- What is the nature of our soul?
- Is life everlasting?

Finally, at the end of the book is an inspired composition I entitled *Inspired Prose - Creation, Life, Love and Our Future Path,* that I wrote in 2018, nine years after I had written my last poetic verse. It occurred at the culmination of a pinnacle phase in my spiritual journey. It describes the important pillars underlying the journey to a more glorious state of consciousness, the ongoing evolution of our mind and brain, the purpose of our existence, and our relationship to God and never-ending journey toward the Infinite. It also depicts the meaning of creation, the infinite number of creations that exist, and how they all eventually unite in one titanic jigsaw puzzle of Love. It is a truly hopeful and inspiring summary of what has been communicated to me through the living of my life.

During the time period in which the verses and inspired prose were written, I also experienced physiological changes in my body that seemed to coincide with certain changes in my consciousness or awareness. As discussed previously in Part II of the Preface, an Indian sage by the name of Gopi Krishna advanced the theory that the human brain is still in a process of organic evolution. He said different stages of spiritual development or the growth of the human mind, as evidenced by changes in consciousness, are the result of a regular process of biological changes that occur in a person's body and brain. He further postulated that this ongoing process of evolution is bringing humanity to a more profound and expanded new state of consciousness. He termed the zenith of this expanded state of mind "Cosmic Consciousness". My experiences supported this.

As I discuss in this book, I eventually came to embrace this revolutionary new theory. This theory relates the ancient eastern concept of Kundalini to the evolution of human consciousness and the human brain. It also identifies Kundalini as the biological mechanism and Intelligent Life Energy that drives the evolutionary process in human beings.

What do I mean by the Cosmic Conscious mind (Cosmic Consciousness) or a more profound state of awareness? Let me describe it and the evolutionary process of Kundalini this way: the next goal of human evolution, working through biological evolutionary processes occurring in the body and brain, is to expand our awareness beyond the limitations of our five physical senses and intellect. The world of consciousness opens up, a new view of creation appears, and a new source of knowledge becomes directly accessible. The world looks and feels different to the transformed mind - more expansive, light, radiant, beautiful, and joyous.

26

This ongoing process of evolution to the Cosmic Conscious mind may expand the intellectual capacity of our minds, foster the development of new talents and genius-like abilities, and result in psychic and paranormal gifts. It also provides access to new intellectual and spiritual knowledge.

Finally, this process has the potential to result in a profound ongoing inner experience of love, light, beauty, melodious sound, joy, peace and happiness, as well as the loss of fear of death, an enhanced moral elevation and the realization of our eternal nature. In its highest transformation, the human mind may be able to perceive the unity underlying creation as well as the living, loving, conscious, and titanic intelligent presence behind life. **I share some of my own limited experiences of Cosmic Consciousness in Chapter 22 "New Consciousness: My Soul and Mind Awakened".**

The concepts of "Kundalini", "Cosmic Consciousness", and "Intelligent Life Energy" are also discussed in more detail in Chapter 9 "Kundalini Awakening!", and in other parts of the book.

Research on the human brain, consciousness, and the benefits of practices such as meditation, mindfulness, and prayer are particularly hot areas of scientific research today. Some new research, although not universally agreed upon, has shown that the human brain is not static and that it can develop new neurons or cells, even in adults. This process is called neurogenesis. Until the final decade of the last century, scientists had maintained that the adult brain can't change. Furthermore, neuroplasticity refers to the ability of the brain to change its structure and function in response to experience. Recent research has also shown that meditation or prolonged and sustained attention can change the inner workings and circuitry of the brain. Professor

Richard Davidson at the University of Wisconsin, Madison found that mental training made it easier for the brain to activate circuits that underlie compassion and empathy implying that these positive states are skills that can be trained.

In addition, other important work has focused on the conceptual similarities of some ancient eastern doctrines and modern quantum physics. As Gopi Krishna wrote in his book <u>Three Perspectives on Kundalini</u>:

> "...according to the latest concepts about matter, the observer and the observed phenomena cannot be isolated from each other, the conclusion becomes clear that the universe we see around, with all its color, light, shade, mass, speed, inertia, time and space is a product of the senses and the mind and has no reality apart and away from them."

Finally, there is significant new research being done on the benefits of the practices of mindfulness and meditation, and other spiritual practices such as prayer. Time Inc. came out with a special edition issue in September of 2018 entitled *The New Mindfulness*. In the first paragraph it says:

> "Mindfulness has become the goalpost of modern life, the answer to our high-paced, overstretched schedules. Do you know anyone who doesn't want to be "more mindful" in some aspect of their life?"

A few paragraphs later it states:

> "For all the research showing the benefits of mindfulness in treating such conditions as anxiety, depression, and chronic pain, researchers still don't know exactly how it works."

These different research areas are revealing important new insights about how our mind and brain function and the benefits of mindfulness, meditation, and prayer and their impact on the human mind and brain. They are also sharing new information about our future potential as human beings and the real nature of the world we live in.

I believe these areas of research will yield even more important insights when they are recognized as important pieces of a much larger and interconnected puzzle. This larger puzzle has to do with the role of the Kundalini Intelligent Energy and mechanism in human evolution and humankind's preordained ascent to the Cosmic Conscious mind.

There are still many surprises awaiting the human race as to who we are and why we exist. I will say more about these things and the concept of Kundalini as the book progresses. You may think at this point that Kundalini and a new theory of evolution has nothing to do with you and your everyday life, but it does, significantly so, and I will try to explain why in this book.

Although this is my story, I'm sure that some of it may also be yours. I believe the sharing of inspiring life stories like mine and others, will motivate people of all ages to embrace healthier lifestyles and to aim for higher and more noble goals in life. Through sharing my story, I'm hoping it will touch places deep within your mind and heart and encourages you to discover your own story and share it with others. Everyone has a unique and important story to tell. I believe that sharing our stories can help us to see our common humanity and divinity, help us to see past our human dualities and divisions, help us to see ourselves as part of an undivided whole, and finally help us to see more clearly the love in each of us.

I'm also hoping that sharing my story will help you realize you are not alone on this journey of life; that you come to understand that no matter what happens to you in life, and no matter how hopeless and difficult things may seem at times, there is a Guiding Light within each of us. This Guiding Light, a kind of Divine GPS system, can direct us through the turmoil and challenges of our lives and lead us to a life of greater promise and fulfillment. I will share how I came to find and strengthen my connection to this Inner Guidance.

Finally, I want to share my story and poetic verses with you because they reflect who I am and what I believe. I feel they contain my deepest essence and most authentic voice. In writing this, I felt a Higher Intelligence was speaking through me and wanted me to communicate hope and good news to people during these challenging times in the world.

I also believe my life experiences, told here in my story and poetic verses, and my current state of being, show evidence of an expanded state of consciousness, a more peaceful, happy, and sublime state of mind, as well as the gifts of new knowledge, talents, healing, and love that can result from the Kundalini process and our spiritual unfoldment. I think they also provide confirmatory support for certain key premises of Gopi Krishna's important theory of human evolution, which I believe has profound positive implications for the safety, survival, and future happiness of the human race.

When I speak of God in my writings, it is the God of my understanding, the Eternal Existence and Intelligence behind the universe, the Source of our Being. I use many terms in this book, including Higher Intelligence, Divine Intelligence, Higher Power, Inner Intelligence, Intelligent Life Energy/Force...to represent God or some form of the power of God working in this creation and in ourselves.

I have a deep knowing that we all have a *spark* of the Divine within us. I also know that this *spark* can be experienced directly. I've even come to believe that the existence of God or a Higher Intelligence can be proven eventually to each one of us in the laboratory of our own experiences. However, each one of us must take this journey in our own way and on our own time schedule. I also honor that your understanding of God may be very different than mine, or you may not believe in the concept of a God, or a Higher Intelligence at all. It is not necessary that you believe in a God or Higher Intelligence to experience the inspiration, hopefulness, power, beauty, and love conveyed in my story and poetic verses. Whatever your views, I sincerely hope that you enjoy this book and that it helps you to live a more happy, peaceful, and fulfilled life.

*The complete collection of 48 verses may be found in a soon to be published book entitled <u>A Soul's Revelation of Heaven on Earth</u>.

1 – Dark Clouds and Sunshine

I've spent a great deal of my life trying to figure out who I am, where I came from, and why I was put on this earth. From an early age it seemed I had a deep interest in understanding the meaning and mystery of life. I can remember as a child lying on my back looking up at the sky wondering where the sky and clouds came from and where the sky ended. Was there really a heaven up above the stars? Was there a God? Do we go to heaven if we are good, purgatory if we are only partially good, and hell if we are bad? What happens when we die? Does life continue? In what form? Do we have an everlasting soul?

On the other hand, a good part of my search for understanding myself and the major questions of life were probably prompted by the fact that I was in pain and wanted to find ways to alleviate this pain. From an early age, I suffered from a mild anxiety disorder. I eventually realized that in order to get rid of the pain from this anxiety, I had to understand where the pain was coming from. And to do this, I had to understand myself better and the purpose of my life, as well as learn how to heal and love myself. This started a life-long process of healing, recovery, exploration, and discovery which continues to this day.

Early Memories

I have some very strong early memories, some hopeful, and some a little unsettling, that had lifetime implications.

At age 6 or 7, I can remember sitting on my parent's bed looking at the sunshine streaming through the window, feeling so young, happy, and alive. I had my whole life ahead of me and was so excited about the future and the possibilities it offered.

As a child, I used to love to play in my imagination. I would imagine myself as a future professional athlete or I would imitate being a play-by-play radio sports announcer. In the winter, I would shovel the snow off our driveway and play basketball games against myself, pretending I was the star player on both teams. I would dream about one day becoming a professional golfer or basketball player.

On the other hand, there were some disturbing signs. At around age 8 or 9 when I went to bed at night, I sometimes had this fear that when I fell asleep, I would stop breathing; I was also afraid of the dark and would sometimes crawl into bed with my older brother.

At around age 12, I was watching a TV show about a doctor, *Marcus Welby*, and the episode was about a young child who had leukemia. Soon thereafter I noticed red spots on my stomach and chest and began fearing I might have leukemia. For a good portion of my life, I occasionally worried I had some form of cancer or some other disease.

At age 17, I had an attack of anxiety at the boarding high school I attended. I was eating lunch and suddenly couldn't eat my food. My head was whirling, I felt panicky and thought I was going to get sick. I didn't know what was happening. I wanted to run out, yet I was too embarrassed. Shortly after this episode, I remember looking up the definition of the word anxiety in the dictionary and thinking I may have a psychological problem.

Finally, when I was 22, my persistent anxiety led me to see a psychologist. I was uneasy about having to see a therapist and didn't want to go, but the pain and fear were becoming too great. I remember feeling so stained, thinking I was a flawed person. I was given a prescription for a mild dose of the drug Valium. I remember something inside of me saying, "Don't take them," which I soon thereafter didn't. I intuitively knew that I had to heal and grow without relying on drugs. I hoped for a quick solution to my problems, but deep down I knew that I had a long and challenging road ahead. On the other hand, I didn't realize how meaningful facing these challenges would make my life, and also the surprising and exciting places they would take me.

Today - Happy Days

And now fast forward. It is the year 2008 and I'm 50 years old and working on a consulting assignment at the Hillview Apartment building on Hollywood Blvd. in Hollywood, California. My good friend Jimmy, who is the caretaker of the building, invites me one day to go to 565 Cahuenga Blvd to look at the house whose outer exterior was used in the TV sitcom *Happy Days.*

When I was younger, *Happy Days* was one of my favorite TV shows. It was about an idealized Midwestern family and certain teenage friends and their growing up activities during the mid-1950's to mid-1960's in Milwaukee, Wisconsin. It featured Ronnie Howard as Richie Cunningham and Henry Winkler as "The Fonz." It was corny and overly simplistic, but it seemed to emanate such innocence and goodness. It made me feel good and I loved to watch it.

Soon after visiting the house, I found myself writing a poetic verse, which seemed in actuality to be writing me! The joy and happiness that flowed out of that verse was overwhelming and reflects the intense joy, beauty, and ecstasy that flows within me today. It felt like my soul was singing of its unlimited freedom and rhapsodizing about its true universal and everlasting nature.

In one section of poetic verse # 47, entitled "Happy Days" (see complete verse included as #11 in Section II - Poetic Verses), I wrote:

"Happy Days are here again. My heart glows with an appreciation that goes back to the beginning of time. The material world evaporates, replaced by a shining radiance, an overflowing happiness, a gaiety beyond compare…

I leave my body and rush up to the stars. I jump from star to star, Walt Disney's magic inscribed in my heart. I descend into Niagara Falls, dancing with the sprays of joy, floating on waterfalls, heaven filling my heart.

I soar up to the stars at lightning speed, my heart bursting with joy, my mind ablaze with glory, I burst into the universe; I open the door upon a silvery, lustrous, magical, gleaming, glistening fairyland of my heart.

… I am light as a feather, traveling everywhere all at once, leaving terror behind, embracing joy, melting with love, extending everywhere in space. Every pore of my body filled with joy, dancing with glee. I am a whole new person."

What did my early remembrances of sunshine and excitement about the future, yet also anxious moments of uncertainty and discomfort in my childhood and teenage years, represent? Were they telling me something about my future life? On the other hand, what happened in my life to bring me through some tremendous years of struggle to arrive at the exciting life and joyous state of happiness and new awareness that I experience today and express in the verse "Happy Days"? This is what I will endeavor to explain in this story.

2 – Family and Childhood Memories

I was raised in Madison, Wisconsin and come from a family of eight kids, six sisters and one brother. For a number of years, we lived in a village of about 1,500 people called Maple Bluff. We had a house on Lake Mendota. It was one of four lakes that surround the Madison area. It was an idyllic place to grow up. We spent our summers boating and water skiing on the lakes, and swimming and playing golf and tennis at the local country club.

Maple Bluff was like the town Mayberry in the old sitcom, *The Andy Griffith Show*. It was a tight-knit community. Everybody seemed to know everyone else, and it was a safe and nurturing place to grow up. Some notable people I can think of who lived in our little village over the years include actor Chris Farley, wiener mogul Oscar Mayer, as well as Olympic gold medal winners: swimmer Jim Montgomery, and cyclist Connie Carpenter. I had formed the impression the rest of the world was like Maple Bluff. I was in for a rude awakening.

God the Father

We were raised in the Catholic religion. My father was a businessman as was his father. His father rose through the ranks to become General Manager of a wood products company in Davenport, Iowa. My father started in the mail room and climbed the ladder to become CEO of Oscar Mayer and Co. He received the United Way Tocqueville and Catholic Charities awards for service to the community. Our family belonged to the prestigious Madison Club.

My father who passed away in 2017 was a hard-working, honest man. He exuded fairness, integrity, and doing the right thing. On the other hand, at times he was hard to approach and could be distant, moody and critical. He did not readily share what he was thinking and feeling. Sometimes he scared me. In many ways, he was like God the Father. I'm sure the pressure of raising eight kids and running a large company put a heavy burden on him. I often wondered how he did it. Like many fathers of his generation, it was not something he talked about. As my dad got older, the shield of armor he encased himself in slowly began to soften, gradually melted away through the aging process, and the trials and tribulations of his own life. The loving and soft core that I always knew was there occasionally shone brightly.

Happy Memories of Mom

My mom left this world in 2004. She had a deep spiritual sense and was kind and loving. I remember her good heartedness and optimistic nature. She loved children. Like most Catholic wives at the time, she played a subservient role to my dad. She was a homemaker. At her funeral, my father mentioned how she had cooked meals for the family almost every night for thirty years. I remember she frequently played the song "Home, Sweet Home", on the piano in our house. When my brother and I were roughhousing, she would often say, "Wait until your father gets home and you will be in trouble." I remember feeling scared to death waiting for my father. Would he be in a good mood and grant my brother and me clemency or would we face the wrath of hell?

One of my mother's favorite activities for the family at Christmas time was watching the movie *A Christmas Story,* which was a nostalgic view of Christmas in Indiana during the 1940s. It featured a nine-year old boy named Ralphie, whose only item on his Christmas wish list was a Red Ryder BB gun. Everyone including his parents and teacher told him he would shoot his eye out if he had the gun. I believe this movie reminded my mother of how she was raised and how she and my dad raised us kids. As I grew older, I also loved to watch this movie. It reflected my own longing for a close family, and a more simple and innocent life, instead of the fast paced, harried, complex life I was living.

There was no question my father was the head of the family, the patriarch, and provided the economic foundation for our household; but it was my mom's love and closeness to God that was the true foundation of our family. My parents had their human failings like all people. Nonetheless, I am so grateful for my upbringing and for the support my parents gave me my whole life. I love them deeply. I knew my parents tried their best to raise us in a loving and caring environment. Despite not always being able to express it well, I knew they loved all of us deeply. They were honest, moral, and trustworthy, and family was most important to them. And there was always a great deal going on in our family, with lots of humor, fun, and adventure, as well as sadness and misfortune.

Heaven on Earth

Our family was many things but one thing it never was, was boring. Large family reunions, family vacations, celebrating holidays and birthdays, going to church, visiting the relatives, and eating out were family rituals, and seemed to be the glue that kept us together. Many of us fondly and nostalgically remember traveling in the summertime to my grandparent's cottage on the Wapsipinnicon River, just outside Davenport, Iowa. This was a Utopia scarcely to be imagined.

The small cottage, with a pump for running water, a wood fired furnace for warmth, and a forbidding outhouse for a bathroom, a dark hole where one feared falling in and being buried alive under the sludge; seemed like a palace to us kids. The joy of being with all of our relatives; swimming in the river, fishing, chasing frogs, fireflies, and butterflies, having picnics, drinking sodas, picking raspberries, playing croquet, cards, horseshoes and volleyball; gliding through the air on the swing over the mud hole which filled up when the river overflowed and watered the earth; all of this was like heaven on earth.

Family Fireworks

Even though I have many fond memories of family togetherness, it was often a tenuous cohesion; and the challenges of life and growing up frequently threatened to blow our fragile family unity apart.

There always seemed to be some crisis going on and oftentimes one family member was mad at the other, someone felt left out, or one played the role of the black sheep. Communication often flowed in indirect ways and sometimes something you said to one sibling would come back to you from another sibling. Shifting tribes and alliances, like small families within the family, frequently formed and dissolved. Sometimes I seemed to have a moratorium in place on talking to certain family members. But this never lasted long.

My sister and I used to joke that one day we could make our fortune by creating a TV series based on the experiences of our family. It would be a combination of *Happy Days* and *Dallas*. *Dallas* was a show from the 1970's about a wealthy Texas family named Ewing, and their life of power, passion, and intrigue. I thought some of our misadventures were right on par with the goings-on of *Dallas*.

As time passed and I discovered what life was like in other families, I came to realize that our family was not atypical. To this day, I don't know how my parents raised eight children and kept our family together. I think it is a testament to their inherent goodness and the strength of their belief in God. I suppose growing up in the late 1950s and 60s, the neighborhood seemed to function more like an extended family and there was a lot of extra support. Maybe life was simpler back then.

Family - Container for Spiritual and Personal Growth

One of the things I eventually came to realize was that my family, like all the different vehicles in my life, was a great container for personal development and spiritual growth. The goings-on in my family challenged me to grow personally and love in ways I never dreamed possible.

I always had the strong feeling that everyone in our family yearned for deeper love and connection, but we lacked the skills or know-how to bring this about. Oftentimes, it seemed as if conflict and trouble would step in to fill the void, in a perverse way, to try to draw us together. I feel some sadness when I think about this, yet I'm comforted by the fact I could still feel a deep underlying love searching for ways to come to the surface.

I also deeply feel that this hidden or unexpressed love never gives up seeking its full expression and connection. Eventually, whether in this lifetime or some future life to come, this love finally reaches its ordained destination and brings comfort, healing, wholeness, and togetherness.

It took a long time for me to realize that if I wanted the family to change for the better, I had to work on changing myself first, rather than pointing accusing fingers at others. I'm truly grateful for this understanding which came primarily from the 12-step programs. Over time and after a great deal of personal recovery work, I have come to see the goodness beneath the flaws and imperfections of each one of us, and to appreciate the uniqueness and talents of each family member. While I don't always agree with them or like what they do, I do love them in a special way.

<u>Church, School, Sports, and Girls</u>

I was quite shy as a child. I was sensitive and had deep feelings that I kept to myself. Feelings were not freely expressed in our family. Humor, sarcasm, and indirectness, along with silence and occasional bursts of tears and anger, were the main currency of communication. The whole family went to church on Sunday. We would dress up in our Sunday best, all ten of us. My dad would slick back my brother's and my hair with Brylcreem and we would march off to Church looking like the perfect family. Of course, we weren't as perfect as we looked. Often there was distress and currents of discontent flowing just beneath the surface, which often stayed hidden there.

As a child, I felt bored in church. I would daydream and count the minutes until it was over. I wondered if people went to church because they were afraid of dying, not because they loved God. I hated having to kneel, feeling like it was some form of medieval punishment. Despite not liking church, I did feel better after it was over. I never knew if this was because I had just been liberated from prison or if God was truly breaking through my outer shell of cynicism and disinterest and actually touching my soul.

I found it interesting years later that when I went back to visit my childhood church, I noticed that one of the streets leading to the front of Immaculate Heart of Mary Church was St. Teresa Terrace. Both Mother Mary and St. Teresa of Avila were to eventually have deep influences on my life. I think God was planting seeds when I was younger, and patiently waiting for me until I got older and began a search for more meaning in my life.

I enjoyed school, mostly for the sports and social part, and I didn't like to study. I found most academic subjects boring yet managed to do well grade-wise.

I was shy in class, rarely raised my hand, and often was terrified that the teacher would call on me, that my mind would go blank, and that I would look foolish.

For the most part, I was a model student. Sometimes though, the dark and daring side of my personality, always lurking in the shadows, waited for its chance to break through the innocent facade I showed to the world. I remember in sixth grade running a dice game out of my desk in the back of the class while the teacher's head was turned. One time in junior high, some rogue classmates and I exploded cherry bombs in the school toilets on the last day of school. My brother and friends would sometimes "borrow" flares, and other materials from the local trains, and we would build small homemade firecracker style bombs, which we would then explode in the nearby lake.

I really enjoyed playing sports, particularly basketball and golf. I loved to spend time alone with my thoughts and realized later, that practicing sports by myself was an early form of meditation. Playing basketball in particular allowed me to dance and express my creativity and different parts of my being, which I had a hard time doing otherwise.

I was afraid of girls when I was young. On my first date in 9th grade, I brought my friend along. He even made the phone call to set up the date. I often wondered what the girl, Sue, who was a cheerleader for our basketball team, thought of all this.

A Soft Heart

At this point in my development, I was an empathetic person with a soft heart that, for the most part, I kept hidden. As one example, I remember when we were on a family vacation in Daytona Beach, Florida. I was concerned that this nice older couple, who owned the souvenir shop across the street from our hotel, did not have enough customers. As a result, I went over to the store several times and counted the number of customers. I wanted to be sure that they were getting enough business.

On the other hand, I didn't always display "saint-like" tendencies. Once when I was young, some friends and I drowned a mole in a jar with the lid on it. My mom yelled furiously at us, and I felt devastated when I became aware of what I had done. I felt sad for the mole and wondered how I could have done such a horrible thing.

Another time when I was around six or seven, I was caught stealing some candy and gum at the local Sentry food store. Mr. Bullis, the store manager, asked in a polite but firm voice, why I had put the candy and gum in my pockets. I told him I had too much to carry with my hands. These two incidents left deep imprints and have stayed with me my whole life.

In general, I was a kind and thoughtful person. I had a strong desire to be liked and to conform to people's expectations. I became a people pleaser and, as a result, lost part of myself at an early age. However, I would later reclaim this lost part, as well as find many new hidden gems, through years of personal and spiritual development work.

3 – Rise: Freedom Journey and Early Work Life

After graduating from the University of Wisconsin with a business degree and majors in marketing and accounting, I decided to move to Southern California. This was where I was sure I would find my freedom and a new and better way of life. The sunny and warm weather, gorgeous beaches, promise of greater freedom of expression, and perhaps most importantly, the exciting night life and the beautiful California girls offered the potential for a more adventurous life. The Midwest, its history, its traditions, and its existing way of life felt too boring and confining.

Outward Directed

At this point in my life, the world didn't seem like a trustworthy place. Frankly, I had no idea of who I was and what I wanted to do with the rest of my life. I was outward directed in my actions and had almost no connection with my inner thoughts, feelings, and desires. I was more interested in having a good time and living the fast life, which included going to the beach, drinking alcohol, and partying.

Some of my behavior was a continuation of behavior I practiced during my high school and college years. I had a large group of close male friends through my high school years into my late 20s. Nightlife activities, watching and playing sports, dreams of high achievement and material success, and having a good time, bonded us strongly together. Drinking alcohol helped us occasionally to let down our guard and show our deep affection for one another.

Now I was heading west where my dream was to eventually make a great deal of money and do work that would be even more prestigious than my grandfather as General Manager and my father as CEO. I would climb the ladder to stardom. That is where I thought I would find my security and freedom.

I believed the person who made the most money or achieved the highest position was one of the winners in the game of life. God or a Higher Intelligence wasn't on my radar screen. I would accomplish great things and that would say I was a successful and worthwhile person. I figured that the large sums of money I would make would then provide me an opportunity to become a philanthropist. I would donate money to help humanity, and I would be admired and respected. After that I could find work that I really loved to do and find my true purpose in life. Not surprisingly, God had other plans and a different road map in mind.

CPA, MBA, CFA, and VP

My work path took me first to becoming a Certified Public Accountant (CPA). I saw this work as a good foundation for a future career in finance. I found the work boring and wasn't very good at it. I proudly called myself the leisure accountant. As opposed to advancing my accounting career, I was more interested in reading the Wall Street Journal, going to the beach, and hosting occasional weekend parties at our rented house on the harbor, which my brother Mark gave the appropriate moniker, "The Huntington Harbour Yacht-less Club". You could also often find me heading off to Las Vegas on a Friday night with my friend Jack, where we would drink and gamble the weekend away. This way of thinking and living illustrated my general lack of maturity and direction in life.

One of our nearby neighbors in Huntington Harbour was a man named Roy Nesseth. I met him through playing basketball with his son Jeff. Roy was an interesting character who apparently was a business dealmaker. Jack and I played golf with him frequently. Because of his large stature, and funny and jovial nature, we came to call him the Jolly Green Giant. He would often invite us out to dinner at nearby Captain Jack's in Sunset Beach. He always insisted on paying the bill and would come flushed with a handful of five dollars bills which he doled out to every waiter and waitress he happened to walk by. I eventually found out he was business partners with then automaker John DeLorean. DeLorean in the early 1980s had developed the DeLorean sports car. This car later became popular as the co-star of the *Back to the Future* movie trilogy, alongside Doc Emmet Brown (Christopher Lloyd) and Marty McFly (Michael J. Fox).

One day Roy asked if I was interested in working with him and DeLorean. I was hoping to go back to business school at the time. They needed an assistant. I needed time to think about it. When Roy brought home one of the first DeLoreans on the West Coast, I took it for a ride along the beach. People gawked. I was in heaven. Maybe this would be my first chance at hitting it big. I could become a sports car mogul. This dream blew up when one day I returned from a golf game with Roy to turn on the national nightly news and saw a picture of him with DeLorean. DeLorean was being accused of orchestrating a cocaine drug deal to finance his sports car company. After this happened, when Roy needed to call DeLorean, we had to go down to the corner pay phone because Roy's phone was bugged by the authorities. Well that pretty much ended that career choice, which would not have been a wise one!

I didn't have a bright future at the accounting firm, nor an interest in this line of work, so I decided to head back to graduate school at UCLA and pursue a degree in finance. While growing up in the cold Wisconsin winters, I always found myself looking forward to watching the January 1st Rose Bowl college football game played in the gorgeous Rose Bowl stadium in nearby Pasadena. Without fail, the weather on that day would be warm and sunny with temperatures in the 70s. I dreamed of one day going to school in Southern California and now my dream had come true.

At UCLA, I earned a Master of Business Administration degree (MBA) with a major concentration in finance, and a minor in playing golf during the relaxed second year. I used to say that in accounting, you counted the money other people made. I wanted to go to a place where I could make the money, and this led me into a career in finance and investments.

I used to half-jokingly say to a friend that some day after making my financial fortune, I would return to this area and instead of making the right turn while heading east on Sunset Blvd. into UCLA, I would be making the left turn into the nearby affluent and high-profile community of Bel Air to return to my palatial estate. Little did I know that one day I wouldn't be making a right or left turn but would be heading straight into financial destitution. And the surprising thing about this is that it would actually turn out to be a good thing; but more about that later.

Between my first and second years of business school, I landed a summer internship in corporate finance, investment banking at the prestigious Lehman Brothers in New York City. My time in Manhattan included working for a short time on the 103rd floor of the World

Trade Center, which collapsed 17 years later during the 9/11/2001 terrorist attacks. During those two weeks in 1984, I had an abnormal fear that the building would fall. I believed I had hit the mother lode with Lehman Brothers and figured I was on my way to hitting the big time in finance. It didn't seem to register with me that that whole summer in New York I seemed to be in an anxious trance, dazed by the fast and whirling pace and pressure of the work and city. Was this the dream life and the work I wanted to pursue? What was this alien and somewhat hostile world I had landed in? Something was amiss in my thinking, but I was not yet aware of it.

After completing business school, I decided to become a financial professional with Prudential Capital, a subsidiary of the Prudential Insurance Company. When I look back, I truly feel that Providence (as in the Divine kind) was looking after my best interests when I landed a job with Prudential. The reason is that if left to my own devices, I would have pursued the money, glamour and prestige of a Wall Street investment banking career. This would most likely not have turned out well, as I don't believe I would have been successful in such a fast paced, high pressure competitive environment like investment banking.

As good fortune would have it, I didn't get the job in investment banking and Prudential Capital was my fallback position. Not surprisingly, the Company turned out to be an ideal fit for me. I really liked the financial work and reasonable pace, and also greatly respected the people, who I found to be honest, hard-working, and down to earth.

While at Prudential Capital, I earned a Chartered Financial Analyst (CFA) designation, received several promotions, and eventually became a Vice President of Corporate Finance. When I was promoted to Vice President, my name and a small picture was in the business section of the San Francisco paper. I remember my parents being so proud. However, I also remember thinking that this accomplishment didn't really mean that much to me. In fact, I was actually thinking that now that I'm acceptable to the outside world, I can really figure out what I want to do with my work and life to find true happiness and fulfillment.

4 – The Good Life?

It was now 1990 and I was 33 years old. I was making a good living. I liked the people I worked with and had great friends. I was playing golf, partying some amount, and taking nice vacations. My wife, who I had met at UCLA business school, was a lawyer and a wonderful person. We owned a house in beautiful Marin County, a scenic area of Northern California just north of San Francisco.

I was enjoying the good life. I had found the keys to the kingdom and my security. I had figured out the meaning and purpose of life. I was living the American dream. My life looked good, at least from the outside looking in. The future should have appeared bright. I was supposed to be happy yet strangely enough as the years moved on, I wasn't. Something was missing and rather than finding more meaning and fulfillment, it seemed like I was slipping into a meaningless void; almost like I was entering a dark and gloomy cave. I kept thinking what could possibly be wrong here.

In my work it felt I was swimming upstream against the current. I saw a vision that I was working in a suffocating, stultifying, square metal box. I wanted to use more of my creativity, but this was not possible given the type of financial work I was doing. I had a sense that the problem was deeper than my work.

Key Therapeutic Insights

Because of my general unhappiness, I decided to see a psychiatrist I was referred to by a nationally known therapist John Bradshaw. At that time, I was intrigued by celebrity personalities, including renowned counselors. I had a tendency to project onto others, particularly celebrities, the natural talent and creativity that I had within myself, which was begging for more expression in my life. The problem was I didn't know how to actualize this greater potential. Thankfully, the psychiatrist I was directed to, Carla Perez, was a very wise and caring person, and someone I came to respect greatly. Among many things I learned from her were two simple suggestions which had a profound impact on me:

• I didn't have to do work that wasn't fulfilling and,
• I could find new work where I didn't have to speak publicly, which I was deathly afraid of.

I remember thinking - I don't have to do work I dislike and that involves public speaking? I actually have choices and can do something different? It was the beginning of breaking out of this collective trance I had been in since an early age.

Becoming Internally Directed

I started keeping a journal and began to become more internally, rather than externally directed. I knew it was time to discover who I was and not what my upbringing, family history, and collective society said I was supposed to be. It was time to find out the real purpose of my life and why I was put here on this earth.

These realizations seemed to release a flood of emotions and I found myself crying rivers of tears as many repressed feelings poured out. I knew I was crying not only for myself, but also for past generations. Life not fully lived was mourning its loss, yet, at the same time, the emotions released were cleansing me and opening up clear pathways to allow a new, more fulfilling life to emerge. The stage was being set for my future life to be expressed in a more creative, unique, and expansive way.

Around this time, I expressed in one of my verses the need to listen to my heart and inner voice and extricate myself from the binds of collective society and thinking, and the materialistic and rationalistic tendencies of the times. I wrote the following in poetic verse #2 entitled, "God is Within - Inner Guidance":

"Let the music flow in life and don't fight, flow! There is a harmony of which our inner voice mirrors and leads. Will we listen? The payoff is great.

We can make great music in this life. We only need to listen to our soul and not let the soils of culture tell us that our hearts are wrong.

Make music, whether it is being a janitor cleaning the floor, a violinist, or garbage collector. We all make music in different ways. We cannot let the "enlightened" culture make snobs of our hearts. Remember at the heart of this can be an elitism that wants to assume the throne but is not entitled to the throne.

There is only one God and he is not us. We are angels following in her light. The key to life is in making our own music; not listening to a world based primarily on technology, rationalism, and materialism, which may heap judgment on how we need to make music."

5 – Entrepreneur, Golf Clubs and My Father

I developed the courage to leave the corporate financial world and found what I thought would be my dream work. I had become an entrepreneur, starting a new investment company with my friend Steve, the former head of the West Coast office of Prudential Capital. We had a wealthy financial backer by the name of Howard Leach. Howard was a very successful businessman and man of high integrity and reputation. At one time he was Chairman of the Board of Regents of the University of California, and also was later the U.S. Ambassador to France during the George W. Bush administration. We were going to source investment opportunities for Howard, as well as invest in companies ourselves. Most importantly, we would get paid to do this! I thought, "What could be a greater opportunity than this?"

Steve and I creatively came up with the name DHI for our firm, comprised of our last name initials followed by the word investments. Our new address was 101 California Street, 43rd floor, San Francisco, CA. We were located in the heart of the financial district. The potential of making large amounts of money now seemed real. I was poised for a financial breakthrough. I could see and feel my impending liberation and freedom that I was sure that wealth would one day bring. When I had graduated from business school, I had dreamt of one day doing the work I now would be doing. I had so many reasons to be excited, yet, strangely enough, I wasn't. This again baffled as well as frustrated me. Why I was feeling this way required a greater understanding of who I really was and what I was called to do in life. At this point, however, I still didn't have answers to these questions.

One of our first investment attempts was to buy a date business, as in the fruit kind, and not the romantic, located in the Palm Springs area of Southern California. I remember wondering at the time, wasn't the date tree, the "Tree of Life" in the Bible? I also discovered that the Deglet Noor variety of date, meant the "Date of Light". These facts held great symbolic meaning. I began imagining that through these symbols, God was communicating to me that he or she was endorsing this opportunity, and that it could fulfill both spiritual and material aspirations. Deep down, I knew my goals were primarily material in nature, i.e., to make my financial fortune and secure my future. However, I knew there was a deep spiritual reason I was being led in this direction, and the full extent of why this was so, has only recently become apparent to me. The sharing of the rest of my story will shed light on this.

Ultimately, we weren't successful in buying the business. Little did I foresee that my numerous failed attempts over the years to make my entrepreneurial fortune would end up serving as another container for personal and spiritual growth. Yes, heaven has a profound sense of justice and wisdom. It could not be outwitted by what I proudly thought of as my "keen" business and entrepreneurial sense. In actuality, this "keen" sense was representative of my somewhat blind, fear based, and overreaching ego, which was looking for immediate entrepreneurial success and financial security. More to the point though, I believe God was teaching me important spiritual and life lessons through my struggles. These were lessons that I would have most likely been oblivious to if I had achieved immediate business and financial success. I believe God also had a deeper purpose in mind for my life as well as was showing me who was really in charge.

Thankfully, all was not business failure and concomitant personal and spiritual growth. I wasn't ready to be a monk or take a vow of poverty yet! We did have our share of financial successes at DHI. We were the financial advisor on two buyouts of companies aggregating to $95 million; we raised approximately $5 million of equity capital for two venture-capital transactions; and sourced $29 million of debt financing for an aquarium that was built at Pier 39 in San Francisco. (We were financially involved with both the aquarium at Pier 39 as well as an aquarium at Mall of America in Bloomington, Minnesota, and both are still in operation today.)

In 1994, my then partner Steve was offered and accepted a position in the aquarium business so I took on a new partner, Mark, a close friend since high school. Once again, our creative juices flowed, and we got rid of the D and added a G and DHI became GHI. We had to face the hard decision of whose name came first in our company name. Putting my own ego aside, we decided that the person's whose last name came first in the alphabet won out. We had made our first major decision.

We were very excited about our new business. Although we had lost our financial backer as the original agreement had expired, we were confident of our ability to make our own money quickly. Our guiding mantra became we would make investments in companies where we believed in the people and the products or services, and which were located in areas of the country that we felt attracted to.

Mark and I loved to network and were both marketing and people oriented. We had a flair for finding exciting business opportunities. At times, our efforts bordered on the edge of mania. Our selection criteria often driven more by prestige of opportunity, greatest financial gain possible, and the "excitement factor", rather than by business acumen, common sense, and financial prudence. We quickly became involved in a flurry of potential deals; some were successful, some were not. A couple of the more interesting opportunities included the following:

We did some work with a PGA professional golfer named Tommy Armour III, who eventually introduced us to the Avid Shirt Company. We set up a corporate distribution business that included selling Avid shirts. This endeavor never caught fire. We began by building a very solid information, customer contact, and accounting system infrastructure for the business. However, we did a poor job in one important area, getting initial sales! Lesson #1 was we vowed that in our future endeavors, we would first focus on generating sales, then build the business infrastructure. We also were trying to find other opportunities simultaneously and neglected focusing enough attention on operating this one business successfully. We had failed the basics of business and entrepreneurship 101.

We unsuccessfully tried to buy an indoor professional soccer team, the San Jose Grizzlies. Our half partner in the team would have been the National Hockey League franchise the San Jose Sharks. While the courting period was underway, I remember my two partners and I being invited to attend one of the Shark's hockey games in the owner's suite. A lavish buffet spread of food was provided that we feasted upon like locusts. Our potential partner probably did not realize at the time that we lacked the investment money that it would take to buy the half share ownership interest in the Grizzlies. We were confident we could quickly raise the money. As it turns out, our confidence was misplaced.

Although being a bit reckless at times, we didn't lack for courage in trying new things. This was both a blessing and a curse. On the one hand it made things exciting, gave us more opportunities for entrepreneurial success, and also provided many different kinds of entrepreneurial learning experiences. All of these things would benefit us in the long run. Our overall approach was high risk, high return. Of course, this kind of focus didn't result in a financially stable and secure business and didn't lend stability to our personal lives either.

Finally, we were successful in raising capital for and invested a significant amount of our personal money in a very unique custom fitting golf club company called Henry-Griffitts, Inc. ("HG"). HG was the pioneer in custom fitting golf clubs on a large scale. My partner and I loved golf. It seemed like a perfect fit. However, like everything else during this time period, the HG investment would turn out to present its own challenges and would be no walk in the park.

HG's headquarters was located in a small building with a large open field in front, near Coeur D'Alene, Idaho. Initially I was sure this location and investment would one day become my own version of a "Field of Dreams". My partner as well as my father and I would make the trek up to this gorgeous part of the world many times during our 13-year involvement with the company. This beautiful setting and seemingly innocuous small company investment opportunity would turn out, however, to serve as another important container for my personal, spiritual, and business growth. At times, it functioned more like a chamber of horrors than the fun little golf company investment and "Field of Dreams" I had envisioned.

The challenges of the HG investment continued for the entire 13 years we were involved with the Company. There never seemed to be a period of respite. The pressure was intensified by the fact we were responsible to a large group of investors, most of whom were family or friends. So many times, the Company was close to running out of money and dangled on the edge of bankruptcy. My partner and I wanted to scream, throw our hands up and quit, but the universe would not provide any avenue of escape. We were eventually able to look back and be proud of the fact that we worked hard, never gave up, looked out for our investors and the Company's interests to the best of our abilities, and we persisted through all the challenges. The Company was eventually sold in 2008 to another golf equipment company and we received a small potential ownership position in the new company which eventually turned out to have no value.

The whole experience with HG was very humbling. I learned many life lessons including the need to be patient and persevere in the face of difficulties, to always keep an open mind to other people's views, to know that what I thought was not always right, and to learn from my mistakes. In addition, it taught me how to forgive and be easier on myself when things weren't going well. I eventually came to appreciate the whole experience as well as all the people involved with the Company. This was despite the fact that my partner and I were sometimes at odds with our HG partners, and occasionally, it seemed like we were adversaries more than partners. In the end, I came to believe that everyone was doing the best they could. These were hard things to learn but once again invaluable and enduring life lessons.

<u>Working with My Father</u>

The HG experience also gave me the opportunity to work with my father, who joined Mark and me on the board of directors of the Company. In looking back, this was a deeply meaningful and important life experience. I had never really worked with my father and realized I didn't know him outside of our own family. I was uncomfortable at first with this arrangement. Eventually though, this experience gave me the chance to understand my dad in a whole new light and it will always be something that I treasure. His integrity shone through. I also admired his quick thinking and his ability to penetrate right to the core issue of a problem or situation, as well as his decisive decision-making ability. He became more human to me as I saw he had his own foibles and shortcomings. In the HG experience, I think I was able for the first time to see him outside of his role as my father and the image of perfection I had always held him in. This was truly a blessing as it allowed me to see him as a fallible human being like myself, and this brought us closer.

On a lighter note, we discovered my father had a hard time relinquishing his standard dress apparel, a business suit. We told him this was a small golf club company in a small town and people dressed informally. Nonetheless, we always found when we picked him up at the Spokane, WA airport that he was attired in his suit. My partner and I chuckled about this, but we came to accept him for who he was, and to respect the more formal business environment from which he came.

One enduring memory I will always have of my father from this experience was on an occasion when Mark and I were dropping him off at the Spokane, WA airport. It was during a particular rough time of the HG experience. He leaned into the car and said with a very quiet voice:

"Be sure to always take care of your loved ones."

Despite my father's difficulty with expressing his feelings, I knew how much he cared about Mark and me, and our loved ones. I also knew how unselfish he was and how deeply he cared about his own family and others. In the end, my experiences at HG with my father confirmed what I already knew, that my father was a kind, decent, caring, honorable, yet imperfect man. His involvement with HG enriched my experiences beyond measure, and his presence was a true gift from God. From my perspective, this experience with my father was clearly

one of the important reasons why I was led into this challenging
business opportunity.

6 – Spirituality and Life Turning Point

Although I was following primarily a business and financial work path during this time, I was also quietly and persistently developing a deeper and richer inner spiritual life. Since my early 20s, I had been interested in subjects pertaining to self-improvement, psychology, religion, and spirituality. I read voraciously and did various practices and workshops in all these areas.

I became particularly interested in the psychology of Carl Jung. As opposed to Sigmund Freud, whose psychological thought seemed coldly analytical, materialistic, and void of a connection to a higher spiritual purpose or meaning, Jung's psychology felt more life affirming. His writings seemed to embrace the profound mystery and potential of the human mind and the mysteries of life. His thought and writings dealt with the inner person and human psyche, and he spoke to the deeper symbolic meanings of human experience and behavior. His writings confirmed my deep intuitive knowing that human beings are more than a collection of atoms and molecules that disappear permanently upon death; and actually, have transcendental reasons for existing. In verse #41, "Everlasting Life", I wrote:

> "We are not just tiny man and woman, clods of sod,
> melded to the earth, to live and die, unaware of our
> eternal existence…There are layers upon layers of
> creation. We never stop existing. New glorious planes
> of splendor are our future inheritance."

I also became interested in the writings of Episcopalian theologians and Jungian analysts John Sanford and Morton Kelsey. Their work and thought, though religious in nature, was in tune with much of Jung's psychological thought.

I was particularly interested in their books having to do with dream analysis and the inner meaning of the sayings and teachings of Jesus. One area where Jung seemed to have a strong influence on Morton Kelsey was in the area of dream analysis. Kelsey believed that dreams were a way in which God was speaking to humans. Jung believed that the unconscious, and what could be found there, connected the individual to a spiritual reality. I began to intensively analyze my dreams. I grappled to understand what my dreams were symbolically trying to communicate. There seemed to be a purpose and intent in their content. Through this work, it slowly began to dawn on me there was a much Higher Intelligence guiding me to a richer, nobler, and whole life. I had to painstakingly, and to the best of my ability, learn the language and understand the meaning of the symbols that this Higher Intelligence was presenting in my dreams. I spent years doing this practice and the harvest gained was well worth the effort. I will speak about some of these dreams and analysis in Chapter 10 "Psychic Experiences/Powerful Dreams".

Sanford and Kelsey's interpretations of some of Jesus' sayings and teachings really opened my eyes to a greater depth and richness that was present in Jesus' thought and the New Testament of the Bible. I began to see that there was a universal meaning to what Jesus was communicating, applicable to all human beings, independent of the institutional religious structure that his teachings were eventually set in. I instinctively knew this was true of all the major religions and the teachings of their founders; that there were similar profound core truths to be learned from all religions; that all these founders needed to be honored for their inspired teachings. I also knew that by limiting myself to the teachings of one religion or one founder, I was depriving myself of other profound wisdom and teachings that could expand my mind and breadth of knowledge. It could also limit my understanding of other people who were adherents of these other faiths. Worst case, it could even lead us to view each other as adversaries, instead of fellow travelers being guided to a glorious destination.

My interest in these subjects had become all-consuming around this time. Whenever I was flying on a business trip and wasn't preparing for an upcoming meeting, it was likely that you would find me reading something about psychology, religion, personal growth, or spirituality.

Michael Murphy and a Turning Point in My Life

Around this time, I also began to develop an interest in the idea of human consciousness, although I wasn't sure exactly what the term meant. In early 1995 at the age of 37, I met Michael Murphy at a golfing event in Pebble Beach, California. Among other things, Michael was well known for writing a best-selling spiritual book about golf called Golf in the Kingdom. He was also known by many as a pioneer in the human potential movement and in the study of human consciousness.

One interesting thing I discovered about Michael was that he and Howard Leach knew each other when they were younger. Howard was the wealthy investment backer of DHI mentioned previously. I found this fascinating as these were two extremely influential people in their particular spheres of expertise and knowledge yet seemed to me to be operating in somewhat opposite worlds. Howard Leach's efforts were concentrated in the political, university, business, and financial worlds, while Michael Murphy's efforts were more focused on human development and the world of the mind and consciousness. Both were men of high character and integrity. I thought that if the two were put together in one person, you just might have a specimen of a near perfectly balanced man. Maybe this is the model of what I was also striving imperfectly to become.

On a more personal level, meeting Michael and my subsequent involvement with him on a project was illustrative of my own ongoing gradual shift out of the business world into the world of spirituality, consciousness, and human development.

It turned out Michael was the guest speaker at this golf gathering I was attending at the historic and elegant Pebble Beach Lodge. After the event, we happened to sit next to each other in the lounge. While I was sipping one of many beers, Michael mentioned that his dream was to develop a new form of health club that would facilitate both healthy physical development as well as the further development of human consciousness. I told him of my entrepreneurial activities. A few days later I found myself walking up the steps of Michael's Victorian era style house in San Rafael, California to meet him and his long-time partner George Leonard.

The meeting was to discuss whether my partner and I could assist them in raising money for such a venture. I remember the meeting and setting had a feeling of mystery and intrigue; like we were discussing a profoundly important subject while treading on sacred ground.

Michael was also one of the founders of the Esalen Institute in Big Sur, CA. The Esalen Institute was founded in 1962 as an alternative educational center. It was devoted to the exploration of what Aldous Huxley called the "human potential", the world of unrealized human capacities that lies beyond the imagination. Esalen is considered by some people to be the birthplace of the human potential movement. Both Michael and the now deceased George had been long-time leaders and participants in this movement. They were also very fine people of sterling character, kind and thoughtful, and thinkers of the highest caliber. We felt very privileged to have a chance to work with them.

It did not surprise me that we met both Michael and George shortly after a large financial deal, involving the acquisition of a New York Stock Exchange traded drug store chain, fell apart unexpectedly. It was appropriate that we had given the transaction the name "Fantasy Deal". It was a deal worth several hundred million dollars. It was going to bring a significant financial fee and small ownership position to my partner and me.

Here's the chain of thinking that immediately formed in my mind as I considered what this potential deal and fee could mean to my life: the money earned would finally provide the seed capital needed to build a large investment company; this in turn would eventually lead to my goal of being independently wealthy, and to being a philanthropic pillar in the community. I would in turn then be widely respected, and maybe most importantly, free to pursue my true dreams in life.

Frankly, we thought the deal had progressed to the point where it was certain to happen. Little did we realize that we were committing the cardinal sin of counting our money and thinking of the ways we were going to spend it before the deal closed. It was then that we received the fateful call.

It was the day after Christmas in 1994. It was a beautiful sunny day in Southern California. My partner and I were driving to the golf course in a jovial mood, anticipating the arrival of a very bright future, when we received a phone call from a friend. The friend said he had just heard on CBS radio that another drug store chain had come in at the last minute and made an offer for our company and were successful in "stealing" our "sure" deal. We were stunned. Our sunny day quickly turned dark. Once again, Heaven had surprised me, even tortured me, as events had taken an unexpected negative turn. Although I had come tantalizingly close, the financial independence as well as honor and prestige I was desperately seeking continued to remain out of reach.

In looking back, I saw that these two events, which occurred a short time apart; my meeting to discuss working with Michael Murphy and George Leonard on the financing of a new pioneering type of health club, and the "Fantasy Deal" falling apart, as "connected" watershed events. They marked a turning point in my life, and I saw the fingerprints of a Higher Intelligence all over them.

It was as if my life's focus and destiny changed from being primarily a pursuit of material gain, prestige, and business success; to one of finding my deepest purpose in life, furthering the development of my own consciousness, as well as embracing the profound spiritual life that seemed to be inexorably calling me. It was as if I had no choice, except at my own risk and peril, but to follow where this Higher Intelligence was leading me. I had to learn to surrender fully. The financial cushion and security that I had lived with most of my life seemed to evaporate from this time of my life forward. I knew my ongoing security was now dependent on my relationship with this Higher Intelligence.

My partner and I collaborated with Murphy, Leonard and others in 1995 to try and raise funding for a Center for Integral Transformative

Practice in the San Francisco Bay Area. The Center, as mentioned previously, was to be a new form of health club that would facilitate human development, both physical and mental, and the development of individual human consciousness.

The guiding principles of the Center revolved around the idea of assisting an individual to develop a balanced and integral set of healthy human development practices incorporating the body (e.g. physical exercise, healthy diet, yoga); mind (e.g. reading and discussing books/articles on relevant subjects such as psychology, spirituality, the mind, and human and personal development); heart (e.g. group processes such as group sharing/counseling, community activities); and soul (e.g. meditation, imaging, journaling). These were to be done regularly as part of a long-term personal development practice.

After about six months of work on the potential Center, the HG golf club opportunity was presented to us by an investment banker friend. It was just too good of a dream opportunity to pass up. At the same time, the Center had surfaced some investor possibilities, which made our services no longer necessary. I later found out that Murphy's and Leonard's Center for Integral Transformative Practice project did not get successfully off the ground, although I believe they continued the practice in other forms and vehicles. I was grateful for what these two great men taught me in our short time together. To this day I remain a deep believer in the idea of a balanced and integral personal development practice.

I furthermore believe it is important that such a practice be done out of a container that fosters humility and surrender to the guidance of a Higher Intelligence, or something greater than one's own self. Such a container and guidance can help lead an individual to the appropriate mix of human development practices to be used to optimize a person's development at any given time. I incorporate such an approach in my own spiritual and personal development practice and use the 12-step programs of recovery as such a container and endeavor to follow the guidance of a Higher Intelligence. I will talk more about the 12-step programs of recovery in chapters 15 and 25.

7 – A Spiritual Mission and Collision Course

Around this time, I found myself repeatedly writing in my journals, "Divinity is within." I also wrote that there was a spiritual purpose to my life and that I had a spiritual mission to fulfill; that my life's path would not be easy from this point on, but it would bring greater meaning and deeper fulfillment.

At times, I wondered whether my thinking was becoming unbalanced. I knew deep down that it wasn't. I knew I was being forced to yield control of my life to God. This brought a great amount of unease and trepidation as well as confusion. I would write from time to time that I felt trapped between two worlds, the spiritual and the material. It seemed as if I had one foot in one, and one foot in the other.

Stirred by Christian Saints, Mystics, and Great Leaders

I then began to develop a deep interest in reading about Christian mystics and saints, as well as books on the historical Jesus and Mary. I studied the writings and lives of many of these saints and mystics, including St. Therese - The Little Flower, St. Teresa of Avila, St. John of the Cross, Dorothy Day, Julian of Norwich, Hildegarde of Bingen, and St. Francis of Assisi.

My intense study as well as my own personal experiences with spirituality, mystical consciousness, and paranormal activity allowed me to deeply relate to their writings on both a conceptual and experiential basis. Each one spoke to me in a unique way, as well as taught and inspired me. They also spoke to me across the centuries of history.

I loved the humility, childlike nature, and the simple way of late 19 century St. Therese - The Little Flower. Her spirituality focused on doing the little things well and with great love, whether it was performing her daily tasks or interacting with people.

I felt the deepest identification with 16th century mystic, St. Teresa of Avila. St. Teresa was at home in both the inner and outer, or the spiritual and physical worlds. She had deep religious and mystical experiences, yet she also lived an active outer life. She suffered incredible trials and tribulations in founding many new religious convents and was in a sense a businesswoman. She also had a wonderful sense of humor. I have a beloved wooden plaque with a large picture of St. Teresa on it made by Robert Lentz and on the back of the plaque it says:

> "Her foundations were small, poor and strictly disciplined, with emphasis on contemplative prayer. Yet the nuns [of her convents] danced in their times of recreation, and Teresa herself played drums and the tambourine. 'It is not a matter of thinking much,' she told her nuns, 'but of loving much. So do whatever most kindles love in you.'"

I loved 16th century mystic St. John's lyrical poetry and could relate to his "Dark Night" poem and experiences in life. He worked with and was very close with St. Teresa of Avila.

20th century Catholic Dorothy Day was the founder of the Catholic Worker Movement. She was a hard and tireless worker for the poor and the outcast of the world. Her autobiography was entitled The Long Loneliness. I related to her words:

"We have all known the long loneliness and we have learned that the only solution is love and that love comes with community."

I recently discovered my great-aunt had worked with Dorothy Day.

I could identify with the teachings and experiences of 14th century mystic Julian of Norwich, who had visual and auditory experiences of Christ, and she wrote of these in her book Revelations of Divine Love. (I speak of my own visual and auditory experiences of Jesus, Mother Mary, Mother Teresa, and others in Chapter 10, "Psychic Experiences/Powerful Dreams").

12th century mystic Hildegarde of Bingen had a deep sense of the unity of creation and was often was referred to as having been illuminated by a Divine or Living Light. I also have experienced a Divine Light in my life and many of my poetic verses, including #16, "The Living Light", speak of this Light.

Finally, beloved 12th century mystic St. Francis of Assisi was a lover of animals and nature as well as all of creation. He was raised in a wealthy family and initially lived a life of pleasure seeking and luxury. Some people believed he lived during a time where the desire for money and power had corrupted society and religious life. I can see parallels with what is going on in today's society. St. Francis gave it all up to live a more religious and simple life.

I could relate to his experience of financial poverty and living a simple life, although his financial poverty was said to be voluntary while mine was initially involuntary. St. Francis also experienced many failures and setbacks during the course of his life. This struck a chord in me because of my own failures and setbacks. One thing St. Francis did not fail at however was in his living of the spiritual life, and with this I felt some kinship.

I began to study the lives of mystics, masters, saints, yogis and founders of different spiritual and religious traditions. Although clothed in different language and symbolism, there seemed to be much commonality to their core experiences and teachings. This insight would have greater meaning for me in the years to follow. In verse #31, "The Eternal Fount of Joy", I wrote:

> "The two are one, the one eternal, the eternal our home.
> This is the great secret, this is the treasure, this is the
> pearl. This is the key hidden from the sight of
> humankind. It is our future inheritance.
>
> It is what all true religions herald; the Christ Child,
> Buddha, Mohammed, Moses and others, all pointed to
> this; the eternal light, the fount of joy and happiness,
> the eternal you and me."

Interestingly enough, around this time I also found myself reading a large number of books on the American Mafia. It was almost as if I had to balance all my spiritual striving and seeking of light by reading about its counterpart of crime and darkness.

Psychologist Carl Jung might have said I was projecting my own unacknowledged darkness or Shadow self, onto the Mafia. The Shadow is that part of our being, both our unacknowledged light as well as our darkness, that we project onto others like film and sport stars, or figures like the Mafia: "Look at that bad man or woman over there!" where we point a finger and don't realize we too have the capacity within us to do dark things. I wanted to work on becoming conscious of my Shadow side so I could come to see myself more clearly. This is one way that we can grow in consciousness. Chapters 14 and 15 describe some of the healing work that I did in this area.

I also became fascinated with and studied the lives of Mahatma Gandhi and Martin Luther King, Jr. Gandhi's humility, and King's courage, as well as their deep spirituality, wisdom, activism, and adherence to the principles of non-violence, moved me deeply.

These words from King in the book <u>The Autobiography of Martin Luther King, Jr.</u> particularly spoke to me:

> "I have always felt that ultimately along the way of life an individual must stand up and be counted and be willing to face the consequences whatever they are. And if he is filled with fear, he cannot do it. My great prayer is always for God to save me from the paralysis of crippling fear, because I think when a person lives with the fears of consequences for his personal life, he can never do anything in terms of lifting the whole of humanity and solving many of the social problems which we confront in every age and every generation."

This saying by Gandhi, cited in James D. Hunt's book <u>An American Looks at Gandhi: Essays in Satyagraha, Civil Rights and Peace</u>, touched me deeply:

> "Whenever you are in doubt, or when the self becomes too much with you, apply the following test. Recall the

face of the poorest and weakest man whom you have seen, and ask yourself if the step you contemplate is going to be of any use to him. Will he gain anything by it? Will it restore him to a control over his own life and destiny."

I was also deeply interested in the lives of Abraham Lincoln, as well as John and Robert Kennedy, whose words and actions stirred my soul. I used to live near Washington D.C. and loved to take walks around the monuments and museums and visit various historical sites. I noticed inspiring quotes. At the Lincoln Memorial, engraved on the wall behind this huge statue of a sitting Lincoln, are these memorable words:

"In this temple, as in the hearts of the people for whom
he saved the Union, the memory of Abraham Lincoln
is enshrined forever."

Etched in a granite wall at Arlington Cemetery near John F. Kennedy's grave, marked by the eternal flame, are these words spoken by the president at his 1961 inauguration:

"In the long history of the world, only a few generations
have been granted the role of defending freedom in its
hour of maximum danger. I do not shrink from this
responsibility - I welcome it...

Finally, whether you are citizens of America or citizens
of the world, ask of us the same high standards of
strength and sacrifice which we ask of you. With a good
conscience our only sure reward, with history the final

judge of our deeds, let us go forth to lead the land we love, asking His blessing and His help, but knowing that here on earth God's work must truly be our own."

Not far from the president's grave at Arlington Cemetery, is Robert Kennedy's grave, marked by a simple white cross on the hillside. Incised in another granite wall near this grave, set above a reflecting pool of streaming, rippling water, are these inspiring and moving words from Robert:

> "It is from numberless acts of courage and belief that human history is shaped. Each time a man stands up for an ideal or acts to improve the lot of others or strikes out against injustice, he sends forth a tiny ripple of hope, and crossing each other from a million different centers of energy and daring, those ripples build a current that can sweep down the mightiest walls of oppression and resistance."

Civilization on a Collision Course

I read these words over and over again and continue to be inspired today. I ask myself, why do the lives, actions, and words of the mystics, masters, and saints as well those of Lincoln, King, Gandhi, and the Kennedy's, resonate so deeply? What are they saying to me? As I reflected on this, I began to see that Western civilization and its freedoms are at risk today. Our way of living and behaving has put us at risk, and I believe civilization is heading in certain vital areas in a perilous, downward direction. The Titanic may have, so to speak, hit the iceberg.

I discuss the reasons why in more detail later, but it mainly has to do with our overly materialistic way of living, and excessive focus on our physical bodies and outer way of living and behaving. This has resulted in our neglecting the inner needs and growth of our minds and souls. We've become smart, rich, and powerful, but lack humility, morality, wisdom, and balance.

I feel our generation needs to come together immediately in a worldwide effort to avert this potential disaster. But what does that mean? What could bring us all together? We can pray and ask for guidance, but we must also take action. What actions do we need to take? What can any one individual do?

First of all, I believe the transformation must begin within each of us as we awaken to a deeper understanding of personal responsibility. We must do the work to change and purify ourselves and become who we are meant to be. The following quotation is from Gandhi in Trudy S. Settel's book The Book of Gandhi Wisdom:

> "The spiritual weapon of self-purification, intangible as it seems, is the most potent means of revolutionizing one's environment and loosening external shackles. It works subtly and invisibly; it is an intense process though it might often seem a weary and long-drawn process. It is the straightest way to liberation, the surest and quickest, and no effort can be too great for it..."

We must learn to lead a conscious, meaningful, and moral life. On a sign posted at the George Washington Carver National Monument may be found these words from Carver:

"No individual has any right to come into the world and go out of it without leaving behind him [or her] distinct and legitimate reasons for having passed through it."

We must create peace and harmony within ourselves so that we can bring peace and harmony to the world. As we change and purify ourselves, this can have a ripple effect and lead to positive change in others and the world. I share more on how I've worked to change and purify myself, as well as lead a more meaningful life as the story progresses.

It also seems many answers or solutions put forth to solve today's monumental problems fall along the left/right political divide; often with one side saying it has the correct answers and behaviors while accusing the other side of being in the wrong. I believe this approach, instead of leading to positive results and more unity and harmony, is leading to more problems and increased division.

It's as if we have a civil war happening in our thinking and behaving, particularly in the Western world. There is so much division, partisanship, and polarization. We fight or accuse each other while the "beast", our collective aberrant thinking, behaving, and way of living goes mostly unnoticed.

We desperately need new inspiring leaders, based on the leadership models of such giant historical figures as Abraham Lincoln, Gandhi, Martin Luther King, Jr., and Nelson Mandela, to name a few. We need leaders who have the ability to unify people and their collective actions behind a common purpose. We also need more unifying ideas, non-violent solutions, and peaceful actions and words that can begin to heal the divide.

I will share more as my story unfolds about how the confirmation and acceptance of the Kundalini theory of evolution is one idea that could be a catalyst for revolutionary positive change in ourselves and the world. It is an idea that could unite the people of the world behind a common purpose and effort.

All of the foreboding is also speaking to my need to take concrete action immediately. This is one of the reasons I have written this book. I suppose I've always wanted to sit safely on the sideline and not take the risk of sharing who I am and what I have come to know. It took me a long time to brush aside all the "what ifs" and negative thoughts and proceed with this book.

I felt God had been quietly imploring me for years to share my story, but I basically ignored these admonitions. I kept seeking outside counsel, rather than listening to the still quiet voice within. Eventually the constant promptings took on a more forceful urging. It began to seem like God was saying I had no choice in this matter if I wanted to be at peace with myself.

The interesting thing I have discovered is that when I take the plunge outside of my comfort zone; when I take the jump into the unknown and trust God; when I express my deepest essence and yearnings; the result is always favorable. The actions taken may not be easy and the path rough at times, but invariably, I find my life expands and becomes more fulfilling and meaningful.

For me this means telling my story, sharing the poetic verses, expressing my fears around the current negative direction of civilization, helping to advance this new Kundalini theory of evolution, and sharing this amazing new state of consciousness and the good news and great hope that this theory brings to humankind. I know the risks of following this path are great, both financial and personal, but I also know the risks of not doing so are even greater.

Returning to these leaders: Lincoln, Gandhi, the Kennedys, and King, all of them possessed unique qualities of thought, personality, character, and leadership. They are in a different class of human beings. Their words and actions penetrated to the deepest core of my being.

I also found it striking that each of these great leaders had been assassinated. I asked myself was there a reason for this, maybe a hidden purpose known only to God? Was the world not yet ready for their deep wisdom and inspiring leadership actions? By their tragic deaths, their powerful lives as well as words and actions, became etched more deeply into our memories. We will never forget them, and what they came to teach us. And at critical future times and places, new leaders possessing some of the same qualities, and inspired by the force of their character, actions, and teachings, will once again step forward to put the core of their principles and teachings into action to help improve civilization and move it in a more positive direction.

8 – Fall: Dark Night of The Soul

The years 1996 through 1998 were my "dark night of the soul" years. Frankly, they were years from hell. I was approaching 40 years of age. I remember reading somewhere that the number 40 generally symbolizes a period of testing, trial or probation. I would frustratingly muse to myself that maybe, like Jesus and others, it was my time to be exiled to the desert.

Ending of My Marriage

My marriage had been suffering for some years as personality differences not fully evident before our marriage, were slowly moving my wife and me apart. I think we both felt that the other was a fine person, but maybe we just weren't meant to be together on a day-to-day basis.

Despite marriage counseling and other attempts at reconciliation, eventually we separated and finally divorced in 1998. This broke my heart. I felt I had failed. My Catholic upbringing told me I had failed. On some level, I couldn't believe this was happening. My dream had always been to have four children and live a 1950's type of ideal life like the Cleavers in the old sitcom *Leave It to Beaver.*

My family was a great source of comfort and support during this challenging time. One of my favorite activities was going to visit my parents in Madison, Wisconsin for a Wisconsin Badger football game or for the Christmas or Easter holidays. I also loved visiting family for the sun and fun in Santa Barbara or Palm Desert, California.

In the end, my marriage was a blessed gift from God. Even with the subsequent divorce, I feel things happened exactly as they were supposed to. Despite some of the struggles and difficulties, the relationship allowed me to spend time with a truly wonderful, warm hearted, and beautiful person. I continue to this day to remain close with my ex-wife and her family. They are all fine people.

Outer World Collapsing

I loved the 1997 movie *Good Will Hunting*. There is a poignant scene in which Sean (Robin Williams), who is a therapist to a young genius named Will (Matt Damon), says to Will in relation to some of the hard things that he experienced in his growing up years: "It's not your fault." He keeps repeating this while holding him tightly: "It's not your fault." Will initially has a hard time accepting this and pushes Sean away. Eventually though he breaks down crying and begins to hug Sean.

This scene of forgiveness resonated deeply with me and brought some measure of relief during the constant challenging and soul-searching times associated with my divorce and subsequent financial and other struggles. Despite making my share of mistakes, I always felt deep down that these difficult things were happening for a deeper purpose and that only the passage of time and unfolding future events could make clear.

My divorce was definitely a wound that cut deep. However, it was not the only trouble spot at the time. It seemed like everything I was doing in business was starting to go wrong. I was a managing partner for several investments that were struggling financially, and my partners and I were responsible to a large group of investors. Most of these investors were friends, family, or friends of family.

At one point in early 1998, El Nina was deluging Northern California with torrential rains and I had some negative news to deliver on the HG golf club company investment. It seemed appropriate that I had just watched the Titanic ship sink in the 1997 movie by that name. I telephoned the investors one by one, explaining the bad news. Each time I spoke with one, I made the sign of the cross in my journal. It felt like I was being slowly crucified. I felt terrible about what was happening and deeply responsible.

Three different investments I was involved with had substantially depreciated in value and one of the companies eventually went bankrupt. I stood to lose almost all of my own invested money, which was a significant amount. Managing these investments took a great deal of time. In the beginning, we received some management payments, but as the years dragged on, these payments stopped. At the same time, my income had dropped off dramatically, partly due to the significant time I was spending managing these investments.

My financial struggles were intensifying and starting to snowball. I sold my house and I moved into an apartment. I started borrowing money to stay afloat. No matter what I did, I was unable to stop the deluge of negative financial events. I had a BBA, MBA, had been a CPA, investment banker, CFA, a Vice President of Corporate Finance, and now an entrepreneur. I started my career by working one summer on the base floor of a meatpacking company in the hog cut department, then as my business career progressed, I climbed to higher floors of achievement - floor 12, then 44, 103 (two weeks during summer of 1984), 27, 36, and 43. And then my financial fortunes began to reverse and I dropped down to floor 13 and then suddenly, I was in the elevator heading toward the basement. The life I had known and expected to live was fast crumbling. I had many credentials and accomplishments, but they were nothing against the downward force of this onrushing tsunami. **Just like civilizations, the higher you rise, the faster you fall when you begin tumbling in the wrong direction. This can happen when a person or civilization is not following their ordained path in life.** Eventually, many years later, my financial troubles would lead me into personal bankruptcy. This was not a place someone with my credentials and work history was supposed to end up.

In addition, partially due to the pressure we were experiencing in the HG investment, the relationship with my business partner had deteriorated. We eventually decided to go our separate ways.

Finally, to top it all off, my health was suffering as I contracted shingles, and I kept getting repeated bouts of tonsillitis and the flu.

A Dark Night

This was a very dark and difficult period in my life. My entire outer world was falling apart. I felt like a dying star that was flaming out and collapsing under its own weight. It seemed that everything I believed in, had accomplished, and that said I was worth something, was disappearing. I no longer could define myself by what I had achieved. I tried to be a good person and wondered why this was happening? When my ego-self began to disappear, I asked myself: Who am I really? Was I still worthy of love and respect? Did I still matter as a human being? What was I now being called to do in life? I realized that I had to find the answers to these questions.

Deep inside I knew I was on a spiritual journey of recovery and discovery. And these so-called failures, trials and tribulations, were taking me off my path and directing me to a new one, the road less traveled. This new path eventually provided me much greater meaning, security, peace, and happiness. Yet at the time, it didn't feel like this. I felt I was dying and undergoing a holocaust of the soul. I had been pushed off the cliff and didn't know if there was going to be a net there to catch me.

My poetic verse #3, "A Dark and Light Night" (see complete verse included as #2 in Section II - Poetic Verses), was written near the end of 1996, when I visited the Salton Sea area of southeastern California.

The Salton Sea is a fertile oasis in an otherwise stark and hostile desert. There are majestic mountains and beautiful groves of date palm trees nearby. It is not far from the affluent and glamorous Palm Springs area of Southern California. It is a solitary and mysterious place where I once wrote upon visiting, that I felt I was back at the beginning of time and of creation. I felt a deep spiritual connection to the area, and it reminded me of an ancient biblical place like Israel's famous Dead Sea. The barrenness of the nearby desert and the solitary feeling that it invoked captured some of the feelings I was experiencing during this "dark night of the soul" period.

At the time, I was terrified of facing the darkness that seemed to be enveloping me. I tried to ignore it and hoped it would go away. Other times I ran. I knew however, that I must eventually face it. Facing this darkness would be life transforming. I described this acceptance at the end of this verse when I wrote:

> "So now we meet. Our souls embrace. I feel the nothingness, emptiness. Your pain greets me, leaves its

mark. I now understand it moves on. I do not die; I die to old ways!

I accept you are not the enemy. You are the reverse side of the face of God. I now see that wholeness embraces both lightness and darkness. Out of both, lives are transformed. I mourn the past to let new life begin. This is how creation proceeds. I let go. I learn to accept."

Treasure Map

One incident during this time period really stood out in my mind. I was about to board a plane for a trip to Orange County from San Francisco. I was talking on the phone with my business partner who shared some further bad news. One of our investment projects (the investment in aquariums at Pier 39 and the Mall of America) was in trouble and could possibly go bankrupt. It eventually did. I was absolutely stunned. Only a year before, the investment was valued at a significant amount of money.

When I got to the Orange County airport, I noticed something was drawn on the top of my black briefcase. I could barely see it as it was in dark blue ink. I held my briefcase up to the light and realized that someone had drawn the picture of a treasure map. This made me laugh but also had meaning.

I felt like God was sending a message of hope through the treasure map, that despite all my current troubles, everything would be okay in the end.

I frequently heard my inner voice say, "All will be well: You are on a treasure hunt to find the true gold or divinity within yourself; and while you feel you are being brought to nothing, and despite the current troubles, your path will take you to a place of much happiness and peace." Despite occasional periods of deep doubt, I held this hope in my heart. It eventually proved to be true but reaching this place and state of mind was many years away, and there were more valleys that needed to be endured, and more mountains that needed to be climbed.

<u>Finding a Spiritual Center</u>

What I came to realize is that the way I was living my life kept me blinded from a greater prize that was ordained for us all. Focused primarily on outer things and events, I lacked an inner spiritual center. I equated security with material possessions and wealth, and I equated self-worth with the attainment of power, position, and prestige.

I had clutched tightly to my then reality and lifestyle, and God was helping me to let go so I could discover a new reality and way of living and being. Life itself was freeing me from the sensual prison I had unknowingly built so that I could discover a simpler and more harmonious way of living; one that could bring me deeper meaning, happiness, creative expression, and peace of mind, as well as begin to reveal the wonder of my own soul.

Unfortunately, but also necessarily, it took much pain and struggle for me to eventually relinquish control and birth a new awareness. In the end, the struggles were well worth it. I realized that in many ways, by being brought to nothing, there was nothing left for me to rely on other than God; and this turned into a gift beyond comprehension. But at this juncture, the big question on my mind was: Where am I heading? What an unexpected and life jolting answer I received!

9 – Kundalini Awakening!

Near the end of 1996, as the turmoil and turbulence in my life was picking up steam, a new and dramatic development occurred; one that was destined to change my life forever.

One day while meditating and praying, I began to feel a bubbling sensation in my lower spine. It felt and sounded like bubbles popping or Rice Krispies crackling. At the same time, this tremendous energy began to course through my body. It was as if a powerful new force had become active and my body's energy flow had instantaneously risen to 50,000 watts. The energy surged up my spine into my head. My body had become a live wire and my head was filled with streams of luminous light. Simultaneously, I felt an intense suction-like effect emanating from my reproductive area and extending up into my throat. It was like a powerful vacuum cleaner was sucking something upward into my head. At this same time, I experienced heat throughout my body and could feel the flow of a soothing liquid substance coursing through it. Whatever this substance was, it seemed to be acting like a coolant.

I knew something profound was happening but had no idea what it was. I also knew it was different from anything I had ever experienced. I did not know at the time that I was experiencing a Kundalini awakening. **It would be three years before light was shed on what had occurred.**

As the story progresses, I will share more about Kundalini and its impact on my life, as well what I believe are its profound implications for humanity. However, because it is so important to the rest of my story, I'm going to give some background on Kundalini and Gopi Krishna.

In the late 1960's, the Indian sage Gopi Krishna (1903-1984) advanced a new groundbreaking theory of human evolution. It has to do with our further evolution as human beings, as well as the continuing biological evolution of our brains. It posits that human evolution is planned and that individuals and the whole human race are evolving to a more expanded and profound state of consciousness. This is coming about through the actions of a biological mechanism and Intelligent Energy in the human body called Kundalini. The zenith of this expanded state of consciousness was termed "Cosmic Consciousness", by Dr. Richard Maurice Bucke in his 1901 landmark book, Cosmic Consciousness - A Study in the Evolution of the Human Mind. I share some of my own limited experiences of it in Chapter 22 "New Consciousness: My Soul and Mind Awakened".

Generally speaking, Kundalini is an ancient Eastern concept. It means "coiled energy", and it is sometimes referred to as a "serpent" because this power reservoir of energy is said to be coiled up like a snake at the base of the spine, waiting to be activated to a more powerful functioning. This more powerful functioning can be present from birth or it can be activated during one's life through an applied practice of spiritual, physical, and mental disciplines, or as a result of spontaneous occurrence. This can result in the opening of a new center in the brain which is fed by this more enhanced energy and eventually the birth of a new man or woman with an expanded consciousness. The functioning of the Kundalini mechanism and Intelligent Energy impacts the whole human body, and its most powerful activity involves the organs, nerves, brain, nervous as well as reproductive systems.

I use the terms "Intelligent Energy/Force", "Intelligent Life Force", "Inner Intelligence", interchangeably to denote a supreme or divine energy. Other names commonly used to describe this energy include Bioenergy, Life Force, Prana, Orgone, and Chi.

Traditionally the process of Kundalini in a human being is held to be responsible for various special states or manifestations of mind, including inspiration, talent, and creativity, paranormal or psychic experiences, genius, religious and mystical experience, higher states of consciousness, including the Cosmic Conscious mind, as well as different forms of mental illness.

The concept of Kundalini is fairly new to the Western world. I didn't practice yoga or Eastern meditation, nor did I know much about Eastern spiritual traditions at this time. As a result, my experience with this Intelligent Life Force and mechanism in my body was a very unexpected development. Because it had such a tremendous immediate impact on my body and mind, and eventually my whole life, I tried to learn everything I could about it. I particularly studied the teachings and writings of Gopi Krishna. Here's how I came to know him.

On Christmas Eve in 1999, I ventured into a bookstore in Boynton Beach, Florida. My inner voice guided me straight to <u>Living with Kundalini: The Autobiography of Gopi Krishna</u>. For years my inner voice often directed me to the next book I needed to read as I progressed on my life journey.

Gopi Krishna experienced profound and permanent changes in his consciousness through a full-blown Kundalini awakening. The book explained what this mechanism and Intelligent Force was, how it worked, what impact it had on a person's body, brain and mind, and also how it was responsible for enormous changes in a person's awareness and understanding of life.

While reading his autobiography, I realized he was offering a comprehensive explanation for many of the psychic and psychological experiences that had occurred in my life, as well as the recent physiological changes in my body. He was offering explanations that neither psychology, religion, physiology, medical science, or for that matter, any other branch of knowledge was able to provide.

Gopi Krishna was born in Kashmir, India and had his Kundalini awakening at the age of 34. He lingered for 12 years on the edge of life and death. Eventually the awakening stabilized and resulted in a massive transformation of his consciousness.

The following is an account* given by him of the state of Cosmic Consciousness that he experienced as a result of his Kundalini awakening:

> "In the middle of the meal... I had gradually passed off, without becoming aware of it, into a condition of exaltation and self-expansion...
>
> The marvelous aspect of the condition lay in the sudden realization that, although linked to the body and surroundings, I had expanded in an indescribable manner into a titanic personality, conscious from within of an immediate and direct contact with an intensely conscious universe, a wonderful inexpressible immanence all around me. My body, the

chair I was sitting on, the table in front of me, the room enclosed by walls, the lawn outside and the space beyond, including the earth and sky, appeared to be most amazingly mere phantoms in this real, interpenetrating and all-pervasive ocean of existence which, to explain the most incredible part of it as best I can, seemed to be simultaneously unbounded, stretching out immeasurably in all directions, and yet no bigger than an infinitely small point.

... The shoreless ocean of consciousness in which I was now immersed appeared infinitely large and infinitely small at the same time - large when considered in relation to the world picture floating in it, and small when considered in itself, measureless, without form or size, nothing and yet everything.

... I was intensely aware internally of a marvelous being so concentratedly and massively conscious as to outluster and outstature infinitely the cosmic image present before me, not only in point of extent and brightness, but in point of reality and substance as well.

... at the point of the deepest penetration, assumed such an awe-inspiring, almighty, all-knowing, blissful, and at the same time absolutely motionless, intangible, and formless character that the invisible line demarcating the material world and the boundless, all-conscious Reality ceased to exist, the two fusing into one; the mighty ocean sucked up by a drop, the enormous three-dimensional universe swallowed by a grain of sand, the entire creation, the knower and the known, the seer and the seen, reduced to an inexpressible sizeless void which no mind could conceive nor any language describe."

For a great number of years, he rigorously observed his own physical and psychological transformation as a result of his Kundalini process. He also studied extensively some of the historical religious, spiritual, wisdom, and occult literature of humankind. He came to the conclusion that this mechanism was known in ancient times in many parts of the world and is described in some of the ancient religious, spiritual, wisdom, and occult literature of the world.

By the time of his passing in 1984 he had written many books on Kundalini and his experiences. He also participated in several film and audio interviews. Most of these materials are available today. His books and interviews are a valuable resource. However. most of the world is still unaware of and does not yet comprehend the importance and implications of this incredible gift that Gopi Krishna has shared.

*From Living with Kundalini: The Autobiography of Gopi Krishna, by Gopi Krishna, © 1967, 1970 by James Hillman. Reprinted by arrangement with The Permissions Company, LLC, on behalf of Shambhala Publications, Inc., Boulder, Colorado, www.shambhala.com.

10 – Psychic Experiences/Powerful Dreams

Shortly after my Kundalini awakening, I began to experience many different types of psychic or paranormal experiences.

As one example, I would go to sleep at night and witness a dream, then sometime later the events of my dream would happen in my waking life. I discovered these are called precognitive dreams.

To illustrate this, one night I dreamt I was in a city in a certain location with a person whom I did not know. Some weeks later, I found myself with the person in this city in what seemed to be the exact situation. At the time of the dream, I didn't know I would be traveling to this city. I had forgotten about the dream, but when it later appeared in my mind, I actually gasped out loud.

Probably like many people, I was skeptical about this sort of thing. If it had happened just once, I might have dismissed it as a freak occurrence. But these precognitive dreams happened time and time again. I felt that conventional science or physics couldn't explain these experiences. They seemed to indicate the existence of a level of reality different from normal human experience as well as conventional time and space.

Before my Kundalini awakening, I also witnessed powerful dreams that announced the arousal of this potent force in my body. These included dreams of tornadoes, a holocaust, a hurricane-like waterspout, and a great wind sweeping the earth. I also experienced other significant dreams that suggested that revolutionary changes were going to occur in my life and spiritual outlook.

One of the most powerful dreams happened while I was visiting my mother-in-law in Ocean Ridge, Florida. It was just before Christmas in 1996. The dream began with seeing a great number of fish swimming near the surface of a large body of water. In the next scene it shifted to being with friends in an affluent section of San Francisco. Suddenly clouds rolled in and a great ball of fire engulfed us. A huge nuclear-like holocaust had hit the area. I held a friend and said goodbye thinking we were going to die. Somehow, we managed to survive, and I then found myself traveling in a car with my friend.

I was then taken prisoner by ancient Roman soldiers. In full view of my friend, three solders tortured me at the direction of a commander. They slashed me three times on my face with a small knife as I pleaded for them to stop. Then the commander took a larger knife and stabbed me in the middle of my chest (which is often said to be the location of our spiritual heart). The wound gushed blood. He then applied a square cotton pad and salve to my chest to soak up the blood and stop the bleeding. I was woozy from the loss of blood but knew I wasn't going to die. I awoke from the dream feeling shaken and had a deep knowing that this dream had enormous implications for my life.

That day I drove to Key West, Florida, the southernmost point in the Florida Keys, to spend a couple of days on vacation. Along the way, I stopped at a beach in the town of Marathon, which is in the Middle Keys. The calm ocean and the clear sky were a pure blue color and seemed to meld together. I could see forever. It looked like a scene out of paradise. This was in sharp contrast to the dark and frightening dream I had just had the night before. Somehow, I intuitively knew these two contrasting events were the Alpha and Omega points of my spiritual journey. I was just at the beginning and had a long way to go to experience these sunny skies and blue waters.

The next morning while in deep meditation in my hotel room I felt jolted by a sudden force and simultaneously I saw a vision that I was in a birth canal and was being born amidst much shaking and turbulence. After the vision ended, I got up and walked over to nearby St. Paul's Church and prayed. A variety of symbols and pictures in the church (the life of Jesus, the Apostles, the cross, the stain glass windows, etc.) spoke to me in a new and powerful way. Everything felt connected and had meaning. My inner voice said I was being spiritually reborn.

When I reflected on this dream and my experiences in Key West, I felt they were pointing to a profound spiritual awakening, as well as a spiritual mission for my life.

In my dream interpretation work, the appearance of fish normally symbolizes that something psychologically or spiritually important is clamoring to be brought to the surface of awareness. In this case the great number of fish seemed to point to this Kundalini awakening and spiritual rebirth. I felt that the arrival of the holocaust with the clouds and ball of fire were also pointing to the revolutionary impact that Kundalini would have on me as well as indicating a spiritual mission for my life. Finally, I felt the fish, clouds, and fire were all portending an awakening, which would result in a deep change in my consciousness, spiritual bearing, and the way I lived my life.

In a larger context, I also felt that the collection of these symbols was pointing to a revolutionary change that would soon occur in our present-day society, and that such change would be driven by the workings of a Higher Intelligence.

At Odds with Western Society

I acquired a deeper spiritual outlook and began to feel at odds with the way Western society functioned and what I perceived as its overly materialistic, complex, fast paced, entertainment and leisure focused, technologically driven, ego dominated, and excessively glamorous way of life. The Roman era soldiers brought up associations with ancient Rome and its imperial governing and military structure. I thought of the material excesses and moral depravities present in Roman society just before its fall as a civilization. From this, I saw parallels between the experiences of ancient Rome and the negative things happening in our society today.

The three slashes to my face and the plunge of the large knife into my chest represented different sufferings I would endure in my life; in a sense they pointed collectively to a crucifixion-like experience. These experiences would forever change my countenance or the face that I showed to the world.

I thought the slashes might represent my approaching painful divorce, the future difficult financial challenges I would face, the intense purification ordeals I would be called to endure, as well as my later feelings of disassociation from the existing work and societal structure. The final plunge of the knife into my spiritual heart, the pouring out of blood, and woozy feeling portended a greater surrender to God, and the subsequent birth of a deeper spiritual awareness. It also showed me the initial disorienting effects of experiencing this new awareness. In verse #21, "Surrender to Love", I wrote:

> "The final plunge, the assimilating of all; a deepening
> into the earth; a seasoning of all that is, and makes all

that is to be, possible; a moistening of the soil for the resurrection of new life.

The old life dies and the new emerges. The two become one. Now we are no longer separated. The veil of tears is torn asunder, the glory of God is revealed...

There can be no ascension without the surrender, the deepening when all is made one..."

Salvation

I had a deep knowing that the sufferings I would endure, which were foreshadowed by the sufferings in the dream, would help to purify me, both spiritually and emotionally, and lead to a greater surrender to God. I also knew that these things would eventually lead to my "Salvation". I felt that my ego or surface persona would be diminished, and a larger Self and awareness would slowly rise. This larger Self or higher awareness would emerge due to the effects of the continuing Kundalini process which accelerated my spiritual and personal development work and change in consciousness.

In the dream, this Salvation was represented by the symbol of the square shaped cotton pad and salve applied to the gushing blood from my wound. In my dream interpretations and in real life, cotton represented something comfortable, healing, and soothing; and a square shape represented a symbol of wholeness in life. Collectively these symbols were pointing to the fact that I would survive these ordeals, a profound healing would occur, I would be deeply transformed, and a more balanced, conscious, and loving personality would slowly emerge.

This dream along with my birth visionary experience in Key West, pointed to a spiritual rebirth that I would experience in my life. Verse #4 entitled, "Ground Zero - At the Salton Sea", was composed on the last day of the year in 1996, a few weeks after I saw the dream. In the last stanza, I wrote:

> "I can expand God's creation through expressing the divinity within me. I must fully experience the dark night of the soul to complete the painful rebirth. I need to be reborn again from within."

A Huge Energy Force

Another dream that had a significant impact found me standing on a sandy beach on a gorgeous, sunny day. I was mesmerized as I watched large and exotic fish swimming near the surface. Suddenly I saw a powerful waterspout coming toward the shore. I ran and hid behind the pillar of a large pier where I remained safe.

After I awoke from this dream, an inner urge led me to draw a picture of the waterspout in my journal. As I drew, I found the picture metamorphosing into a smiling face. This dream and subsequent drawing actually brought feelings of relief as I felt they were telling me that this energetic force was benign.

I know this all may be difficult to comprehend for someone who has not done dream analysis work or experienced a Kundalini awakening. However, after the premonitory dreams of a holocaust, tornadoes, a hurricane-like waterspout, a huge wind sweeping the earth and then the actual arousal of this potent energy force in my body, I was feeling afraid and vulnerable. I knew something significant had happened within me. It had a tremendous physical impact on my body, as well as resulted in substantial psychological and spiritual effects within my mind and heart. I didn't know what it was or what it meant. Frankly, I feared that it might eventually kill or drive me insane. I also knew it was something completely out of my control.

As I analyzed the symbols of the dream, the fish and the waterspout, it spoke to me again of the Kundalini Life Force rising up from within. The pillar supporting the pier under which I sought safety connoted to me that my inner connection to God was the foundation that would keep me on safe ground during all of the subsequent upheaval. The sunny day in the dream also said to me that I would survive the impact of this awakening and that there would be a happy ending.

<u>Something Enormous is on the Way</u>

Another significant dream occurred a couple of years later in November of 1999. It was a short but powerful dream, that had a lasting impact. It occurred one month before I found Gopi Krishna's autobiography. I knew these two events were connected in a meaningful way. In this dream, I was once again observing a large number of fish in the water. I suddenly looked over to one side, and could see underneath the clear water, a huge whale's tail protruding out of a nearby underwater cave. The whale's tail was gargantuan.

I woke up from this dream breathless and had a deep intuitive knowing that this dream had a monumental meaning for my life. I could see just a small portion of the tail and it seemed to represent the idea that I was being given a glimpse of something titanic that was going to enter my life. It immediately struck me that the dream was pointing to an enormous change in my future awareness and being, way beyond any change that had been engendered to date by all the psychological and spiritual healing work I had been doing. As time passed and additional events occurred, I came to understand that this dream was foreshadowing these great changes in my life due to the effects of this Kundalini process.

As far as the meaning of the cave in the dream, the thought that came to mind was that from the "darkness" or "dark cave" of my current consciousness and the "dark experiences" of my life, a new and more expanded awareness was being birthed through the development of a "sixth" sense. It made sense that what I had perceived through my five physical senses in my normal level of awareness, could now be likened to being shut up in a dark cave.

I also recently learned that there was a more literal and physical interpretation of the cave symbol i.e., that this new powerful energy that had been stirred to activity had found its way into the fourth ventricle of my brain. A friend in medicine shared that this fourth ventricle is sometimes referred to as "the cave".

When I was very young, I saw in a dream that the world, in the form of a large globe, was sitting on top of my head. The dream evoked a feeling of carrying a gigantic weight that had the potential to crush me. I remember being terrified after this dream and then going to my dad for comfort.

It's interesting that this same crushing feeling that the dream evoked would continue to arise occasionally during my college years, as well as in my late 30s and early 40s. I associate that feeling with the immense pressure I would later experience from my challenging life, as well the activity of the Kundalini process and the emergence of an expanded awareness. It was as if my body and mind were intuiting years in advance, the weight and strain of all the subsequent experiences of this new and powerful consciousness. I believe the globe also represented the fact that the concepts of Kundalini and higher consciousness were bringing something of great value to the world.

Finally, I also made a connection from this dream to the Walt Disney Feature Animation movie, *Fantasia 2000*. I found this movie fascinating and I watched it repeatedly.

In particular, there is a scene in the movie where a large number of whales are suddenly able to fly, evidently due to a supernova that occurred in the sky. Amidst flashes of lightning, the whales emerged from the water and eventually soar into space and swim toward a large white star. The musical score "Pines of Rome" accompanied the breathtaking scenery and this entire scene evoked feelings of wondrous awe as well as great peace and serenity.

My interpretation of this segment was that the lightning flashes were representative of the flow of luminous energy in the body, as well as the inner illumination and sudden seeing of a glorious new spiritual reality that can occur as a result of a Kundalini awakening; the large white star represented both the inner guiding light of God as well as our ultimate divine destination; the whales represented the possibility of a titanic shift in consciousness after the successful consummation of a Kundalini awakening; and the soaring into space and peace and serenity, as well as the beautiful music and scenery, all combined, are a small sample of what a person experiences in the highest levels of expanded consciousness. Verses #44 and #47, "Cosmic Consciousness" and "Happy Days" respectively, portray different expressions of this expanded consciousness. They are shown as verses #10 and #11 at the end of Section II - Poetic Verses.

I realize my dreams and interpretations may only be meaningful to me. I am careful with such interpretations and use them, along with other practices, to glean insights about myself, and my life's direction. I try and gauge how deeply a particular dream experience and interpretation resonates, and also whether it fits into a particular pattern with other insights that I am having. In the end, it is only the future unfolding of events that will confirm whether a particular insight and interpretation was true and beneficial for me.

In sum, all of the dreams left a deep impression and seemed to be pointing to meaningful changes and important events that would subsequently occur. I found them inspiring, informative and a little bit scary, as I felt they were painting a vision of my future. One thing I deeply knew was that my life was going to change in a dramatic way.

And it has, as the further unfolding of my story will evidence. It is my experience that we do sometimes receive hints, messages, and visions about our future through our dreams. Furthermore, I believe that the events in my life and changes in my awareness that have unfolded have confirmed the messages delivered in my dreams.

Visionary and Auditory Experiences

In addition to significant dreams, I also began to have many different types of visionary and auditory psychic experiences following my Kundalini awakening.

One of the first experiences occurred in early 1997 as I was flying from Orange County to San Francisco. As I was writing in my journal, I happened to look out the plane's window when I noticed a bright light. At first, I thought the light was attached to the airplane's wing but soon it became clear that it wasn't. I saw a rainbow near the light and followed the light for about ten minutes. Suddenly I heard an inner voice say, "It is gone" and it disappeared. I looked down and saw that the journal I was writing in said "Angels" on the front cover. Near the page I was writing on was a picture of an angel with many bright lights in the night sky. The page had a quotation on it, the ending of which said:

> "Like Angel's visits, short and bright; Mortality's too weak to bear them long."

This experience caught my attention. It was not only intriguing but amusing. I knew immediately something out of the normal had happened. It felt like some psychic force was trying to draw my attention to an experience, which was not part of my ordinary daily life.

Another time I was hiking in Hawaii on the island of Maui. It was a beautiful sunny day. I came out into a clearing and suddenly saw the face of Mother Mary on a nearby cliff. Her face filled the entire side of the large cliff. This was not something I was necessarily seeing outside of myself, but rather seemed like an inner image projected from me outward onto the cliff. I viewed it with great reverence. I knew it was a real experience. Mother Mary has always represented to me purity and mercy and the birthing of the Divine.

On another occasion, I saw a vision where an image of Jesus, enclosed in a bright flame, suddenly became engraved in my heart. Again, it was so real and inspiring. At the time, I had the feeling some significant spiritual transformation had occurred within myself.

Another day in September of 1997 I was hiking in the beautiful redwoods in Muir Woods, just north of San Francisco. Suddenly, I saw an image in my interior of Mother Teresa. This was shortly after she died. She looked like a middle-aged woman in the vision and had a grave and solemn appearance.

With my inner hearing (i.e., this was not an actual voice coming from outside of me), I heard her say:

> "The system needs to change; that she had worked in saving individuals, but that more individuals could be saved if we changed our human systems."

This image of Mother Teresa seems to be permanently engraved inside of me as it is still present in my interior today.

Another day I was hiking at Jack London Park near Sonoma, California. I was looking at the burned down remains of author Jack London's famous house, "The Wolf House." As I was walking around the house, I heard a voice from within say:

> "Repair my house."

It also said:

> "Finish my dream."

I didn't know exactly what these references meant at the time, but I definitely felt they had something to do with my spiritual calling in life. I also knew future events would provide more clarity and they have.

I believe they were speaking of my calling to do my small part to help bring awareness of this new Kundalini theory of evolution to people; to express the view that the human race is experiencing profound problems and its future is at risk for many reasons including its ignorance of the requirements of the aforementioned Law of Evolution, as well as its violations of still unknown or misunderstood spiritual laws that govern it. These transgressions are placing the health of the evolving human brain at risk. This in turn is forcing "Intelligent" Nature to respond in unpleasant ways to clear away the blockages and set us back on the right path of healthy evolution.

These references were to also call attention to the good news that there is a "dream" destination awaiting the human race at the next stage of its evolution. This, however, requires that we repair and reverse some of our current unhealthy ways of living, thinking, and behaving.

Another time at the park while visiting Jack London's grave, an internal voice said:

"The soul is eternal."

I have now come to realize that this saying is really true; that as our brains evolve and our consciousness grows, and a new level of creation appears, we begin to realize that the permanent part of us, our awareness, never dies. Yes, the body will pass away, but our souls will live on. This is one of the great gifts that Heaven has provided as an incentive for us to live a moral and ethical, service oriented, love filled, and mentally, physically, and spiritually healthy life. This is necessary so that our bodies, brains, and minds can continue to evolve in a healthy manner, and we may reach this

next state of consciousness where the truth of our eternal nature becomes evident.

On yet another day, I would look up at the sky and it appeared as a sheer, otherworldly blue color. Occasionally, I would see square rainbows on clear days. These square rainbows seemed to occur at important junctures in my life. Often meaningful life events would soon transpire thereafter. I also feel they were announcements of some sort. My inner voice said, "Open your eyes, a new reality is starting to appear."

One day in 1998 I was standing just beyond my backyard looking at my house when I saw a wave or current of energy ripple through it. It was as if my house had completely lost its solidness and was composed of vibrating light waves.

Sometimes I found myself experiencing visions of future scenes or objects, and other times found myself wandering in past historical times. Here are two examples of these experiences and what they meant to me:

1) One day I was in Richmond, VA for a weekend visit and I took a walk to the nearby James River. I suddenly found myself back in Civil War time, shortly after the destruction of the city of Richmond. I could deeply feel the sorrow and anguish of the people. It weighed very heavily on me. I felt an immediate connection to then President Abraham Lincoln and thought about how his leadership had helped heal the nation at that critical time of this country's history. I also thought of how today we have another civil war playing out in the United States between the deeply polarized Right and Left factions in our country. I would

even call it a deep split in our human psyche. It also occurred to me how I believe proving Kundalini will one day lead to events that will help heal this split and division.

2) Finally, about ten years ago, I had a vision where I was suddenly able to see the surface of the moon from what seemed like a position slightly above it. Like the Mother Teresa experience, this image remains permanently etched in the interior of my mind. Many years later as I watched the 2019 movie *Apollo 11*, which was about the first landing and walk on the moon in 1969 by U.S. astronauts Neil Armstrong and Buzz Aldrin, I gasped again as I saw a picture of the same surface of the moon in the movie. In the last chapter of this book, I talk about the momentous historical nature of the Apollo 11 moon landing, and how I believe the verification and acceptance of Kundalini theory will be a similar momentous event in human history! Frankly, I think it will have even greater ramifications because its implications are directly relevant and meaningful to the present-day life of every person.

Again, I saw these visionary and auditory experiences as something that were not happening outside of me, but it was as if there had occurred a change in my inner organs of seeing and hearing. I felt I was seeing and hearing things at a more subtle level of existence. I could only attribute these experiences to the effects on my body and mind from this Kundalini awakening and the enhanced Intelligent Energy flow.

All of these psychic or paranormal experiences have had a lasting and meaningful impact on me. I knew the experiences were real, maybe even more real than what I had thought of as "so called" normal experiences. I knew I was sane, yet I also knew if I told some people about these experiences, I ran the risk that they would think something was wrong with me.

I trusted my deep inner knowing which said that I was treading in an area that was real, but not yet understood by the mainstream of humanity or medical or physical science. Eventually I learned that many people have experiences of this type.

It soon occurred to me that these experiences were primarily for my benefit. They told me there was something beyond the reality of ordinary time and space; that there was more to the world and this universe than what I had always assumed, also that greater potentialities existed in my body, brain, and mind. However, I also realized that sharing these experiences with people sometimes seemed to have a distancing effect. Oftentimes they seemed to make people feel uncomfortable. This is understandable given that these are not normal everyday experiences, and if a person does not experience this layer of reality, it is hard for them to relate. I learned I had to be selective with whom I shared this information.

Proceed with Caution

A wise friend and long-time supporter, Gene Kieffer, said something I consider critically important. He mentioned that when a person has a powerful Kundalini awakening, it will often be accompanied by psychic and paranormal experiences, the development of other new gifts and talents, as well as, in rare cases, profound permanent changes in consciousness. He cautioned, however, that due to a host of reasons including an unhealthy lifestyle or living environment, defective heredity, poor mental and physical health practices, deficiencies in a person's physical body system and organs, various physical injuries, etc., the Kundalini energy may become tainted or impure. As a result, a person is susceptible to becoming unbalanced in their thought and behavior. They may also suffer from physical and mental disturbances or mental illness. In other words, Kundalini, which I mentioned previously is sometimes referred to as a "serpent", because this powerful reservoir of energy is coiled up like a snake at the base of the spine, and may, when activated, "sting" a person. This can occur when their body and mind are not in proper condition to facilitate a healthy awakening.

I listened closely because Gene has been advancing the work of Gopi Krishna and studying Kundalini and accelerated energy changes in the human body for almost 50 years. Gene edited and published some of Gopi Krishna's books and Mr. Krishna in turn referred to Gene as his spiritual son. Over the years, Gene became a mentor to me and has provided a great deal of help and support. Another person who I must signal out for their general support on my journey is long-time friend Susan Grace, who has been involved with Kundalini work since the late 1980s. Both Gene and Susan were from the Midwestern U.S., like myself, and I consider them to be kind, thoughtful, and grounded individuals. I learned that it was healthy for me to be around these types of people as my awakening progressed.

Gene also said that there are things we can do to assist the ongoing Kundalini process to proceed in a healthy fashion. He said to eat nourishing food, exercise, get lots of sleep, practice spiritual disciplines, keep stress to a minimum as much as possible, and, in general, live life moderately and in balance, and in accordance with the basic ideals stressed in all healthy forms of religion and spirituality.

He said it was important to stay grounded in my thinking and actions and emphasized to not get too sidetracked by a fascination with psychic or paranormal experiences. He mentioned that preoccupation with such experiences could even act as a hindrance on the spiritual path as it could lead to ego inflation and create an unhealthy imbalance in one's personality and actions.

He said to stay away from watching too much violence on TV and movies, as well as in the news media, as that could taint the enhanced energy that was now flowing in my system.

Finally, Gene mentioned mysteriously that if I continued to progress on the path, there was even a much greater prize possible beyond psychic and paranormal experiences; and that was to be able to experience the power, beauty, and wonder of the liberated human soul and a new consciousness. He added that Kundalini can lead to the development of higher levels of creativity, a more powerful mind, glorious levels of inner happiness, love, bliss, peace and serenity as well as expanded states of consciousness. At the time, I wasn't exactly sure what he meant by all this, but I did have a deep knowing that there was something significant to what he was saying.

I also understood that it was absolutely critical for me to live in a healthy manner and stay grounded and measured in my thinking and actions. In verse #19, "A Message of Hope" (see complete verse included as #5 in Section II - Poetic Verses*)*, I wrote:

> "There is magic in the air, the stars will forever be lit
> up. The angels will be dancing, as I soar into eternity
> with my feet on the ground."

11 – Titanic and Resurrection

I also began around this time to experience a phenomenon where happenings and events in my life, which were seemingly unrelated in a normal cause and effect way, appeared to be meaningfully connected. I developed a new ability where I could piece together a series of seemingly unrelated events and discern a meaning associated with the events. This meaning encompassed, yet transcended, the meaning associated with each individual event. In turn the meaning uncovered, the knowledge gained, the guidance discerned, as well as the subsequent actions taken, all related to events happening in the physical plane of existence but the ultimate meaning from the collection of events seemed to belong to a different universe or new level of creation. This new universe is definitely more mental, holistic, interconnected and permanent than the normal physical reality we all experience.

I later learned these occurrences are called synchronicities and that actually many people have experiences of this type. These synchronicities seemed to be guiding me in my life, and also confirming that I was heading in the right direction. Oftentimes they highlighted that there was a particularly important meaning to something I had experienced.

Titanic Movie

Let me give an example of a series of synchronicities that extended over a period of many years that had to do with the 1997 movie *Titanic*. I first saw the movie in the theater on February 4, 1998. This was about a year after my powerful Kundalini awakening. I have seen the movie countless times since then both in theaters and on television.

119

The first time I saw the movie it held me absolutely spellbound. It also jolted me to the core of my being. I felt this incredible stillness and awe. I wasn't sure why I was having such a reaction. I remember being so impacted by one series of scenes that I could barely catch my breath. This was the part of the movie where the ship was beginning to sink. Water from the ocean was rushing in and beginning to fill the decks. People were panic stricken, running frenetically in every direction, some were swimming in the water, while various objects were sliding down the deck. Meanwhile the priest on board was saying prayers, reading from the Bible, and ministering to the passengers.

The priest quoted from the Book of Revelation **"Then I saw a new heaven and a new earth, for the first heaven and the first earth had passed away, and there was no longer any sea... There will be no more death...for the old order of things has passed away."** The ship's band also continued to play. One story is that the last song the band played before the ship sank was **"Nearer, My God, to Thee."** As the ship sank, I felt like I was physically and emotionally going down with the ship.

After watching the movie, I returned home and began reading a book entitled Jesus, A Revolutionary Biography by John Dominic Crossan. One of the first pages I read that night was about St. Paul and how he believed the end of the world had begun. It also said that St. Paul believed in the general resurrection at the end of time and that Jesus' resurrection was the start of the general resurrection. Crossan goes on to say on page 164 about St. Paul's views on the resurrection:

"... That is why he [St. Paul] can argue in either direction: no Jesus resurrection, no general resurrection; or, no general resurrection, no Jesus resurrection. They stand or fall together, and Paul presumes that only the mercy of God delays the final consummation, the ending of what has already started. The *Titanic* has, as it were, already hit the iceberg, and Paul's mission is to waken the cabins as far and as wide as possible, while God gives time."

Interestingly enough, one of the first psychic visionary experiences I had after my Kundalini awakening in 1997 was of St. Paul's shipwreck on the island of Malta. St. Paul was a Jewish citizen who persecuted Christians before converting to Christianity and becoming one of its most important missionaries. This conversion happened after St. Paul, in a flash of light, saw and heard the risen Jesus on the road to Damascus. **In fact, I believe St. Paul's seeing of Jesus was actually a Kundalini visionary experience, an experience of Cosmic Consciousness.**

St. Paul subsequently became an Apostle to the Gentiles, or the non-Jewish people, and some historians believe that his efforts helped Christianity become a world religion.

At the time of the shipwreck, St. Paul was reportedly being transported to Rome to face Roman rulers related to charges that Jewish authorities had leveled against him for inciting riots and showing disrespect toward the Jewish Temple. This shipwreck is described in Acts 27 in the New Testament of the Bible. One afternoon while I was driving along the cliffs and rocky coves on Highway 1 in Bodega Bay, which is about an hour and a half north of San Francisco, I suddenly had an inner vision of this shipwreck. Again, it was so realistic, like I was back in this time period observing this shipwreck. It had a very powerful impact on me. I soon thereafter found myself reading many books on St. Paul including all the passages attributed to him in the New Testament.

As I reflected on the meaning of the passage in Crossan's book, I related it to my vision of St. Paul's shipwreck and to the scene in the film where the Titanic was sinking, and the priest was quoting from Revelation. There were also other events in my life having to do with the themes of "fall and rise" and "death and resurrection". This whole series of unrelated events yielded a profound meaning. Let me explain.

"Resurrection"

I became interested in the concept of the "Resurrection" around 1990. I was uncomfortable growing up in the Catholic religion and what seemed to me to be its overemphasis on the Crucifixion of Jesus. The sight of Jesus nailed up on a cross in the front of the church was a depressing sight to view and reflect upon in terms of a central theme in the religion. I felt it was high time to have a scene of the Resurrection in the front of the church. I knew the Resurrection was also important in Catholic theology, but it seemed to be emphasized far less in my view.

I was fascinated by John Sanford's book "The Kingdom Within - The Inner Meaning of Jesus' Sayings", which I read in the early 1990's. I remember thinking at the time that I knew I was going to go through a symbolic crucifixion in my own life, but that my life eventually would be about a resurrection.

At the end of the book, Sanford mentioned how many readers had written asking him to write a book specifically on the inner meaning of the Resurrection. Sanford said at the time that he didn't intend to write this book, but that it was a book that one day should be written. I had an intuition that maybe one day I was meant to write such a book. In a sense that is what this book represents. However, my story is not written from a religious point of view, but rather from a universal healing and growth in consciousness standpoint.

Messages of the Book

I don't feel the end of the world is near (as St. Paul believed; therefore, his perceived need to awaken people to believe in Jesus Christ and be saved before it was too late), but I do feel humanity, like the sinking Titanic, is heading downward in many critical areas. I believe people need to be powerfully awakened, as quickly as possible, to the enormous divine and biological potential that exists within us all. I feel we have the possibility, to one degree or another, to be resurrected to a new way of thinking and living, and also to a more advanced state of awareness and peaceful and harmonious way of being.

This is one of the messages I am delivering in this book. I'm also bringing the message that a biological process with a normal rhythm and progression, exists as a divine-like potential in the human body. It is responsible for not only individual spiritual transformation or "resurrection", but also in a more general sense, is the engine behind human evolution and humanity's collective ascent to a higher and more glorious dimension of consciousness and the eventual birth of a New World of unimaginable peace, joy, adventure, harmony and love.

The amazing gifts to an individual that can arise from such a resurrection or transformation have not yet begun to be understood. Rather, I feel they are shrouded in misunderstanding and misconception. Being grounded in a biological process that

involves the human brain and body will put this human and spiritual potential on a solid footing. This will allow both science and individuals to eventually empirically prove this biological potential that exists in the human frame. This is why I'm so excited about understanding the potential of Kundalini.

Like St. Paul's efforts which helped Christianity become a world religion, I feel the concept of Kundalini will unite the main world religions one day, because it will show each founder or prophet had the same transformative power of Kundalini awake in them and spoke their wise and prophetic teachings from a higher state of consciousness. Just as importantly, it will also bring together science and religion/spirituality behind the empirically provable idea that the whole human race is predestined to reach a divine like state of consciousness through the biological workings of Kundalini.

I watched the movie *Titanic* numerous times over the years, including the night I returned home from a trip to Nashville, Tennessee, where I had been for a weekend business seminar. It was the night of Sunday, September 19, 2004. I remember that date because it was my sixth anniversary of having joined a 12-step program. I should have been in a buoyant frame of mind having just finished an uplifting workshop. However, on the flight back to Washington, D.C., I remember having a sense of foreboding, like something wasn't right. I was afraid the plane was going to crash.

I was glad to make it home safely that night and then was excited to discover *Titanic* was on television. My inner voice whispered that something important was going to occur during the story and to pay attention. This sort of thing happened frequently and over time, I learned to heed such promptings.

There was a scene toward the end of the movie where one of the main characters, Rose, a Titanic survivor, and now a much older lady (Gloria Stuart), was on board the ship that salvaged the wreck of the Titanic. Earlier in the story, a much younger Rose (Kate Winslet), was engaged to be married to a wealthy man she abhorred. She felt she would be confined, unhappy, and dreaded her future. She threatened to commit suicide by jumping off the stern of the Titanic. She was saved at the last moment by a young free spirit named Jack, who was from Wisconsin (Leonardo DiCaprio). She fell in love with Jack who inspired her to live a more free and expansive life. Unfortunately, Jack died during the sinking of the ship. But Rose survived, escaped her planned marriage, and lived a full and happy life. In a sense, she experienced a symbolic resurrection in her life.

Near the end of the story on a beautiful starlit night, the older Rose walked alone to the stern of the salvage ship. As she reached it, she opened her hands to reveal a large blue diamond necklace, known as the "Heart of the Ocean". She had mistakenly received the diamond when her despised fiancée gave her his coat before the Titanic sank. He had forgotten the precious diamond was in one of the pockets.

As she stood at the stern all these years later, she dropped the diamond necklace into the ocean. For some reason while watching this scene I found myself focused intently on Rose's ankles and feet as she walked toward the stern of the ship. I remember thinking at the time that the older Rose looked so much like my mother.

That night I awoke with a startle as the phone rang around midnight. I dreaded receiving calls at that time. I felt it was going to be bad news. My sister said that my mother was in the hospital, had some worrisome physical symptoms, including swollen ankles and feet, and might have a serious health problem.

We soon discovered she had pancreatic cancer and she would eventually die six weeks later, appropriately in my mind, on **"All Saints Day", November 1, 2004.** I was devastated. I remembered the scene in the movie where I fixated on Rose's ankles and feet as she walked to the stern of the ship, thinking she looked like my mother. I believe I had a premonition of my mother's impending troubles.

I then remembered another scene in the movie that grabbed my attention. It was the ending where the young Rose is reunited with her lover Jack at the top of the Grand Staircase of the *resurrected* Titanic. They are kissing and are surrounded and cheered by those who had died on the ship that night. I felt this scene was speaking of the theme of resurrection.

I wrote the following in my journal the next day after hearing about my mother's illness:

> "Last night the movie *Titanic* was on television. At the end, the older lady walked down the back of the salvage ship and it showed her feet and ankles. She then dropped the big diamond [Heart of the Ocean] into the ocean. Last night, my mom's ankles and feet were swollen. This was a synchronistic connection. In the movie, they show the ship decayed at the bottom of the ocean. They then show the ship resurrected and all the

people who died on the ship resurrected too. I believe these scenes were showing me:

- The connection to my mom and her feet and ankles.
- The Heart of the Ocean diamond going into the ocean was to show me my mom would be returning to the ocean of eternal being.
- The sunken ship represents our submerged [surrendered] egos/intellects.
- The resurrected people on the ship were showing me that we are all healed in the end; that everything is resurrected and brought back to fullness.
- **They also represent the potential for us to transcend our egos/intellects [while alive] and be resurrected to a higher dimension of consciousness where eternal life swims into view."**

Two days after my mother died, in verse #39 entitled, "Mom's Death and Resurrection", I wrote the following:

"You have given a gift to us with your life: your kindness, goodness, and motherly love. Your life has deep meaning, an eternal presence. You let everyone know that death is not the end, but a new beginning. That death is not an extinguishing, but a transformation. That death marks a holy transition from the human to the eternal. This is the gift that you leave with the living, that you leave with the world. May God bless you and hold you. We all love you deeply and will love you forever."

In another event pregnant with meaning, my mother just happens to be buried in *Resurrection Cemetery* in Madison, Wisconsin.

In the end, these series of synchronicities related to the concept of death and resurrection were deeply comforting. Although it was sad in the movie to receive a premonition of my mother's impending troubles, I also felt that God was communicating to me a deeper, more hopeful and lasting message. And this was about the reality of the Resurrection and the impermanency of death; and that one day I would see my mother again. I end verse #39, "Mom's Death and Resurrection", with the following:

> "So have the [Wisconsin] Badger game on, the little wieners cooking, the egg rolls in the oven, the card table and snacks ready, the Christmas tree lit, Grandma and Grandpa singing *Silent Night*, family, relatives, and friends nearby.
>
> For soon we will be saying hello again, for eternity."

When my mother died, six siblings, myself and my father were present at her bedside. At the moment of her passing, I saw in my interior my dad's father taking her by the arm. She was crying and telling my grandfather she didn't want to leave us kids. My grandfather was kind and soothing with her, yet by his gentle actions, let her know it was time.

Today I know she is at peace. Through inner messages, she conveys the following to me:

> "There is nothing we have to worry about."

I can look inside myself and see my mother. I see her in two main places:

In one place she is smiling and standing in bright sunshine in a bubbling fountain of joy, against the background of the beautiful local beach. The beach is near the country club where we were members, not far from the house we grew up in. There are large sparkling waves gently rolling ashore on the beach. There is a gorgeous view of the State Capitol building in the far distance, framed against a clear, pure blue sky.

In the other place she is sitting on a bench with her mother at my paternal Grandparents' cottage on the Wapsipinnicon River in Iowa. Their faces are calm and serene, and full of kindness and deep humility. They are always comforting and say:

"Finish your life. All is well."

These are gifts God has left permanently etched in my interior to remind me of my mother's eternal presence and our eternal nature.

One of my favorite days to celebrate every year is Mother's Day. In 2010, it fell on May 9th.

On this day, I wrote in my journal:

"To solve the mystery of life and death, we must wake ourselves up from being asleep. We must shake ourselves out of the bewitchment and entrancement we all live in. It is possible to be resurrected while living."

That night I turned on the television and what movie was on? Why of course, *Titanic*!

Sone people may feel these events and experiences are just a series of coincidences and might draw other conclusions. From a rational point of view, I can understand this. However, from my experience, synchronicities have always spoken to me in a very personal way and leave little doubt that there is a deeper meaning to these occurrences; a meaning that transcends rational understanding.

What was also striking to me was that these synchronicities seemed to occur almost every day in my life for a significant period of time. I was able to constantly make new connections from them as well as draw fresh meanings. I continue to experience such synchronicities today.

In truth, I knew the universe was speaking to me in a new way, from another dimension of consciousness, from a deeper level of connection, and I was struggling to comprehend. This was because I hadn't yet fully developed this new sense, and didn't fully understand what the symbols meant, what the alphabet was, and how this language of our souls, conveyed meaning in this new reality.

In poetic verse #41, entitled "Everlasting Life", I wrote:

> "We are immortal, everlasting specks of glory. Our eyes gleam, our hearts dance, we touch the ether of everlasting life. We see a new paradise, dedicated to the proposition that all men and women are created equal. We see a new universe. It is the universe within, spacious, glorious, full of everlasting life.

We are purified, pristine, sparkling jewels of everlasting worth. A new paradigm is born, a new creation, a new language of God, spoken from the heart, filled with glory, love's new language. The universe speaks to us a glorious new truth. A new model of life awaits us.

We are not alone. We are here to speak a new language, sing a new verse in life. Our souls are great, everlasting, immortal; specks of light from the eternal splendor, conceived in love, dedicated to the proposition that love is all that endures."

12 - Vision, Body, Mind Changes and Intense Purification

This potent energy that was flowing in my system also had an effect on my vision. At night I noticed large luminous clouds surrounding streetlights, stoplights, and other lights. Some lights sparkled brilliantly like diamonds. Other lights, such as Christmas tree lights and other strings of decorative lights, had a richness and intensity that I found mesmerizing. These were new experiences as I had never seen lights in this way.

Years ago, I loved to visit the Rocks and Minerals exhibit on the second floor at the Smithsonian National Museum of Natural History in Washington, D.C. Some of the rocks and minerals on display emitted this otherworldly metallic glow that I found fascinating.

Nearby was the Hope Diamond exhibit. The Hope Diamond is a massive blue diamond that was purportedly found in India a long time ago. It is said that the Heart of the Ocean diamond mentioned previously in the *Titanic* movie was modeled after the Hope Diamond.

The exhibit explained that over a billion years ago, the Hope Diamond was formed miles beneath the earth under conditions of extreme temperature and pressure. I thought this was a great metaphor for the spiritual journey; where under conditions of extreme pressure and heat. (i.e., life's sufferings and purificatory trials), human beings can metamorphose into more pure and joyful spiritual beings.

Another change I noticed was in my field of vision. It was as if the lens of my mind has been widened and the frame upon which I view the world expanded. I would liken it to the view you have when you are perched upon a high cliff overlooking the ocean and you gaze out toward the distant horizon. You can see further and in a more expanded way from this elevated position.

At first, this new condition made it more difficult to drive a car. This was especially true when traveling on busy city freeways. The fast-moving cars and intense traffic, combined with my expanded field of vision, required that I maintain a greater distance from the cars in front of me. Not surprisingly, this increased need for spacing seemed to infuriate other drivers. This was particularly the case when I drove on the Capital Beltway in the fast paced, power driven area of Washington, D.C., where speed and aggressiveness and getting somewhere fast seem to be the law of the land. Eventually I got used to this new condition, but it took a fair amount of time.

Intense Purification Activity

One of the functions that this more powerful energy was now performing in my body was one of intense purification. The energy appeared to be working in an accelerated fashion to clear away psychic and physiological impurities present in my mind and body.

As embodied human beings, we carry certain levels of psychic and physiological impurities in our minds and bodies. I would imagine that the level of these impurities is affected by, among other things, our heredity, the environment we live in, the way we think and behave, as well as more generally, how we are living our lives. It seemed likely that I had accumulated a significant number of impurities or toxins over the years due to some unhealthy living practices. These included some mild substance and other forms of addictive and dysfunctional behavior patterns.

For as long as I can remember, I have had a deep spiritual thirst. Unfortunately, I found growing up in the Catholic religion that the teachings and practices of the Church were inadequate in fully assuaging this thirst.

Although I have a deep and healthy respect for the Catholic Church and all the major religions in general, I felt I needed other different and healthier forms of spiritual sustenance.

Just as human beings have imperfections and frailties, so do the institutional structures of our major religions, as they were created and run by fallible human beings. I found that although I benefited from some of the teachings and practices of the Catholic Church, I found that others were unhealthy for me. I found certain of the Church's teachings and practices to be deeply shame and guilt inducing, and these included the doctrine of original sin, the condition or state of sin into which each human being is born, as well as what I considered to be their negative view toward sex and the human body.

I was also not comfortable with the level of control exercised by the authorities of the church, the mediation of God by the priests as opposed to encouraging direct experience with God, and finally the absence of women as pastors.

As a result, my mind to some degree became tainted and my spiritual development somewhat stunted. Gopi Krishna wrote the following in a letter in 1976 to a weekly news magazine in India:

> "Healthy spiritual food is as necessary for the proper development of the human mind as healthy nutriment is necessary for the body to function and live."

I believe as our minds and brains continue to grow, we will continue to need new and healthier forms of religious and spiritual sustenance. As I will talk more about later, I found the 12-step recovery programs provided me new and very healthy spiritual food.

One of my shortcomings was that when I was in pain or felt depressed or lonely, rather than deal with the uncomfortable feelings and pain, and uncover the underlying causes, I sought easier avenues of escape. These made me feel better temporarily, but it didn't take long before they eventually created greater problems in my life.

Some of my favorite escapes included drinking too much alcohol, smoking cigarettes when I drank, gambling, excessively trading stocks, drinking too much coffee and soda, occasionally overeating, and most recently overusing my cell phone and computer. I also found that I was driven by an intense need for success and acclaim, and this was also a form of dysfunction.

I didn't realize that some of these unhealthy tendencies were probably in my genetic makeup, courtesy of my ancestors. They too must have felt similar longings and pain, and also sought avenues of escape. Over time, my mind and body became filled with greater amounts of toxins and impurities from these unhealthy behaviors.

In addition, I had stored up large amounts of fear, anger, and grief, which I did not know how to discharge in a healthy way. These feelings had come about partially as a result of living a life that was not in harmony with who I was, what I needed to do to stay healthy, or what God intended.

Clearing Toxins and Impurities from my Body and Mind

By this time my inner guidance was an immense source of comfort and wisdom. I began to realize that answers to my problems resided within myself. Slowly, I became proficient at tapping into this guidance. This inner guidance showed me how to use the force of this potent energy flow to feel and purge the large amounts of frozen anger, rage, and fear, as well as other toxins and impurities that were stored inside of me.

I was intuitively guided to do what I call a "blowing technique". I press my upper teeth against the outside of my lower lip, creating a pressurized, suction-like effect. I then take a deep breath and forcefully expel the breath through my mostly closed mouth.

I found this practice helped to release the anger, rage, fear, toxins, and trauma stored in my physical cells, nerves, and tissues throughout my body. The clearing work started predominantly in my lower abdomen and progressively moved up my body over the years toward my head and neck area.

I was surprised by how clearly stored up emotions like rage, fear, and grief, as well as other mind toxins and impurities, had an actual physical presence in the body.

Renowned psychologist Sigmund Freud once said:

> "Unexpressed emotions will never die. They are buried alive and will come forth later in uglier ways."

Throughout the years my head has been occasionally battered by this enhanced flow of energy. Sometimes I experienced some minor concussion-like symptoms. At other times, it seemed like a forest fire was burning in my head, or a volcano was erupting. I sometimes heard a crunching sound in my head. The strangest experience was one time it felt like an Alka-Seltzer tablet had been dropped into my head and was fizzing. To say the least, dealing with the ramifications of this energy flow over the years has often been challenging at times, but I would also say always manageable.

Effects of Violence and Noise

Another change connected with this enhanced energy flow is that my body has a negative physical reaction when I'm exposed to any kind of violence. This was especially true for a period of time after the initial awakening. For example, if I saw violence on television or in the movies, these images and energy in my head area felt immediately toxic. I also felt increased pressure in my head.

I have also become more sensitive to noise, especially harsh, loud, or strident noises. My body and mind shudder and feel as if they are being attacked when these types of noises occur.

Reduced Body Temperature/Increased Metabolism

When I experience an illness, say the flu or a cold, this energy activity becomes more pronounced. The healing processes in my body begin to work more expeditiously to expel the toxins and pathogens that have arisen from the illness. I use this blowing technique to help expedite the clearing of the toxins and pathogens. I also have noticed when I become sick, I no longer get an elevated body temperature.

Finally, the metabolic activity in my body (pulse, respiration, flow of blood, etc.) as well as some of my bodily functions, including my digestion and elimination processes, have sped up. Once again, these changes were more pronounced in the initial years after the awakening. My body often felt like a chemical laboratory working at a feverish pace for extended periods of time. Over time my body has gradually adjusted to the Kundalini process. As a result, some of the changes in my metabolic and bodily functions have become far less pronounced. And my ability to feel the energy coursing through my nerves and body has also diminished significantly.

Emotional and Physical Illness

Since this energy awakened, I have gone through brief periods where I experienced an increase in anxiety and depression. In the early years after the awakening, I felt like I may have exhibited some mild symptoms of bipolar disorder. I say this because I had some significant mood swings, as well as occasionally experienced confused thinking, and in one or two instances, some mild paranoia.

These experiences made it clear to me that there is likely a connection between some forms of mental illness and the Kundalini process, when the process is not functioning in a healthy way.

I also experienced more frequent occurrences of physical illness (shingles, flu and colds, repeated bouts of tonsillitis, sore throats, sinus infections, etc.), as my body struggled to adjust to the flow of this more powerful energy current and the accompanying physical changes.

Other Body/Mind Effects

A few days after the initial awakening, my body began to feel like it had been scalded or burned up from within by this new powerful energy. It took me awhile to recover from this. For the next few years,

I intermittently had difficulty concentrating and I lost my stamina. At times, it was hard to do normal work and complete everyday tasks. I often tired easily and had trouble reading for any lengthy period of time. Occasionally I was forgetful. Sometimes my body, particularly my legs, felt very heavy and other times my hands mildly shook, and I felt stabs of pain throughout my body. I also found I had to cut back on my practice of meditation as it would put too much strain on my body and mind. I learned to listen to my body and inner guidance and curtail any practices that seemed to be affecting me in a negative way.

For some time after the initial awakening, whenever I meditated or focused my attention inward, I would feel the energy flowing even more strongly throughout my body and into my brain. Soon thereafter, I often found that new ideas and original thoughts would flow into my mind. This increased energy flow had apparently stimulated my brain and thinking process in some way. The next day I would feel like I had been run over by a truck. One other thing I noticed was that after I shed tears, new thoughts and original ideas would also often flow into my mind. Somehow the crying seemed to have had a cleansing effect on my mind, in a sense acting like a windshield wiper, and this enhanced my thinking and brain activity.

I slowly came to realize that the Kundalini energy was working tirelessly in my body day and night. It seemed to be making changes down to its deepest cellular levels, with the apparent goal ultimately being to fashion a new expanded consciousness. This is a massive change to be undergoing in one's bodily system which is so finely balanced. It definitely had some negative effects on me both physically and mentally and took a significant period of adjustment.

At times, my condition got so bad that I felt like I was dying. I railed against God for what was happening and felt abandoned. Also, not surprisingly, it was very difficult to explain to family, friends, doctors, and even my spiritual director, what I was going through. People just couldn't understand and most times, couldn't even take in what I was saying. Oftentimes, I felt like I had been set adrift at sea and was completely alone.

The good news is that as the years have passed, these negative effects on my body and mind have diminished significantly and are almost non-existent today.

For twenty-five years I've lived with this accelerated energy operating in my body. I have meticulously observed myself over this long period of time. There is not a doubt in my mind that the changes that have occurred in my hearing and seeing, in certain physical bodily processes, in some of my physical, emotional, and mental states, in my overall level of consciousness (experiences of psychic and paranormal phenomena and the eventual onset of a new sublime consciousness - more on this in Chapter 22), as well as the development of some new talents (sudden ability to compose poetic verses and think more holistically); are all connected to the actions of Kundalini and this new enhanced energy in my body.

I am by no means unique. Many others around the world report similar experiences of dealing with a more potent flow of energy, new biological symptoms in their body, as well as changes in their consciousness. Unfortunately, people oftentimes have no frame of reference or access to trustworthy information sources to help them understand and cope with the changes that are occurring. They also may not know where to turn for reliable help or treatment. I know I have struggled greatly to understand these experiences and cope with the changes that have occurred in me both physically and psychologically.

I am sharing my story at this time because I want to help others who may be struggling with some of the same symptoms or experiences. I want to let them know they are not alone and not crazy. I also wanted to share some of what I have done to help deal with the changes and heal and transform myself.

Finally, I wanted to provide hope, as this process has led to incredibly amazing positive changes in myself and my life. The benefits of these changes have far transcended the pain of the challenges and struggles.

13 – Institutions' Shortcomings and Rise and Fall of Civilizations

I'd like to divert from my story for a moment and share some comments related to some of the developmental challenges I encountered. Having the benefit of looking back with hindsight, I realize some of my early life challenges and struggles were exacerbated by growing up in institutional structures that were unable to optimally facilitate the healthy development of my mind, body, and spirit. These institutions included: religion, family, school, work, and the medical and mental health systems.

This is not to place blame on anyone, particularly my parents. I feel most fortunate to have grown up the way I did and am deeply grateful to my parents. This was also reflective of where society and its institutional structures were at that time. Lastly, some of my struggles and troubles were the result of my own choices, personal failings, and normal human shortcomings.

Nonetheless, I feel this is an important point to make. I believe my physical, spiritual, emotional, and mental developmental needs were not met in a healthy manner by the way these prevailing institutional structures functioned.

These institutional deficiencies included: an outdated religious model, which left me with a deep coat of shame and guilt, as well as feelings of inadequacy and a discomfort with my body and sex; an excessively patriarchal family system, where open communication and thoughtful listening were lacking, and expressing one's full-range of human feelings was not modeled or encouraged; an educational system, in which intellectual and rational thinking dominated, unique expression was often not encouraged, and experiential learning was minimal. This hampered my ability to learn organically, and to adequately develop and use my deep sense of intuition; an overly hierarchical business and work system, which lacked equality and mutual interaction, where I often felt pressure to conform and not free to use my intuitive abilities; and finally, an illness model of physical and mental health, which failed to teach me how to live a healthy life to prevent illness, and instead, focused on what was wrong with me, often treating symptoms, and not underlying causes.

Another way the prevailing societal paradigm had a negative effect on my development was its excessive emphasis on achieving material gain and power, in an overly fast paced, perfectionistic dominated, and excessively competitive and less cooperative system. In such an environment, one person's gain often came at the expense of another person's loss.

As a result, my personal development became unbalanced and somewhat stunted. I developed some unhealthy psychological symptoms and behavioral characteristics including mild anxiety, depression, and fear; a lack of self-confidence and self-esteem; as well as mild addictive behaviors. These addictive behaviors in turn created additional psychological and behavioral problems. I believed the fault was fully mine. I felt flawed as a human being. Never did it dawn on me that the way these institutional systems functioned may have contributed to some of my troubles.

It is also true that finding fault and blaming self or others is never helpful. The journey is about growing in self-awareness, about becoming more conscious. I believe this is my life's destiny and that events were meant to happen exactly the way they did, that I was meant to overcome these challenges to later be able to share with people what went wrong, what I was able to learn, and how I was able to change, heal, and become a more balanced and better human being.

Nonetheless, during moments of deep frustration, I angrily felt the real culprits for some of my troubles were going unnoticed, i.e., the unhealthy way society and some of its institutional structures were functioning at this point in time, and that they too were in need of healing, change, and recovery.

Etched into the wall of the Jefferson Memorial is the following quote from Thomas Jefferson:

> "I am not an advocate for frequent changes in laws or constitutions. But laws and institutions must go hand in hand with the progress of the human mind. As that becomes more developed, more enlightened, as new discoveries are made, new truths discovered and manners of opinions change, with the change of circumstances, institutions must advance also to keep pace with the times."

Over time I came to believe that the healthy growth of many of our institutions and systems hadn't kept pace with the ongoing needs of our evolving human minds and brains. For many people, some of these institutions and systems had begun to function more like prisons, rather than healthy support systems. I feel this has contributed to increasing physical and mental health issues for a greater number of people. Understanding this issue better will help us to look at the increasing rates of mental illness as not just an individual problem, but also as pointing to deficiencies in the composition of our systems and institutional structures and ways of living. These deficiencies in turn are creating mental health problems on a large-scale level. The culture has become the patient.

I think this is why there is a great deal of dissatisfaction today with our political, medical, education, business, legal, law enforcement, prison, and religious institutions, to name a few.

For the most part, I don't believe this is the fault of any one individual or group of individuals. No matter who is currently in charge of the various institutions or systems, the leader will eventually fall into disfavor. This is because of the need for far reaching structural changes in our institutions and systems. This is particularly true, for example, of the United States political system where today, the partisan division between the Republican and Democratic parties has become extreme. There is also much public unhappiness with the various branches of government as well as Washington, D.C., in general. The unfortunate result of this is that the opposing sides are often tearing each other apart, which hurts everyone, while the real problem of needed peaceful, well thought out systemic and institutional change, does not receive the bipartisan attention it needs. Again, what I see as needed is a growth in conscious understanding.

I am again reminded of something I mentioned earlier where Mother Teresa appeared to me in a vision and said:

> "The system needs to change. I worked in saving individuals, but more individuals could be saved if we changed our human systems."

In Chapters 25 and 28, "New Hope, Intelligent Evolution, and Children", and "Dinosaurs and a New Positive Asteroid" respectively, I further discuss some of the issues surrounding needed institutional and systemic change. I also address some important qualities that I believe will be needed in future institutional structures and leaders. In Chapter 25, I emphasize the important role I believe the 12-step programs of recovery and their main principles, steps/traditions/concepts of service, and organizing forms, will one day play in informing the makeup of future institutional structures.

Rise and Fall of Civilizations

As I reflected on some of my initial family, school, marital, work, and financial successes in life (I called this my period of "rise"), and then some of my subsequent marital, work, spiritual recovery, Kundalini, and financial struggles (I called this my period of "fall"), I noticed something interesting. My life was following in a microcosmic way the historical precedent of the macrocosmic rise and then eventual fall of successful civilizations, families, and individuals.

Gopi Krishna often talked about the rise and fall of civilizations in his writings. He wrote in the book <u>Kundalini: Empowering Human Evolution</u>:

> "Civilizations rose and fell, families prospered and then went to ruin; individuals rose to power and then mingled with dust, because of the ignorance of the cosmic law ruling the life of man."

He discussed how too much luxury and excessive wealth and leisure can act like a poison on the brain and eventually stunt an individual's, a family's, and civilization's development. He wrote that something like 14 to 16 civilizations have risen and fallen in the last 3,000 to 4,000 years for many of these reasons - including civilizations such as the Egyptians, Indo-Aryans, Chinese, Persians, Greeks, and Romans.

He also said similarly in his book <u>The Way to Self-Knowledge</u>:

"... Every culture of the past, which favored luxury to enjoy the fruit of labor, hard and fast, Nature took good care to destroy.... This did not happen once or twice, but hundreds of times...."

Around 1970, Gopi Krishna wrote the following in <u>The Biological Basis of Religion and Genius:</u>

"The ancient civilizations, cultures, and empires, after attaining a certain level of ascendancy, fell victims to decadence as the lives of the people did not conform to those standards - political, moral, and social - that were demanded by the mental stature attained as the fruit of evolution at the time they touched the zenith of their career. The sudden or gradual eclipse of the ascendant nations of the last few centuries was also brought about by the same causes. The degenerative tendencies that have now set in among almost the whole of mankind as the consequence of modern defective ways of life, incommensurate with the present evolutionary stature of the race, owe their origin to the same factors. No amenities provided by science, no spate of inventions, no psychological cures, and no amount of education can arrest the growth of this canker unless the evolutionary demands are fulfilled. The danger to the race from a continued neglect of these conditions in the present state of technological development is too plain to escape the notice of even the least observant. But the reason why effective measures are not employed to end it, is that the present habits of thought have become too ingrained to be changed, a last symptom of decay."

As we become more materially advanced and mentally evolved, Gopi Krishna believed it was necessary that individuals and societies develop a simpler, natural, slower paced, less materialistic, cooperative, spiritual, and ethical way of life. This is necessary to stay in harmony with the requirements of evolutionary laws.

Gopi Krishna saw that despite all the incredible progress in the world in the last few centuries, our civilization is poised for a fall, like all the civilizations that have fallen previously. He felt this is due to humankind's ignorance of the evolutionary requirements of the human brain - placing the needs of the body ahead of the needs of our minds, brains and souls.

I asked myself questions such as, "What is this cosmic law (i.e., Law of Evolution)? And what are these spiritual laws or laws of consciousness, ruling the life of humankind that Gopi Krishna wrote about? Was I, after an initial period of rise, falling into ruin like past civilizations, families, and individuals? Was I having an inordinate amount of life problems because I was practicing unhealthy ways of living and ignorant of and in violation of the demands of these laws? Was I unknowingly off the path of healthy evolution ordained by the needs of our evolving brains that Gopi Krishna wrote about? Was I off 'the path', off 'the way' that Buddha, Lao-Tzu, Christ and other spiritual luminaries taught and spoke about? If so, what did I need to do to find the path of healing and rise again?" I will share more about these things in the next chapter.

Warning Signs and Problems of Civilization

In the 1970s and early 1980s, Gopi Krishna often asked why at such times of great material prosperity and technological advancement in the world, and the West in particular, have such serious warning signs, threats and problems developed? I believe these dangers are even more pronounced today. These include widespread feelings of discontent and foreboding in people, large amounts of suffering, and institutions that are functioning less effectively. Some of these serious warnings, threats, or problems include:

• Significant loss of faith in governments, the media, and journalism.
• Serious financial issues including high levels of government, institutional, personal, and school debt.
• Political and corporate business leadership scandals.
• Ongoing problems with our medical system.
• Sexual scandals and problems within some of our places of worship.
• More division and partisanship in our political process.
• More dissatisfaction among young people with our current business, religious, political, and other institutional structures.
• High divorce rates and family structure breakdowns.
• Sexual harassment/sexual assault issues, particularly related to women.
• Continued threat of terrorism and a nuclear, biological, or chemical holocaust.
• Continued global unrest and threat of World War III.

- Civil and racial unrest in many countries, including the United States.
- The prevalence of workplace, school, places of worship, and other mass shootings.
- High rates of mental disorders and brain diseases.
- High attention deficit disorders and autism rates in our children.
- High rates of addictions - drugs, alcohol, food, gambling, sex, etc.
- High rates of cancer and other illnesses.
- COVID-19 pandemic threat.
- Despite the connective power of the worldwide Internet and social media such as Facebook, YouTube, and Twitter, in some ways people feel more estranged from each other.
- Environmental problems such as pollution, water shortages, and possible threat of global warming.
- Overpopulation problems.
- Catastrophic hurricanes, tornadoes, floods, tsunamis, volcanic eruptions, forest fires, and oil spills.
- Immigration and border safety issues for some countries.
- Vast disproportions in the distribution of wealth.
- Many people seem to have lost touch with what is the purpose and meaning of their life.

I could go on! What's going on in the modern world? I realize the world has always had serious problems. I also realize we have made great progress in many areas of life such as medical advances, better health care, improvements in communications, technology, and transportation, increased standards of living, longer life expectancies, to name a few. I will talk more about the positive developments in Chapter 25. Yet the question remains: why do these severe problems persist, and why are some of the problems getting worse? Why are we still at risk of a nuclear, chemical, or biological holocaust? Why during these times of relative economic prosperity, certainly by historical standards, does it seem like society could be breaking apart at the seams?

Moving Against Nature and our Brains

I feel some of the serious problems we are facing in society today are related to our excessive striving for material success, power, and prestige. This in turn has helped fuel the development of a society that is overly fast paced, technologically and materially/consumeristic driven, self-seeking, as well as excessively glamorous, entertainment focused, and leisure seeking. Our ethical and moral behavior, although in some ways it has advanced significantly, in other ways it has not kept pace with our material progress. We've become unbalanced as a people and society. This has had negative consequences for our healthy evolution.

I further believe our current environment, especially given our advanced stage of material and mental development, is anathema to the harmonious working of the inner evolutionary processes, and to the further healthy evolution of our body and brains. In poetic verse #41, entitled "Everlasting Life" I wrote in 2005:

> "Nature calls urgently to humankind. Reform your misguided ways, life is not meant to be lived so brazenly, so harshly, so quickly, with so much self-seeking. Rather life is to be lived simply, graciously, unselfishly, in harmony with nature. Humankind has to live a lifestyle befitting of its glorious stature, its' eternal nature."

In Time Books publication <u>100 Events That Changed the World</u>, event #73, "A Restless Planet Is Decoded", began with the following:

> "For countless centuries, humans struggled to survive in a world whose workings they did not understand. Erupting volcanoes, destructive earthquakes and overwhelming tsunamis killed hundreds of thousands in cataclysmic events that seemed spontaneous and unrelated. It was a German meteorologist, Alfred Wegener, who first proposed that these seemingly disparate natural disasters were all threads of a single tapestry. His audacious proposal: the continents we stand upon are in constant, slow motion across the surface of the planet."

In a similar vein, I believe the increased troubles we are experiencing today, have a common or root cause and reflect civilization's divergence from nature's intended path. We are in violation of evolutionary laws, and this has resulted in a malfunctioning evolutionary mechanism. The Intelligence behind this universe is trying though the vehicle of nature and this Law of Evolution, to bring the whole human race to a happier and more profound way of living and being. Many of us remain unaware of this truth and are putting up obstructions to this glorious, ordained future by the unhealthy ways we are currently living our lives. This, in turn, is forcing Nature to respond in unpleasant ways to clear away the blockages and set us back on the path of healthy evolution. As a result, there is this feeling of uneasiness in many people today. People are nervous with the direction society is headed. Evolution has become distorted in a negative direction. The evolving human brain is suffering.

Gopi Krishna also wrote the following in the aforementioned 1976 letter to a weekly news magazine in India:

"A wrong social or political environment can stunt or distort the evolutionary growth of the adult brain as surely as a wrong or adverse family environment can disrupt the harmonious growth of a child."

He talked about how nature is screaming warning after warning that it is time for humanity to change. He felt nature is trying desperately to protect our evolving brains from ruin, as has happened time after time to civilizations in the past. Gopi Krishna wrote the following in 1978 in the book The Real Nature of Mystical Experience, which I believe is just as applicable, if not more so, to today's world situation:

"Since it is hard to accept that an All-Knowing Intelligence controls the destiny of humankind, we are prone to ascribe the present overhanging threat of a global war and the precarious condition of the world to a chance combination of certain factors or to a rapid advance in technology and entertain the hope that the crisis would pass off with a proper handling of the situation by the political leadership of humankind. But we never ascribe it to the imbalance created by disproportionate growth of the human personality … The reason for the menacing condition of the present world lies in the imminent danger of disproportionate evolution, which if not corrected, would be fatal for the race."

When speaking of the disproportionate growth of the human personality, Gopi Krishna often alluded to humanity as having an overly developed intellect at the expense of an underdeveloped sense of wisdom, an insufficient moral sense, and an undisciplined and self-seeking will.

Oftentimes I think about those idyllic days I spent as a child with my extended family at my grandparent's cottage on the Wapsipinnicon River, and the simpler, communal, slower, austere and natural way of living. In many ways they were more representative of the type of environment and lifestyle needed to facilitate our further healthy growth as human beings.

My experiences and those of untold countless others serve as a warning that unwholesome, unbalanced, overly sensual, fast paced, self-seeking, and materialistic lifestyles are hurting the healthy evolution of our brains, ourselves, and our societies.

14 – Rise Again:
Healing Practices and Insights

Eventually the pain became so great, I realized I needed to change the way I was living my life. I felt a strong impulse within to move toward wholeness and health. I was yearning for a greater personal and spiritual expression. This program of change and growth began in my early 20s when I saw a psychologist for anxiety. It sped up around 1990 (age 33), when I began to feel mildly depressed with work and life. Finally, it became a full-time job after my Kundalini awakening in 1997 (age 40). This program of working on myself continues unabated to this day.

I thought it might be beneficial to share some of the more important practices and activities which have helped in my personal development, spiritual growth and in dealing with the Kundalini process. Each of us has a unique path to follow but, hopefully, some of these ideas may be of assistance to you.

One of the first things I did was to open the door to my inner being. I wanted to learn more about myself. I wondered: who am I? Who is this knower inside of me? What is the purpose of my life? What do I need to do before I die? What do I like to do? What makes me happy? What makes me sad? What gives me trouble? What are my strengths and weaknesses? I reflected upon these questions and searched within for answers. I also talked with others and participated in various types of self-improvement workshops.

I completed different kinds of self-assessment questionnaires. I found answers to such questions as: what are my skills, values, and interests?

What does my job history say about me? I also took personality tests including the Myers-Briggs. All these things helped me to appreciate my uniqueness as a person.

I also found that prayer, meditation and keeping a journal, helped me to stay centered and peaceful. Going to movies and walking in nature brought nourishment to my soul, exercise to my body, and rest to my brain. My mind seemed to be working at a feverish pitch due to the effects of the accelerated energy on my brain. It often felt like it was on overload and close to short circuiting. Escaping to see a film and sitting in the darkness or walking in peaceful nature acted like a soothing balm. Often new insights and inspirations about my life and work would flash into my awareness. Eating large amounts of popcorn and peanut M&M's during movies also brought much pleasure, but probably not much healthy nourishment.

Slowly I learned to express what I was thinking and feeling in my journal. This in turn helped me to better express what I was thinking and feeling to people in my everyday life. This deepened my connection with people and also allowed me to release tensions, thoughts, and emotions locked up inside of me. This releasing in turn helped me to become calmer and less reactive.

I used to think of emotions as something negative, to be swept under the rug. For example, I thought expressing anger was wrong, and that it was weak to express fear or cry. I hadn't realized tears are the water of life that help to soften the ground of our being. If I expressed joy and happiness, I thought that was being full of myself and besides, there were others who were suffering. The cultural message ingrained in me from an early age was, I must maintain a strong, stoic male disposition. However, as I healed emotionally and grew spiritually, my emotions slowly became my teachers. I once read that emotions are energy in motion (e-motion).

Fear taught me that I had more to learn and new ways to grow. I realized I was afraid of many things and this was keeping me from living a full life. I was afraid of change, even good change. It felt easier to stay in the same routine. Sometimes I felt afraid of the future. Surprisingly, I was terrified of success. At some point, I had gotten used to the struggle and leaving it behind frightened me. I was afraid of discovering who I really was and how powerful I could be. I was afraid of love and closeness with others. I was afraid of getting too close to a Higher Power as he or she might make me do things I didn't want to do. I was also afraid of getting close to myself. To change took hard work. I had to learn to feel comfortable feeling uncomfortable. And slowly I realized the greatest danger to achieving peace and happiness was from trying to stay the same.

Sadness and grief taught me that I was hurting or missing something or someone. I missed the people I loved who were now gone or some part of me that had been lost along the way. These vestiges of losses from my past were still clinging to me, like barnacles, not having been fully felt, mourned, and let go of. I needed to become aware of and feel my sadness and grieve the past. Sometimes I was afraid to do this because it meant saying goodbye to old relationships, memories, places, or ways of living. It felt like the faster I grew, the more intensely I needed to grieve. This was necessary however, to allow new activities, people, and new life to enter more quickly. I found growing in awareness and learning to shift my perception was never easy.

I gradually learned to feel fear, loss, and pain in my life. I realized to develop more courage, I had to ask God for guidance and strength, then face my fears and take action. Intuitively I learned various exercises, which helped. To practice, I would imagine a situation which brought anxiety (such as visiting the doctor or making a business presentation to a formal board of directors). I would hold my breath and feel the fear for a period of time. I would do this repeatedly, just like in physical exercise repetitions.

To feel and work through the pain of loss, I would once again hold my breath and imagine a painful loss, such as the time an old girlfriend left me, my failure to date more when I was younger because of fear of rejection or recalling the memory of a dear loved one who had passed on.

Finally, if I was irritated with someone and felt I might explode in anger, I would sit, breathe slowly, not react, and absorb the powerful energy for a period of time. Simultaneously I would ask God to transmute this energy into inner peace, strength, courage and love. This helped to avoid venting it outwards onto others in improper and harmful ways and served to strengthen me.

I also recognized that legitimate pain and suffering helped to lessen my ego and bring me closer to God and others. I realized that when I had previously sought refuge in addictions, or other avoidance behavior, this did not allow the natural cleansing process to provide healing as well as to diminish my ego.

After doing more difficult forms of exercises, I nurtured myself by doing some consoling inner imagery work. For example, I would imagine myself sitting on a beautiful sandy beach with the Sun of God warming and nourishing me.

I also did supportive inner dialogue writing in my journal that included conversing with different parts of myself - the angry Scott, the happy Scott, the fearful Scott, the ego filled Scott, etc. I dialogued with myself at different ages (for example 7, 12, 21, 35, etc.). I freely expressed whatever was on my mind; never censoring, always encouraging and accepting myself. This was very powerful work in terms of learning how to listen to and support myself.

As part of my routine, I also imagined situations where I felt the emotions of love and compassion, and I sat with these feelings for a period of time. I envisioned God as humility, love, beauty, radiance, and sublimity and absorbed this vision and the feelings they evoked into my being.

I found over time all of these practices made me stronger, and I felt calmer, lighter, and happier. They helped to strengthen my spiritual muscles, much like a person does physical exercises to strengthen physical muscles. Very gradually, much of the fear, pain, and loss I was experiencing was transformed into feelings of greater inner peace, joy, freedom, and love.

My anger taught me that something was not right either within myself or in my outer life circumstances. Sometimes I brought into my conscious awareness anger that was festering inside of me, searched for the underlying reasons, and then worked through the feelings. Other times I needed to change how I dealt with someone or some situation. Oftentimes I needed to confront a person or address a situation related to some perceived wrong. I found I had stored up large amounts of anger and rage over my life because I had been mistreated and hadn't adequately addressed and worked to heal it. Instead, I often turned my anger and rage inward, essentially mistreating myself, or it would come out in inappropriate or indirect ways, often hurting others. I also learned that anger turned inward can lead to depression.

I was angry that I wasn't living the life I wanted to be living and fully using my unique talents and skills. I was angry at being a doormat for others at times, not standing up for myself, giving my power away. I was angry at not feeling like I deserved good things in life. I was angry that I had been a people pleaser, a conformer, and a victim. Anger taught me that my personal boundaries had been violated. Sometimes I realized that I was angry because I wasn't being listened to and getting my needs met. As a child, I wasn't responsible for this, but as an adult, I knew this meant I wasn't listening to myself and meeting my own needs.

I learned over time to express my anger in safe and healthy ways and to listen to what it was telling me. Anger became my friend and confidant. I honored it. Among other things, I learned to release it by screaming in a safe place, pounding a pillow, writing in my journal, and by using the aforementioned blowing technique. I've also learned how to respect myself and my needs, set appropriate boundaries, express my truth, and to live the unique life my inner voice had been urging me to live.

I've slowly begun to understand how to conserve, control and channel the powerful force of anger in a healthier direction; one that allows me to move my life and dreams forward in a positive way. This includes, directing the anger I experience with the negative things that happen in society: the excessive violence, the injustices, the extreme partisanship in politics, and the unkind way people treat one other, into the more productive and immediate uses of working to improve myself and moving forward my work on Kundalini and this book! As a result, the negative anger and rage long frozen inside of me, has begun to slowly melt away, while the more positive aspect of anger has become a fuel for healthier uses in my life.

As far as my current daily routine, I begin each morning with a half hour prayer and meditation session, asking God to guide me in my actions for that day. I also stretch or do yoga several days a week, as well as occasionally practice memorization exercises to strengthen my mind. I pray for empathy, gratitude, love, compassion, fearlessness and courage. I also ask God to help me love my family and others, as well as people that are difficult for me to love. I pray that any negative, unkind, and critical thoughts toward others, as well as my own self-pitying and fearful thoughts during the day, be immediately transmuted into love, faith, compassion, mercy, hope, and courage. I ask God to then help heal the part of me that needs healing.

I do my best to serve God throughout the day, asking for help with problems or situations, or for guidance on next steps or course of action.

I also challenged myself with many new activities. I overcame lifelong fears by taking an acting and a voice expression class. My singing voice had been frozen since primary school, when I got a D in music class. Like the tin man from *The Wizard of Oz,* I was slowly becoming unfrozen. I oiled myself with these practices, giving a greater voice to my feelings, thoughts and talents.

For a period of time, I saw a nutritionist who taught me healthier eating and shopping habits. She helped me to overcome my overly carnivorous, excessive rice and noodle consuming, obsessive sweets devouring, and deficient fruit, vegetable, and salad eating tendencies. I discovered organic foods, and products such as goat yogurt, brown rice, flax seed, different varieties of nuts, and tofu, became new additions to my diet. At the same time, my inner guidance also directed me to the foods I needed to consume to stay healthy and feel better.

I am also grateful that a referral from theologian Morton Kelsey led me into five years of spiritual direction counseling at the San Francisco Theological Seminary's Lloyd Center. Reverend Kelsey referred me to a spiritual director by the name of Carol Saysette. Carol is a gentle, wise, and humble soul who helped me tremendously with her patient listening and loving presence. She never told me what to do, but rather gently encouraged me to look within myself to God for answers. I then completed one year of formal spiritual direction training at the Mercy Center in Burlingame, California to become a spiritual director. I was then led into the 12-step programs of recovery and Speaking Circles®, both of which I will discuss more in-depth in the next chapter.

The spiritual direction counseling, 12-step work, and Speaking Circles helped me to stay sane during the long periods of upheaval I underwent. They provided great support and taught me how to let go of my need to try and control events in my life and surrender more fully to the guidance of the still voice within. They also helped to purify my body and mind of unhealthy thought patterns and behaviors.

Slowing Down and Doing Less

All of these practices helped me to slow down, and I developed a better sense of what the next right action was in my life. I was also improving at staying present to God. If I felt anxious or in a hurry, I made an extra effort to meditate and stay still. Sometimes slowing myself down was nearly impossible. It also was uncomfortable, yet I learned to simply sit, metaphorically tying myself to the chair, breathing slowly, and feeling the discomfort until I settled down.

I would often say to friends that today's fast paced society moved at a speed of 78 RPMs, yet it seemed I needed to live life at 33 RPMs to stay healthy. God also seemed to speak to me at 33 rpm's, therefore I needed to slow down to hear God's still quiet voice. Constantly asking for guidance and help throughout the day was my way of praying unceasingly or practicing mindfulness. In verse #12, entitled, "God is Always Present", I wrote:

> "God is waiting in the moment.
> When I flee the moment, I flee God.
> When I stay, the moment turns into eternity.
> When I flee the moment, I vote for fear, rather than trust, thinking safety comes from the world, rather than from God."

I also noticed that by slowing down, I was hearing and seeing many things I had previously missed. As an example: I began to hear and comprehend the words to songs. All my life I loved to listen to music, particularly oldies and holiday songs, but I wasn't aware of the lyrics. I loved the melody or harmony of a song but didn't connect the words with their meaning, at least consciously. This new ability has made music much more enjoyable and meaningful. This has also made me wonder what other experiences I have missed in life because of rushing around and my inability to slow down and focus.

Letting Go of the Need to be Perfect

I also learned that I needn't be afraid of failure and making mistakes. I needed to let go of my all-consuming desire to be perfect. I learned it is okay to make a mistake and learn from it. Even to admit I made a mistake. In the old sitcom *Happy Days*, the tough guy with the heart of gold named Fonzie used to say, "I was wrrrr…" He couldn't say he was wrong. I always had a good laugh at this, but it slowly dawned on me that this too was me!

I slowly began to realize that my mistakes and so-called failures, rather than being a confirmation of unworthiness or deficiency, were actually a good thing. They helped me to grow and accept my full humanity. I saw they could propel me to a better life if I was able to accept them as part of a natural learning and spiritual unfolding process. Perhaps most importantly, they humbled me and opened me to new sources of knowledge, new ways of learning, and a deeper connection to God and others.

Compassion for Self and Others

I also developed compassion for the vulnerable and troubled parts of myself. Over the years, it dawned on me that my losses, wounds, troubles, and confusions were the cracks that allowed more healing and a stronger presence of God into my life. My verse #8 entitled, "Quasimodo - God is Truth and Love", begins with the following:

"Who are you Quasimodo?
I am the vulnerable part of you, the crack that lets God in. I have a big heart. I am sweetness. I am kindness.

My heart expands when I see you. Love comes cascading out like a waterfall. I am moved to tears, to tears of compassion. I know you are so close by. I can't see you with my eyes, but I see you with the eyes of my heart. You are my breath, my life. You sustain me."

I gradually learned how to be compassionate with the vulnerable, weak, imperfect, failing side of myself. This helped me to better accept all of who I am, the light and the darkness together.

Seeing and working through the deep hurt within has allowed me to be more compassionate toward others. It has also freed me to see more clearly that the anger and hurtful actions of others, most likely comes from their own pain and sorrow.

The Importance of Mentors

We all need the help of others. We cannot do life alone. I've had many great mentors and role models throughout my life. They always seemed to arrive when I needed them most. If I really admired someone, I had the courage and perseverance to track them down and ask for their help. I've already talked about some of the wonderful people that have helped me in my journey but here are some additional examples and reflections.

My mom and dad were great role models. My mom epitomized love, caring, wisdom, humility, and kindness. My dad was a rock of integrity, courage, reliability, community involvement, and business achievement.

Sometimes my role models provided both positive and negative examples at the same time. Roy Nesseth, John DeLorean's partner, taught me entrepreneurial drive and generosity, but his experiences with DeLorean also taught me not to chase quick money, take shortcuts to success, or sacrifice ethical behavior to achieve my goals.

John Bradshaw, new age sage of inner child fame, taught me how to listen to myself, my inner child, as well as communicate with different parts of my being. He also introduced me to a very important counselor, Carla Perez, whom I mentioned earlier.

Michael Murphy, who founded Esalen, and was a pioneer in the human potential movement and consciousness studies, taught me the value of having an integral practice for physical and spiritual growth that included body, mind, heart, and soul practices.

I learned humor, alternative health practices, and the need to follow my dreams from Patch Adams, whose life was portrayed by Robin Williams in the movie *Patch Adams*. One night I watched the film in the theater and was so moved, that the next day I picked up the phone and called him. I lived in the San Francisco area at the time. I didn't reach Patch, but I got his warm, friendly, and funny personal assistant Beach Clown (Kathy Crewes). We talked for an hour and immediately became friends. I then moved to the Washington, D.C. area where Patch and Beach lived. One day some close friends and I went on a metro ride with Patch and Beach. They were dressed as clowns and bounced balloons off the heads of unsuspecting people riding that day on the metro. I never laughed harder in my life. I have to admit though that I was afraid we might be in peril from some grim looking passengers (said with a smile on my face), as they sat motionless and emotionless, and tried to fathom what these two crazy clowns were doing.

I once read some of my love poetry to then 96-year-old Heloise Sabin, the widowed wife of Albert Sabin, who developed the oral vaccine for polio. She talked about how she could still feel Albert's presence as if he were still alive. I frequently visited Mr. Sabin's grave in Arlington Cemetery and have become convinced that a vaccine equivalent for mental illness could one day be developed once we understood Kundalini.

I spent four hours one day with former heavyweight boxing champion Joe Frazier, first having lunch, and then visiting his old training gym, the Joe Frazier Gym, which is now on the National Register of Historic Places in North Philadelphia. I was friends with his business manager who set up the meeting.

I'm going to share some detail about this visit because it moved me deeply. We were exploring the idea of doing a film on Joe Frazier's life. After we had lunch, I drove with Joe in his car to the gym. He had first placed his gun, or his "heat", as he called it, underneath the seat. He pretty much ignored all red stoplights on our journey to the gym. He had been in a bad car accident many years earlier which had left him walking with a cane. Now I understand why this may have happened! I was sure I was going to die before we got to the gym. He gave me a tour of his gym, even taking a gentle swing with his famous left hook as I held the old punching bag that was still in the gym.

I had to get back to Washington, D.C that night to watch on television the Wisconsin Badgers play Miami in a college football holiday bowl game. We were set to leave, and Joe had left his keys in his car which was locked. His business manager gave me a ride back to downtown Philadelphia and we had to leave Joe by his car waiting for AAA road service. That is my last memory of Joe Frazier. He died a couple of years later. He had come from a family of 12 kids and an impoverished background. I was moved by how real and sincere Joe was as a person. He was a humble but tough man who taught me about humility, courage and overcoming my fears in this one short visit.

One question I asked was what he was thinking as he sat on his stool in the boxing ring right before the bell sounded for the first round of his Fight of the Century with Muhammad Ali. The fight was held in Madison Square Garden in New York City in 1971 and was broadcast on closed circuit television. I was 13 years old at the time and had watched it that night and rooted for Ali at a local sports stadium with my brother-in-law. Now 39 years later, we were face to face. This time I rooted for Joe. His terse answer was that he had butterflies, but he wanted to kill Ali (said not with a smile on his face).

Finally, one of my greatest mentors I call Sir Walter Henry Doodle, my nephew's Cosmic Conscious 85-pound Golden Doodle god. Oops I got that last word backwards, I meant dog, whom I call the Golden Noodle, who is the kindest, most gentle, humble, loving being I've ever met. Joseph Meyers once wrote in an op-ed: "To err is human, to forgive is canine."

My gentle suggestion, if somebody moves you deeply, track them down and reach out to them for help! They may just respond and end up inspiring you for the rest of your life!

Teachers are everywhere

More generally, I have learned that it is important to be humble and open to learning from everyone and everything - for example from my sister's dog, other animals, younger people, older people, people from other religions and races, people or things I didn't like, nature, etc. I began to understand through my 12-step practice that as I learned more, the less I knew. This was very humbling and almost the exact opposite of the attitude I carried when I was becoming an "expert" in the financial world. I have come to believe that knowledge is infinite and if I am open to learning, all of my life's experiences and circumstances have something valuable to teach me. Verse #43, "Heaven and a Dog's Love for Family", found my Inner Intelligence speaking through the voice of my sister's recently deceased dog, comforting my sister (and myself) with these great pearls of wisdom and light:

> "Live life to its fullest; mourn my passing but move on, new love awaits you.
>
> … Know that I am in the light. It is a light that never goes out. Know that I am held deeply in love, in God's womb, as you are too. In sickness and grief, in sadness and loss, in trial and tribulation, God is always there holding you, loving you, embracing you, comforting you, blessing you.
>
> … Know that the things you have loved are not lost. Nothing is gone forever.
>
> … There is so much more life to be lived. Do not fret. Know deeply in your heart that I am here waiting for you. Time moves fast, move on to new loves. Know that your love will always be emblazoned in my heart, and know that one day soon, we will be together, the whole family, in love, for eternity."

I also learned that how I feel about or react to a certain person or situation, is actually telling me something more about myself, rather than the person or situation. More specifically, I discovered that if I have an intense reaction, this generally means there is something I need to examine inside myself. If I have the awareness and self-discipline to do this, there is a chance for me to learn more about myself and ultimately to continue to grow.

For example, if I have strong feelings of admiration for a person such as Gandhi, this might mean that certain positive characteristics or traits that he possessed, such as humility and truthfulness, might also be present within me as a greater potential to be developed. Conversely, if I have a strong negative reaction to a person or situation, such as being upset with what someone said or did, or having jealous feelings toward someone, then this likely means there is something within me that needs healing or further developing.

In either case, I have learned to take a daily inventory of my most intense thoughts, actions, and reactions. I then ask God to help me understand and develop further positive characteristics, or to heal the personal shortcomings. Over time this practice has helped to lessen the chance that I will impulsively react in a negative way to a person or situation. It also has helped me learn more about myself and feel better about who I am.

The 12-steps taught me how to parent and heal myself. They showed me how to love myself first, which was a foreign concept to me. I thought that was being selfish. For a good part of my life, I was hard on myself. I sometimes berated myself and could never seem to live up to my own high expectations. I learned that until I could learn to treat myself with compassion, kindness, trust, acceptance, and love, it would be hard for me to treat others this way. I slowly became my own father, mother, friend, and maybe most importantly my own grandparents, who were the epitome of unconditional love. I was able to love others in a deeper way because I first learned how to be gentle and caring with myself, and to love and accept myself as I was. This included being able to acknowledge and accept my flaws as well as my virtues.

In summary, I believe we are all an extension of a loving God. I believe the more we are able to learn to love, heal, and purify ourselves, the more we will be able to love and serve others. The more we take on the characteristics that are often ascribed to God, such as love, kindness, truthfulness, wisdom, charity, mercy, compassion, etc., through right thoughts, words, and actions, the more quickly we can facilitate this transmutation into a more loving extension of God. We reward and punish ourselves and create our own reality through the way we live our lives. The more deeply we get in touch with the Power inside of us to guide us, the truer and straighter our paths will become, and the more our lives will unfold in a meaningful and bountiful way!

15 – 12-Step Programs and Speaking Circles®

I feel a deep debt of gratitude to the 12-step programs of recovery. They have had an enormous positive impact on my life. The first time I walked into a 12-step meeting I could hardly breathe. I knew I had come home. I believe they helped save my life during a critical period of time as I struggled with my Kundalini awakening.

Although my Kundalini experiences were not the primary reason for entering the 12-step programs of recovery (at least not consciously), the programs helped me to stay grounded in my thinking and behaving, and in touch with day-to-day reality during the significant upheaval in my mind and body caused by my Kundalini experiences. They also helped me to cope with all the other challenges I was experiencing at this time of my life and provided great hope when it was badly needed.

Finally, and most critically, the 12-step recovery programs have helped me to get more deeply in touch with a Higher Power, which I call God. The guidance and support I have received from God have been indispensable in helping me navigate the perils and challenges of my Kundalini awakening and life journey.

I was especially attracted to the 12-step principle of equality where we all are considered to be equal at a spiritual level or the level of our hearts. In fact, after one year of training to become a spiritual director, I decided to end the training and concentrate solely on my work in the 12-step programs. I just was not at peace with the idea that as a spiritual director, I would be put in an elevated position over the people

I spiritually directed. I also was not comfortable receiving money for such services.

The 12-step programs are universal healing, cleansing, and spiritual recovery programs. Their healing principles and practices transcend differences of race, religion, country, ethnicity, sex, economic and social status, etc.

The 12-steps taught me that I could define a Higher Power in a way that spoke to me but emphasized the need for it to be something greater than myself. If I wasn't comfortable with the concept of God, I could define it as the wisdom of the group, nature, or love, for example. They also taught me that humility and surrender to a Higher Power was an indispensable part of my recovery journey and spiritual path. They emphasized the need to live life in balance taking one day at a time. I do my best to listen to my Higher Power and take the next right step in life, leaving the results of my actions in God's hands. If I had an expectation of a result from an action I had taken, it was a regret possibly waiting to happen.

Participating in 12-step programs helped me to better follow the guidance of my Inner Intelligence. By applying their practices and principles on a daily basis, I was able to take some of the most important precepts and ideals that I was taught in my religious, spiritual, and ethical upbringing, and apply them more effectively in my daily life. These included the need to be honest, to pray and meditate, to take a moral inventory of myself, to forgive, to not judge others, to be patient, to be humble and charitable, to treat others as I wished to be treated, and to love. The focus was on changing myself, and not trying to change others. I was told that by changing myself first, this just might lead to positive change in others.

I became an "Inner Activist", with my goal being to rigorously cleanse myself from the inside out. I thought this would help improve my outer actions in the world as well as allow me to have healthier relationships with people.

The following quotation from Gandhi is in Trudy S. Settel's book The Book of Gandhi Wisdom:

> "The outward freedom that we shall attain will only be in exact proportion to the inward freedom to which we may have grown at a given moment. And if this is the correct view of freedom, our chief energy must be concentrated upon achieving reform from within."

I asked for God's help in lessening or removing my character shortcomings as well as strengthening my character assets. I learned to share my setbacks and struggles but also learned it was just as important to share my accomplishments and victories. I learned to make amends to people for past wrongs and missteps, and this slowly released me from the great burden of guilt I carried. Finally, and maybe most importantly, I learned to laugh at myself and my behavior, realizing that I was imperfect, made mistakes and was human, just like everyone else.

The 12-steps are a community where I can speak my truth. I can be authentic and also ask for help. I learned it was safe to share the "shameful secrets" of my life. This helped to release me from the bondage of shame. I had often heard we are as sick as our secrets, and I have found this to be true. The program encourages me to express my emotions, rather than keeping them stuffed inside. It also taught me that changing my attitudes could aid my recovery. Changing my attitudes was a big deal, because oftentimes I carried negative or self-defeating attitudes without knowing it. Some of these negative attitudes included believing things always had to be difficult, that I didn't deserve good things in life, that my actions or behaviors were often wrong, or that my ideas weren't important.

As my work in the 12-step programs of recovery deepened, my relationship with my Higher Power has also continued to grow. I found that my concept of God changed from a somewhat distant, rule-making, and impersonal being to a much more loving, intimate, and personal Presence. This new God guides me, wants the best for me, and can help me get through any difficult situation.

My Higher Power was no longer above me and at a distance but was beside me and inside of me. All I had to do was ask for help and I received it. The help God provided wasn't always what I wanted or what I thought I needed, but I gradually found out over time it was what was best for me. This Loving Presence was now in a circle of connection with me as were other people. As I grew in humility and was now able to listen to the wisdom and experiences of others, I realized that my Higher Power often spoke to me through other people. This helped me to grow immeasurably. I didn't have to do things alone but had the help of other people in the program.

In the early 1990s, I was flying from San Francisco to Portland, OR. I was reading a book and drinking a beer and observing other people on the plane. I remember thinking at the time how shut off I felt from others. I had no idea who they were or what they thought or felt. I guess I thought I knew what they might be like, based on their outer behaviors and actions. But in reality, I had no clue as to what their inner thoughts, feelings, or motivations were. People seemed distant, and I felt separated from life. My experiences in the 12-step programs have changed all of this.

It's been my experience that as I continue to grow in recovery and deepen inwardly, I feel a growing connection to others. As people share their stories and the challenges in their lives, I see how similar we are and the common heritage we share. We may have different problems and goals in our lives, but the similarities between us - our emotions, feelings, struggles, adversities, challenges, insecurities, hopes, desires, etc. - are much more than our differences. In fact, my experiences in the 12-steps have helped to gradually expand my definition of "family" to include the whole human race. In some ways these deeper feelings of connection are also a natural stepping-stone to the next level of connection, where in the experience of Cosmic Consciousness, one sees the unity underlying creation, the oneness of us all, and that all of life is one's family and part of God.

One interesting and somewhat humorous experience helped to bring home this broader concept of family. It occurred on July 4th, about fourteen years ago. I was flying to Madison, Wisconsin from Washington, D.C. to celebrate the holiday with my father and some of my sisters. I bought an inexpensive ticket where you are given a window of time as to when you might fly that day or night. When I subsequently discovered that my actual flight would arrive in Madison late at night, I was upset. I complained to friends that I was going to be arriving too late to be able to watch the fireworks and spend time with my family.

My flight schedule had me stopping in Kansas City on my way to Madison. The sky was just beginning to darken as we took off for Madison. As we flew north, I began to see fireworks being launched from numerous towns and cities along our flight path. As we approached Madison, there was an incredible lightning show off in the distance which lit up the night sky.

There were only two other passengers on the flight to Madison that night. I sat up front and the airline flight attendant served me hot chocolate chip cookies and pretzels. I was in heaven. When I asked the attendant what her name was and she said "Goddess", I then knew I wasn't in "Heaven" or "Kansas". I was in the "Twilight Zone" or "Oz"!

As it turned out, I wasn't able to watch the fireworks that night with my family in Madison, but instead, got to see many fireworks displays with families in towns across a certain stretch of the midwestern U.S.

That night my inner voice whispered to me, I always take care of you and now you know who your real family is; it is everyone.

When I was younger, I used to go to "Happy Hour" on Friday nights to enjoy liquid beverages and have a good time and connect with others. However, the next morning, I often felt terrible physically and mentally due to overindulgence and staying out too late. I also felt disconnected from myself as well as others. I found the "happiness" from the "Happy Hour" didn't last.

Now I say to friends that that when I go to a 12-step meeting on Friday night or any other time, it is my new "Happy Hour". I go to improve myself and find peace and serenity. I have found going to this Happy Hour actually leads to a deeper, more lasting connection with myself as well as others. There is also the additional gift that this type of peace and happiness lasts and is not fleeting… and I feel a lot better the next day!

In summary, on one hand, I would say my work in 12-step programs broke down barriers between God, myself and other human beings and helped me to live day to day better connected to God and others.

On the other hand, as I will explain in more depth in Chapter 22, I would say my Kundalini or spiritual awakening completely shattered my conception of God. It showed me the immensity of God as reflected in the experience of a new consciousness and picture of the universe, as well as my true relationship to God, the universe, and others.

Speaking Circles®

I'd like to share one other program that has had a deep impact on my life. It is a program called Speaking Circles. A life-long terror of public speaking led me to Speaking Circles in 1998. I was one of those people who would have rather died than speak publicly.

I recall like it was yesterday the memory of my mother taking my hand and leading me down the path next to our house toward the beginning of kindergarten. I felt shy and self-conscious. I was not ready to show my face to the world and reveal who I was. Now this kind of reaction or feeling is not unusual for a young child, yet it is probably a bit unusual when you feel that way for a good part of your life. Flash ahead to sixth grade when I'm attending Lakewood School in Madison, Wisconsin. Based primarily on my ability to read clearly, I had been selected to be the co-lead in the Christmas school play. When the performance came, I felt terrified and frozen, like the Tin Man in *The Wizard of Oz*.

When I looked back at my school report cards, one in sixth grade said:

"Scott does well in class, but I wish he would raise his
hand more often and speak up in class."

I received similar comments in junior high and high school.

At the University of Wisconsin, any class that required a speech or presentation in front of the class was to be avoided like the plague. Imagine my discomfort when I discovered I'd need to take a speech class to graduate. My final year came, and I could no long put it off. I took the class, nervously squeaking through my speeches, sometimes with the help of a beer or two.

Graduate business school at UCLA and work at Prudential Capital brought more of the same. Speeches and presentations were still to be avoided. I felt like I was being hunted and at any moment my insecurities could be exposed. Over time I became more mature and experienced. I took a Dale Carnegie speaking class and excelled with flying colors. I learned to memorize my speeches through repetition, and to project a strong, icy calm, and relaxed presence. However, my speaking often lacked spontaneity and originality. Sometimes I said what I thought my audience wanted to hear, and not what my heart believed.

I gave many successful speeches, yet I remained uncomfortable, and the fear persisted. Any slip or loss of memory during a speech brought the possibility of implosion from within. I lived life on the edge, with possible failure and seeming public exposure and ridicule always waiting nearby. Wedding toasts, church readings, impromptu business introductions; all represented threats that sometimes could not be avoided. At one point, helped along by excessive alcohol consumption, I froze during a wedding toast and confirmed that the threat was real. It was from this background that I found my way into Speaking Circles.

One of the pleasant surprises of participating in Speaking Circles has been that the benefits have gone way beyond learning to speak more comfortably in public speaking situations. It has also helped me to become more at ease in my personal interactions with people in social situations as well as in everyday life.

Speaking Circles has taught me to listen within, to let go of control, and to trust that what I needed to say would emerge out of this silent space. It showed me how to become more present to myself. It has encouraged me to accept myself for who I am and embrace exactly how I am feeling in the moment, anxious, scared, excited, embarrassed, angry, sad, happy, etc., and to speak from this place of authenticity to people.

Speaking Circles said people would be attracted to me if I shared my feelings and authentic self. And I would also feel more connected to people. I have found these things to be resoundingly true. Finally, it encouraged me to maintain eye contact with one person at a time. This would allow me to speak from a place of relationship with each person while receiving their support.

This program has been tremendously healing for me. I highly recommend it to others who are looking to speak more comfortably in public situations, as well as in all areas of life. It has helped me to get more in touch with my inner voice, to be more present with people, and to grow inwardly and outwardly. It is a completely safe and nurturing environment.

The good news is that during this current pandemic with our lockdown and social distancing requirements, Speaking Circles can still happen via Zoom Circles, with people participating from all over the U.S. and sometimes around the world. I have found it to be just as powerful an experience as if in person. Speaking Circles founder Lee Glickstein has begun to frame these Zoom Circles as Luminous Listening Circles rather than Speaking Circles, since the group listening that occurs in these sessions seems to be a particularly critical alchemical agent for personal growth and gaining of self-knowledge.

I continue to this day to journal, meditate and pray, watch movies, walk in nature, as well as participate in both the 12-step programs of recovery and Speaking Circles/Luminous Listening Circles. All these activities have helped to strengthen my inner foundation, my sense of self as well as my connection to God. This in turn has helped me to become more effective, confident, and creative, as well as feel more peaceful and serene in my daily work and life.

16 – Solquest, Letting Go, and A Gift

My Kundalini awakening has had a dramatic impact on my life in many different ways. I've had experiences which I never imagined were possible. Its's completely changed what I thought life was about. Over the last 22 years it has also significantly changed the work I do and the way I live my life.

In 1999, I created a new business called Solquest. The idea was to combine my business counseling, coaching, consulting, and connecting skills (the 4 C's), and use them in a process to help people and businesses to grow and prosper.

The goal is to help a person progress in their inner development and simultaneously become more effective in their work and business. The idea is that inner development creates self-confidence, personal strength and knowledge, and leads to outer development and success. This outer growth and success in turn fosters continued inner growth. The intent is to also help people get more in touch with their own inner guidance and wisdom.

I saw Solquest as a vehicle where I'd finally be able to merge my interests, experiences, and skills in the areas of business and spirituality. Each piece of the business came out of my own work, spiritual, and life experiences. Essentially what I learned and experienced became incorporated into an integrated package of services that I now provide to people today. Combining our past experiences and knowledge in novel ways to serve people is a formula for how our life purpose can always keep moving forward in exciting new and fulfilling ways.

I found it incredibly challenging to develop and market the business in a way that people could understand how they may benefit. I also discovered that many people do not see the value of inner work or the direct link between inner work and outer success.

When I first opened Solquest, I sent a marketing piece to fifty people offering a free consultation. Not one person took me up on my offer. I used to joke that I couldn't even give my time away for free in the beginning! For a long time, I struggled with self-confidence and clarity about what were the best mix of services to offer.

I've consulted with various individuals and businesses since 1999. I've barely been able to scratch out a living and at times, I had to borrow money from family members and friends to stay afloat.

When I look back over the years, Solquest became another vehicle for continuing self-development and spiritual growth. I learned to do many new things, develop different skills, face constant challenges, and endure disappointments. It taught me patience and perseverance. It also served as a vehicle for further stripping away vanity and pride; for learning to rely more on the help of others; and finally, for deepening my connection with God.

It felt as if my spiritual journey had become a full-time job and although I grew tremendously, inwardly and outwardly, I fell short in my ability to earn a sufficient living. I worked hard, yet there was an invisible barrier between earning money and myself. Well-meaning people suggested I find a job. That kind of comment only made things worse. Frankly it drove me nuts because deep down I worried they might be right.

From time to time, I tried to find work in the financial world. The thought of going back into that environment felt like a fate worse than death. Yet, if need be, I was willing to do it. It seemed that door had permanently closed as I received one rejection after another. Deep inside I knew I wasn't called to go in that direction, and that I was meant to endure what I was going through and continue to progress on this new journey.

I did odd jobs here and there to survive. For example, I occasionally did errands for my ex-wife including walking her dogs. She worked for the President of the United States at the time, and I lived in a cheap apartment in what is the second richest county in the U.S. The irony was not lost on me. During these trying times I trusted my inner voice which said that no matter what happened, I would be taken care of. I was also in a vulnerable state from the challenging effects of the Kundalini energy. This made it more difficult to do certain kinds of work, especially work that involved prolonged mental concentration. I needed to be careful because if I made a wrong choice, it could have a negative physical and mental impact that could last for months.

I've lived on the edge of a cliff financially for almost twenty-five years, most times scratching and clawing to survive. I've been fortunate in that I happened to have two close friends, Mark and Fred, who were in similar, perilous positions, and we were able to constantly share the travails and terrors of our journeys. Without their support, friendship and humor, the stress, strain, and worry might have taken a more damaging toll. However, the thing that has kept me going and provided the needed support during these challenging times was my connection to God. I had a deep inner knowing that these experiences were leading me to a better life and were a necessary part of my education. I also knew they were in service of a deeper purpose and would one day help me accomplish my calling. I also knew this calling would involve giving back and serving others.

I knew the best was still ahead if I could hang on. Frankly, my surface consciousness had tremendous doubts, whereas my deeper inner being had none. I felt supported by my work in the 12-step programs and knew the path I was following was built on the foundation of a Higher Intelligence.

Occasionally I had to borrow money from friends and family, and this was a brutally painful experience. From time to time I also had to bring my change jars to banks and supermarkets to obtain living money. I remember one humorous time when I placed my coins in the bucket at the local supermarket, which of course made a loud noticeable clanking sound. I pushed the start button, and the machine didn't work. Somewhat embarrassed, I quickly hauled the change out and went over to a nearby bank and put the money in their bucket. The same thing happened. I quietly slithered out of there knowing it was just one of those days!

Sometimes I had to go through the grueling ordeal of facing eviction from my apartment for lack of rent payment, and, on rare occasions, feel the gnawing pain of hunger from not having money to buy food.

All these experiences, although painful, have also been beneficial. They have allowed me to connect with a broader spectrum of people, and experience people and situations in ways that probably would never have been possible if I stayed in my financially secure way of life. It felt like I was being led to visit different landscapes in the spectrum of consciousness, to more broadly understand and appreciate people, and their different life circumstances.

I now understood what it felt like to face losing one's home, and to have to ask for money and to be dependent on the goodwill of others. It was only when almost everything was taken away that I came to appreciate what God had given me; also, how prosperous I was materially in comparison with most people in the world.

My material needs were significantly reduced, and I learned to feel comfortable living on less. I felt a deeper kinship with people and believe I have become more compassionate, less judgmental, and more accepting because of these experiences. I don't see others as different from me, no matter what their station in life. And I've learned to see beyond surface differences to the connection we all share at the level of our hearts.

The entire process has been extremely humbling and also difficult. Yet, I also feel Heaven's destiny has guided me, and I'm right where I'm supposed to be. I have found that as each layer of material possession has been let go, most times quite grudgingly, I have discovered greater strength within to surrender my trust to the power of the Unseen. Gradually the Unseen has become more known and real than the Seen.

Mountain climber Alex Honnold was filmed in the 2019 Oscar winning documentary *Free Solo,* free climbing the 3,200-foot sheer vertical granite face of El Capitan in Yosemite National Park. Alex was the first to ever do this climb without the security of ropes. In many ways, I felt like Alex in that I was now free climbing my own El Capitan spiritual mountain to a transformed consciousness and new life. I was doing this without my usual security ropes which included financial support, my intellect and self-will calling the shots, and following my normal pattern of living.

No matter how destitute I became or how bleak things looked, Heaven always provided what I needed, which seemed to be less than what I thought I needed. Sometimes money seemed to appear out of thin air when I was particularly desperate. For example, on two occasions, an anonymous person paid my apartment rent at the last minute, or I would have had to face legal proceedings related to being evicted. I later found out who this was and paid them back. Other times, business opportunities surfaced just as dire consequences were setting in.

My circumstances forced me to ask for help from people, which has always been difficult. I felt it was weak to ask for help or I wasn't deserving and had to learn to stand on my own two feet. So many people have helped in so many ways, oftentimes not really understanding why I needed help. Many times, they probably gave out of the charity of their heart, but other times, they probably felt they couldn't say no given my difficult circumstances.

These struggles have been one of the greatest gifts of my life, for I was forced through sheer necessity to learn to rely more on the will of God, rather than my own self-will.

Thirteen years ago, I had little money and few material possessions to my name. I sold one of my last remaining major assets, my beloved 1996 Buick Park Avenue. It had 160,000 miles on it. I felt sad to let it go as it was the one material constant I could rely on. My mechanic kept it glued together for years but finally, the wear and tear and cost of needed repairs made it necessary to part ways.

Initially, I couldn't imagine not having a car and wondered how I was going to survive. For a while, I borrowed a friend's car. This made me uncomfortable as I felt I was imposing. One day I drove over a parking block with my friend's car and scratched the bumper. I knew then that it was time to increase my use of public transportation. I felt like I was back in the 8th or 9th grade again, in the days before I had a driver's license.

An interesting thing happened though, I found myself gradually slowing down and doing less, yet I felt happier and more at peace. Since I didn't have a car, I couldn't jump in and drive off doing whatever I wanted. I had to think about my day and determine what was important and what mattered. I realized I didn't need to do as much and had been wasting time doing unnecessary and unimportant things.

I had tunnel vision then, rushing to my car in the morning and driving hurriedly to wherever I was going. But then it was as if a slower moving, more expansive world opened. As I walked to the bus stop, I heard birds chirping, I gazed at the beautiful trees, flowers, or snow as well as the peaceful looking doves perched above on the telephone lines. I felt the warm sunshine or brisk air on my skin, and I noticed people. As I waited for the bus, I imagined what it must have been like to live during the days when there were no cars or buses. This brought a peaceful, serene feeling and helped me to feel connected to the past.

As each day began, I felt calmer and more relaxed. I often prayed and meditated as I rode the bus to the cafe at the local Barnes and Noble bookstore, which served as a second office. I got to know some of the bus drivers, and many of the workers at Barnes and Noble. I learned about their lives and interests. I found myself talking to more people as I went about my daily life. And I began to feel as if I was part of the natural flow of life again, as well as part of a wider community of people.

At the time, I didn't know how long my car-less status would last. But I realized that although I had lost some mobility and freedom, I had gained more valuable, lasting things. These included the savings from not having the expenses of a car, a deeper connection with people, a slower pace of life, a more efficient use of time, less stress, and a greater peace of mind.

In October of 2017, my deeply loved and respected father passed away at the age of 90. He had always been a huge support for me in my life. My parents final act of support was his passing on a modest inheritance. This allowed me to take care of a good portion of my debts. And it gave me money to live on for a while as I continued to pursue what I felt God was calling me to do.

My physical possessions remained minimal, although I now lease a car. I moved from the Washington, D.C. area to Madison, WI, where I live with a sister for part of the year. I also spend time in the winter in Santa Barbara, CA, where I also live with another sister. These arrangements have helped me get to know my sisters in a different way from when I was growing up. This has been an eye-opening, challenging and ultimately enriching experience.

In addition to a small amount of remaining inheritance, my other assets include the following: this book and my writings, my journals, my life memories, my much loved and appreciated friends and family, my good health, a greater awareness in as well as optimistic outlook on life, a slower, more balanced way of living, a deeper purpose in life, as well as the love and trust I have in my heart for God and the path I'm on. And oh yes, I do still own some other physical assets including a laptop computer, cell phone, and clothing. All of these have greater value to me now.

Today I feel free, safe and cared after, and have such hope in my heart. I feel my future potential is unlimited. At age 63, I feel the best years of my life are still ahead. I know I will never stop growing nor will I ever retire from work. My life has become my work and my work has become my life. New adventures await me. This is what the spiritual path has provided: an inner security and confidence that I didn't have before when I had greater material means, but a lesser connection to the Intelligence within me.

There is a reading in the 12-steps that says:

> "I don't have to give up on my hopes and dreams, my Higher Power is not limited by my lack of imagination."

When I hit the finish line of my life, I will have accomplished my purpose for being here on earth. I will then excitedly look forward to my next life knowing that I moved one step closer to God in this life. I also know that I will start my next life incarnation with an even more glorious destination ahead. This is how I believe eternal life proceeds, if lived in concert with the Supreme Intelligence behind life.

I feel it is important to live in a state of balance between the inner and outer worlds, or the material and spiritual. I don't think it is necessary, nor do I believe God wants me to live again in a precarious financial state. I believe it has served its purpose to get me where I am today in my perspective and approach to life. I believe the remaining amount of my inheritance will get me to the finish line of financial stability and my life calling. When the money starts flowing, I will have some remaining debts to take care of and future obligations and dreams to fulfill. This time, instead of drawing signs of the cross, which I did during my investment loss "crucifixion" experiences, I am quite certain I will be drawing happy pictures of resurrection scenes of giving back and serving.

Update - Closing of Date Deal - A Gift!

As I was approaching the completion of the writing of this book, a very unexpected development occurred.

As fate would have it, a recent financial advisory work assignment had me returning to the Palm Springs/Coachella area of Southern California. It also found me working with the owner of a date fruit company whom I had known for almost 30 years.

Earlier I shared how my initial foray as an entrepreneur had led me into the date industry in the early 1990s, where my goal was to make my material fortune. I wasn't fully aware at the time that such an intention was somewhat hidden under the guise of spiritual aspirations. Back then I thought of it as the beginning of my journey to material security and economic and personal freedom.

Now, I was returning full circle in my journey. Things looked the same, but everything was different. I was different. I had gone through almost three decades of intense spiritual and personal development work. It seemed as if I had been thrown into a wildly churning washing machine and had been "cleansed" to the core of my being. I was now ready to allow a Higher Intelligence to guide me in my work actions and life.

On this project, I assisted the owner and his son in selling their company to new ownership. It was very fulfilling because I was able to use my skills and experiences in the areas of business, finance, interpersonal relationships, and spirituality in a balanced way.

The ironic thing is almost ten years earlier I had helped the owner and president (a close friend) of a different company in the same Palm Springs/Coachella area sell their company to new ownership. Their product lines also included dates! I was due a six-figure fee at the close of this deal in 2011. Unfortunately, I never received the fee. The story is too long and complicated to go into, but after a great deal of soul searching, prayer, and research work, I decided to not pursue the non-payment of the fee.

Although desperately needing the money at the time, I felt in my heart that God did not intend for me to receive this money. I was told by my inner voice that my rewards would come later. It was a heartbreaking blow, yet I trusted God, and in the end, I was able to forgive all parties involved, including myself. I found over the ensuing years that my continuing financial leanness even helped me surrender more deeply and brought me closer to God. I trusted that God's guidance would eventually bring me a brighter, more expansive, and secure future.

Well, that brighter financial future has arrived. On the recent sale of the company, I received a financial fee that was many times greater than the fee I thought I was going to receive from selling the other company in 2011. This income made up for all the money that I hadn't made in the intervening years, including this lost fee. I found myself jubilantly drawing happy pictures of resurrection scenes much earlier than I ever imagined as I paid off all my benefactors and remaining debts. This was a gift beyond compare and left me flushed with good feelings. I also have enough money left to pursue my life dreams which I describe in the next two chapters. What a gift I have received! Yes,

Heaven can be trusted, and one may eventually realize that things that seem bad often happen because they are opening a door for something better to arrive in the future.

17 – New Direction, Lois W., and The Power of Love

These words from Theologian Henri Nouwen's book <u>The Return of the Prodigal Son</u>, probably best describe what I am trying to do with my work and life going forward. He said:

> "But I am grateful as well for the new place that has been opened in me through all the inner pain. I have a new vocation now. It is the vocation to speak and write from that place back into the many places of my own and other people's restless lives… I know now that I have to speak from eternity into time, from the lasting joy into the passing realities of our short existence in this world, from the house of love into the houses of fear."

His words touched me deeply. I am forever grateful for the new place that has been opened within me through the experience of inner pain and outer turmoil. I'm also deeply grateful that the pain and turmoil has been transmuted into an inner state of peace, serenity, happiness and love.

Henri Nouwen's words summarize the main pillars upon which my current and future work rest. I want to serve and inspire others through speaking and writing, as well as through other creative expressions such as films and/or documentaries. I want to share my life story and poetic verses which represent a story of recovery, hope, and resurrection. I want to help people believe in themselves and to help them see and realize their immense divine potential.

I would also like to be one of countless catalysts that help to advance the hypothesis put forward by Gopi Krishna that human evolution works through the biological mechanism of Kundalini; that it is a natural process and potential in all human beings; that the human brain is in an ongoing state of evolution; and that there is a predetermined objective to the next stage of human evolution - the Cosmic Conscious state of mind.

I believe the dissemination of this message and its eventual verification will have a profoundly positive impact on humanity. Frankly, I think it will one day change the world in a powerful way.

I feel it will give people great hope. Many people will see themselves in a more positive light. People will begin to realize that we all are on a path to divine consciousness and eternal life. The new knowledge gained and shared should eventually help to lessen humanity's excessive preoccupation with the material side of life, while increasing its attention on the spiritual and moral side. This in turn will help people to live a healthier and more balanced life, as well as to alleviate much suffering and many inequities in the world.

My goal is to continue to become a more loving person and be able to better express the love and compassion I have in my heart for people and life.

I believe we are ultimately here on earth to learn how to love and serve God, ourselves, and others. We need to develop the capacity to love to its fullest extent and be willing to die for love!

Today I feel a much deeper identification with people - their hopes, aspirations, frailties, and sufferings. I see most of us as wanting the same things in life - happiness, opportunity, freedom, prosperity, peace, good health, connection with others and love.

Vitold Kreutzer said the following at a spirituality conference I attended:

> "In life it is not about getting to the finish line first; it's about helping everyone to get to the finish line."

That really struck a chord in me.

Lois W., co-founder of Al-Anon, and wife of AA co-founder Bill W., wrote in her memoir Lois Remembers:

> "I deeply believe it is love that makes the world go round. God is love, and love is the creative force, the force that ties family and friends together. It inspires us to greater endeavor in all fields of activity, in love of God, love of man, love of ideas, love of self, love of things. The well of love refills itself. The more one gives of love, the more one has to give...I used to believe that thinking was the highest function of human beings. The AA experience changed me. I now realize loving is our supreme function. The heart precedes the mind.

> Gazing at the sky on a bright starlit night, we are overwhelmed with wonder at the seemingly limitless universe. Our finite minds cannot envision its extent and complexity, much less the possibility of other universes beyond. Likewise, our finite minds

sometimes question why a loving God seems to permit apparently God-loving and virtuous people to suffer the tragedies that occasionally befall them.

But our hearts do not need logic. They can love and forgive and accept that which our minds cannot comprehend. Hearts understand in a way minds cannot."

Lois W. also said in the same book:

"I suspect that love, too, is an actual physical emanation as well as a spiritual force."

Gandhi said in Trudy S. Settel's book The Book of Gandhi Wisdom:

"Love is the subtlest force in the world."

"Love is the strongest force the world possesses, and yet it is the humblest imaginable."

The following quotation from Martin Luther King, Jr. is engraved on his Memorial in Washington, D. C.:

"Darkness cannot drive out darkness. Only Light can do that. Hate cannot drive out hate, only love can do that."

Gopi Krishna said in his eBook The Last Discourses:

"The love you give, the service you do, the help you render is the food of the soul. It is immortal."

Walter Russell said in his book <u>The Quest of the Grail</u>:

"If you put love into everything you say or do, love will come back to you in the measure of your giving."

I believe that the universe is powered by love and that love is the spiritual reality behind the universe. I also believe love is a state of being that evolution, through fits and starts, is ultimately propelling humanity toward. We have not even begun to grasp how powerful and real this force can become in helping to effect positive change in society, and to heal ourselves, as well as the world.

Certain individuals such as the esteemed founders of our major religions, certain venerable mystics, saints, and yogis, many unknown, unsung regular people, as well as other giants such as Abraham Lincoln, Gandhi, Martin Luther King, Jr., Mother Teresa, and Nelson Mandela, to name but a few, have given us glimpses, but only glimpses, of the power of this force. To make it a more potent reality in the future, we must all discover how to better heal and love ourselves as well as others.

18 – My Dream Work and Life Purpose

When my father passed away in 2017, I was parentless. It was a sobering and lonely feeling. I soon came to a realization the best way I could honor my parents for all I had received, was to not dwell on their loss, but to live my life with deeper character, truth, and service. I know they would have wanted me to pursue my God-given desires and to finish my dreams. This is how I would best keep them present in my memory. And this is what I am endeavoring to do.

I believe my dream work and life purpose is to use my Solquest business and spiritual skills, knowledge, and experiences, as well as my creative talent and energy, to help advance this Kundalini theory of evolution, and to serve and love people. I have made a commitment to do this work and suspect I will become a hurricane force of focused energy and unbridled enthusiasm. I know it is time to step across the threshold of fear and uncertainty and pursue this path. I also know that finishing this book is one of the important steps on my path. Here is my vision of what some of these work dreams could one day entail.

<u>Books Published</u> - The initial springboard for beginning my work effort is to have this book written and self-published. I also have several shorter manuscripts nearing completion. These include a book of my poetic verses, as well as a small book that exchanges love poetry between myself and a brilliant young, handicapped man from Canada who is unable to speak and slowly going blind.

<u>Public Speaking</u> - The goal is to speak about the material of the books and this revolutionary theory in various public and private settings. As part of my speaking effort, I would eventually like to create a TED talk. I could envision possibly modeling such a talk on the inspiring

speech John F. Kennedy gave at Rice University in September of 1962, about the United States effort to land a human on the moon within that decade. In this case, the talk would be about creating a research project to prove the theory of Kundalini within a similar period of time.

Documentaries - I feel it is important to create a documentary about Gopi Krishna and this theory and disseminate it to the general public as soon as possible. Unfolding world events are confirmation that something has gone awry in humankind's evolution and current way of living and thinking. Quite possibly humanity is on a path to further disastrous events and even significant destruction. The unsettling nature of unfolding world events in turn have made people more open to new ideas. This theory and information provide new answers to why things are happening as they are in the world today and deserve a broader audience.

Another idea for a documentary relates to the film work of Walt Disney. Among the many films Walt Disney did in his lifetime, the content of two different documentaries stand out in relation to my work on Kundalini. Both were created in the 1950's: 1) An animated documentary *Man in Space* which helped build a large constituency for space exploration in the U.S.; in fact, President Eisenhower ordered that it be shown to his rocket experts; and 2) *Our Friend the Atom*, which also had the same effect in creating a consensus in the U.S. behind atomic energy.

In a similar fashion, I envision developing a documentary with the intention of building a large constituency in support of the concept of Kundalini and the inner exploration of the human mind. This time, the goal would be to create a worldwide consensus behind the idea of the exploration of "Inner Space" and the concept that there is an "Intelligent Energy or Electricity", that is responsible for the phenomenon of life; also that this Intelligent Energy is the controlling Intelligence behind the activity of the human body as well as is the driving force behind human evolution and the evolution of the human brain to the Cosmic Conscious state of mind. I believe such a documentary could help accelerate this step inward, and will inspire people, particularly our youth, who could lead the charge in advancing this concept forward.

<u>Feature Film</u> - One short synopsis for a possible movie related to the themes of inspiring life journeys, personnel recovery, and human potential and destiny, is the following:

Through the poignant and moving life stories of several down-to-earth individuals, it would trace their rise to material success and personal achievement, and then their fall into loss and subsequent emotional and spiritual pain. It would detail the reasons behind their rise and fall. And it would then portray the inspiring stories behind their subsequent recovery and rise to not only a more balanced and healthier spiritual and material life; but also, their entrance into a fascinating and wondrous new dimension of mind.

It would be a new type of Horatio Alger rags to riches story. In this case however, it would show how they were able to make the leap beyond materialism to the riches of spirituality, service, love, and personal evolutionary advancement (in terms of achieving a higher state of consciousness), as the primary guiding and motivating factors in their life.

The film would address the revolutionary idea of the continuing evolution of the human mind and brain. It would show that there already exists a potential in the human body and mind (the process of Kundalini) for an individual to make the leap beyond a normal state of consciousness into a more expanded state: the zenith of this potential expansion being represented by the Cosmic Conscious state of mind. The film would also introduce the idea that humankind is hard wired biologically for a more enlightened or Cosmic Conscious state of mind.

What do I mean when I talk about the Cosmic Conscious mind or a more profound state of awareness? As I described in the Introduction to *My Personal Story,* the next goal of human evolution, working through biological evolutionary processes (Kundalini) occurring in the body and brain, is to expand our awareness beyond the limitations of our five physical senses and intellect. The world of consciousness opens up, a new view of creation appears, and a whole new source of knowledge becomes directly accessible. The world looks and feels different to the transformed mind - more expansive, light, radiant, beautiful, and joyous.

This ongoing process of evolution to the Cosmic Conscious mind may expand the intellectual capacity of our minds, foster the development of new talents and genius-like abilities, and result in psychic and paranormal gifts. It also provides access to new intellectual and spiritual knowledge.

Finally, this process has the potential to result in a profound ongoing inner experience of love, light, beauty, melodious sound, joy, peace and happiness, as well as the loss of fear of death, an enhanced moral elevation and the realization of our eternal nature. In its highest transformation, the human mind may be able to perceive the unity underlying creation as well as the living, loving, conscious, and titanic intelligent presence behind life.

What a profound and noble gift this expanded state of mind represents for a human being. I believe the portrayal of this type of story would inspire people. It could serve to motivate many to embrace healthier values and lifestyles, as well as to aim for higher and more noble goals in life. Such changes in behavior and ideals could in turn eventually serve to reduce the immoderate thirst in people for material goods as well as the effects of runaway consumerism that plague not only Western society today, but increasingly the whole world. In addition, it would provide a more positive alternative to the alluring attraction of many dangerous temptresses when used to excess, such as alcohol, drugs, sex, food, and technology.

With the recent civil unrest in the United States in 2020 and 2021 and the call for racial and gender equality, many people, especially our youth, are in search of a healthier paradigm to live and work by. People want equal social and political systems to grow and participate in, and new life affirming stories to embrace, ones that are more in alignment with the continually advancing human consciousness.

I could envision such a movie addressing, connecting, and expanding upon some of the major themes and content of four different popular movies I watched and enjoyed over the last twenty-five years - *The Da Vinci Code*, *Contact*, *Shrek*, and *A Beautiful Mind*.

As opposed to *The Da Vinci Code,* it would unlock the true mystery behind religion and spirituality.

It would expand upon Carl Sagan's movie *Contact* by demonstrating that the Kundalini theory of evolution is one of the greatest discoveries awaiting humankind; that it can serve as the primer to unite science and religion; and that we can find new life and discover new secrets in the universe by "traveling" within our own minds and brains and unlocking the potential that exists therein.

It would follow the wise advice of *Shrek*, a charming ogre, who taught us that we must peel away the layers of our own onions to find the true beauty that lies within all of us. It would teach us that befriending and healing our imperfections and shortcomings are the gateway to God, to finding our true selves, to community with others, to inner peace, and to new potentials and higher wisdom residing within the human mind, brain, and heart.

Finally, it would take a giant leap beyond *A Beautiful Mind* in showing us that both genius and mental illness can originate from the same source, the process of Kundalini. Furthermore, it can show that with right ways of living, thinking, and behaving, with a healthy environment to live in, and the appropriate practice of spiritual, mental, and physical disciplines: that genius, inspiration, talent, and creativity can be cultivated; that the probability of mental illness and brain diseases occurring can be reduced as the human mind and brain continue to evolve; and that the Cosmic Conscious mind represents a true potential for human beings.

This may sound like science fiction, yet I firmly believe the force of truth is in these possibilities. What inspiring and uplifting news this represents for the human race!

<u>Disney Type Projects</u> - Walt Disney and the Disney Company's entertainment work over the years - cartoons, feature films, theme parks, etc. - have always inspired me. I see a connection between the innocence, goodness, happiness, beauty, and optimism embodied in so many of Walt Disney's creations, and this new amazing state of mind and world that await the human race.

I hope this theory and what it represents in terms of the potential of the human mind, a kind of **"Disneyland of the Mind"**, will one day be embodied in future Walt Disney creations (Exhibits at Disney theme parks and various venues, concepts featured in future movies and documentaries, animations, cartoons, etc.) and be the **"Happy Ending"** to the life work of Walt and Roy Disney.

19 – Jack London and My Valley of The Moon

When I worked at Prudential Capital in the late 1980's, I drove south from Marin County over the Golden Gate Bridge into San Francisco. As I crossed the bridge, I often wistfully looked out past the San Francisco Bay to the wide-open spaces of the Pacific Ocean.

I dreamed of one day visiting far-away lands, Hawaii, Tahiti, Australia, and China. I dreamed of pursuing a different life, a more adventurous life. My heart ached for something more. I felt I was living in a gilded prison, slowly suffocating, but not sure how to escape.

On April 27, 2010, I found myself reminiscing how this date represented my 8th year anniversary of moving to Washington, D.C. from the San Francisco Bay Area. The night before in meditation, my inner voice suggested I dig out the book <u>The Valley of the Moon</u>, written by famous author Jack London. I first read the book in the late 1990's. It had been probably ten years since I last read it. Quoting from the Introduction to the book written by Russ Kingman:

"The story is a California romance based on London's youth in Oakland, his experiences with Bohemian artists in Carmel, his four-horse trip to Oregon in 1911, his many adventures on the delta waters off the Sacramento and San Joaquin Rivers, and his ranch in the actual Valley of the Moon, just sixty miles north of San Francisco. These experiences are mirrored in the lives of Billy and Saxon, who, living [sic] behind a

miserable working-class existence in Oakland, embark
on an epic walking journey in search of prosperity,
fulfillment, and a dream ranch they thought could only
exist in a valley on the moon."

Often in the 1990s, I visited the Sonoma Area and frequently hiked at
Jack London Park. I loved this beautiful wine country area of Northern
California with its gorgeous vineyards, gently rolling hills, and
majestic redwood trees. It held a fascinating mystical charm, and I was
drawn to it like a magnet. It truly was "The Valley of the Moon".

When Jack London graduated from grammar school, he immediately
started a job working ten or more hours a day, six days a week. He felt
imprisoned and yearned for something better. He wanted to escape
what he called the "economic trap", and the urban industrial bondage
in which he felt imprisoned.

Returning again to the Introduction in The Valley of the Moon, Mr.
Kingman wrote:

> "But Jack yearned for something better and the books
> he read awakened him to possibilities. In the novel, this
> awakening comes to Saxon through a young fisherman
> on the Bay, whose advice 'Oakland is just a place to
> start from', becomes her strength in leaving behind her
> miserable life there."

Reading the passage reminded me that I had flown out of Oakland
when I moved to Washington, D.C in 2002 to start a new life.

In rereading parts of the book, it struck me how deeply I identified with Jack London, and the way he initially felt imprisoned in his work and life. I also related to how he expressed his own life's journey and search for something more in life through the journey and adventurous travels of Billy and Saxon.

Russ Kingman ended the Introduction by referencing what occurred at the end of the story with the following:

> "And finally, Billy and Saxon turn their steps toward the valley where they will end their journey…Billy and Saxon upon entering the valley, find all the conditions and requirements to be right at last. Their education nearly complete, the wanderers are ready to settle and begin building in reality the life they have been building so long in their imaginations. As they enter the valley, Billy affirms, 'I guess we won't winter in Carmel. This place was specially manufactured for us.' and Saxon: 'there isn't the slightest doubt. This is our place, I know it.'"

Approaching my own Valley of the Moon

As I finish writing this book, I also am entering my own Valley of the Moon. It's been a long, challenging, and fascinating journey to find my dream life and purpose.

I have escaped the gilded prison that earlier in my life kept me imprisoned. I also know my life up to this point has been a beautiful place to begin from and the best still lies ahead.

I'm not certain where my next destination is. As I described in the previous two chapters, I do have hopes, visions, and dreams, but I hold these gently. I no longer look wistfully to the ocean outside yearning for something more; but look expectantly to the ocean within, for directions to my next port of call. I know this ocean of true life is leading me to the fulfillment of my dreams and life destiny.

Finally, I know the journey to my next destination will be life affirming, life enhancing, and life expanding. I pray it becomes a little easier. I'm ready for a little bit of a vacation. I know the universe is smiling as I write this.

20 – Where Am I Today?

So where do I find myself today as I stand on the precipice of a new phase of my life? How have I grown to this point? What have I learned or found? What have I gained or lost?

In general, I have slowly become a more physically and mentally healthy, stable, vibrant, and happy person. The periods of anxiety and constant physical illnesses are almost nonexistent. In many ways, I feel better today at age 63 than I did at 35. Do I struggle and still have bad days? Yes! Occasionally I experience times when it feels as if I'm going backward in my journey. Thankfully I know this isn't true, and these periods are rare and don't last long.

Today I have a deep conviction about the direction of my work and life. On occasion, usually when I've overtired and stressed, the thought creeps into my mind that my work on this Kundalini theory of evolution has been a mistake: a grand illusion or delusion.

I laugh at myself and marvel that this can still occur. However, I take comfort in the fact that one of my favorite persons and mentors, St. Teresa of Avila wrote about this same thing happening to her during her own spiritual journey back in the 16th century. This shows the similarities of our human experiences, as well as the timeless nature of this journey of life we are all on.

I've come to accept that I am both fully human and fully divine, and that I am perfectly imperfect. I've slowly come to learn that in life it is about the journey, not the destination. It is about progress, not perfection.

I've also learned many new positive things.

I've learned how to take care of myself, to better express myself, and to share myself with others, including the good, bad, beautiful, and ugly. I've learned to love, nurture, and forgive myself. I've learned to feel and share my feelings. I've learned that I matter, my life matters, and that I'm right where I'm supposed to be in my life. For most of my life, I've felt I was behind schedule. Today, I know I'm right on schedule.

As I write this today, I can honestly say I've lost many things in my life that I'm glad I've lost. These include most of my self-consciousness, unhealthy addictions, anxiety, grief, and rage. Also, I've healed many fears including fear of flying (that was a big one); fear of dying (that was a bigger one); fear of public speaking (that may have been the biggest); fear of not being enough; and most recently fear of being so called "successful" again. I've learned that all of these things were keeping me separated from my True Self, others, God, and a gracious and meaningful life. I must admit though that I haven't completely lost my fear of doctors or the medical establishment; or of having a debilitating illness; or of being able to successfully finish my Kundalini life work. However, I now see these fears as prompts for further growth.

To a greater or lesser degree, I lost, gained, or found the following:

- I lost my outer security for a period of time and gained inner trust, peace, and serenity.
- I lost thinking I was in control and gained knowing God is in charge and could be trusted.
- I lost who I thought I was and found who I am.

- I lost thinking I was always right and gained knowing only God knows what is right.
- I lost what I thought I'm supposed to do and be and gained my freedom, work I love, and dreams beyond my dreams.
- I lost my childishness, immaturity, and self-criticism and gained childlike wonder, maturity, and self-appreciation.
- I lost knowing what you should do and gained minding my own business and peace of mind.
- I lost fear of dying and gained joy of living.
- I lost fear of flying and gained the freedom to soar in life with my feet on the ground.
- I lost fear of speaking and gained finding my voice.
- I lost thinking I was so different from you and gained seeing you as a new family member.
- I found if I wanted to know something, I could ask God before I went to bed and often the answer was there in the morning.
- I found I could get through any problem or challenge with God's help.
- I found life is an adventure and has meaning and purpose.
- I found life is eternal and forever moving toward greater levels of adventure, happiness, and peace.

I now know that God always provides if I do the footwork. I am not financially wealthy or a CEO of a large company like I envisioned, but I am what I'm supposed to be, I do receive what I need, and most importantly, I am given what is best for me.

I also know God has a plan for me, which will also benefit others. I know I can trust it even when I'm not trusting it or in fear, which is very infrequent these days.

I've learned patience and the need to persevere when pursuing my dreams. I love the below saying from Eleanor Roosevelt. She was talking about her husband, the 32nd President of the United States, Franklin Delano Roosevelt (FDR), and his battle with polio. It appears on a wall at the entrance to one of my favorite Memorials, the FDR Memorial, in Washington, D.C.:

> "Franklin's illness gave him strength and courage he had not had before. He had to think out the fundamentals of living and learn the greatest of all lessons, infinite patience and never-ending persistence."

Most recently, I found Eleanor Roosevelt again speaking to me through the following quote from her book You Learn by Living: Eleven Keys for a More Fulfilling Life:

> "You gain strength, courage and confidence by every experience in which you really stop to look fear in the face....You must do the thing you think you cannot do."

Ugh! I knew in the deepest fiber of my being that this among other things was speaking to my calling to finish writing this book, to share my story and poetic verses with others, and to speak publicly about the truth of Kundalini and its astounding positive implications for the human race!

In the end, I've realized that some of my greatest gifts have come out of my greatest tribulations. Likewise, with many of my failures, I realize God was closing one door, to later open another larger, better door.

I've slowly come to believe that nothing on our journey of life is ever wasted or lost. Rather, I feel everything I go through has a purpose, and any suffering I endure, pain I feel, or loss I experience, no matter how traumatic, has the potential, through prayer and spiritual work, to be accepted and gradually transmuted by God into something of deeper meaning or purpose for my work, life, soul, and future.

From poetic verse #19, "A Message of Hope", I wrote:

> "Soon all will be bathed in love and light. I say goodbye temporarily in the present to welcome a future that will be bright beyond my conception. It is a future born out of a deep trust and love for God.
>
> I step forward, not looking back as I know my future will capture all of my lost pasts. It is a path that winds down a never-ending road into a magical kingdom of life, light, peace, and love."

One of my favorite sayings found in a 12-step book is, "Present joy wipes out past unhappiness."

What I've gradually come to realize is that underneath tremendous grief and loss, a shining new world is being shown to me, and a new and more expanded life is welcoming me.

21 – Kundalini - Why Me?
Dr. Bob and Bill W.

So today, how are my body and mind responding to the effects of this ongoing Kundalini process, and how do I see and experience the world through my consciousness?

Before I describe some of the changes that have occurred, I thought it might be helpful if I first explained why I believe I experienced a Kundalini awakening. And despite all the challenges, why I've been able to grow into a relatively healthy progression of the ongoing Kundalini process.

The short answer to both questions is I'm not exactly sure. I am by no means an expert in this area and am still trying to better understand what the experience is all about. I approach these questions with a deep level of humility as I'm addressing a domain and Intelligence that will always remain far beyond my full understanding. I'd like to share some thoughts and ideas that have come to me out of my own experiences, through discussions with other people familiar with the concept of Kundalini, my in-depth study of Gopi Krishna's books and materials, as well as reading other literature on the subject matter.

First of all, I may have been evolutionarily ripe for the experience. Our minds, brains, bodies, and nervous systems have to be developmentally ready. I believe heredity plays a large part in terms of our readiness for experiencing an awakening and taking the next evolutionary step.

I personally believe that good heredity, the intellectual development of our minds, the practice of moral and ethical behavior, the development of a pure and loving character, living a healthy, moderate, and balanced life, practicing an appropriate blend of physical, mental, and spiritual disciplines, and living a life in accordance with the basic ideals stressed in all healthy forms of religion, spirituality, and human ethical systems are all important elements.

I believe most of the credit goes to my parents and ancestors, as I believe the composite of positive, personal qualities they possessed played a large part in genetically predisposing me to a fairly healthy awakening. For example, my dad was honest, hard-working, had a high degree of integrity, and an intelligent mind. My mother was wise, humble, loving, and kind. Both were unselfish and concerned with the welfare of others.

I come from a devoutly Catholic religious background. My father's side of the family came from the Alsace Loraine area of France, and you can find the family last name on a stain glass window in the local church dating back to the 1800s. There are some extended family members who became priests. My mother's side of the family came from Prague, Czechoslovakia and seemed to have a particularly loving disposition. I think my mystical frame of mind and intense desire to search for the deeper mysteries of life probably have come from both sides of the family. My sister recently told me that she believes one of our relatives, traced through my paternal grandmother's side of the family, participated in the American Revolutionary War and lived in Boonesborough, KY with frontier pioneer Daniel Boone. Maybe this is where the pioneering side of my own personality comes from?

Awakening Process Over Time

When I reflect back on the progression of events in my life, I feel the awakening has been slowly happening since childhood. When I was younger, I believe it was occurring in a more gradual fashion. At that time, I was not able to feel the energy moving, or any of the other physical effects. I don't believe my body and mind were physically and psychologically ready for the experience, and that is why I may have had early trouble with anxiety, and other minor mental instabilities. I also mentioned previously how the environment that existed in my family and society then, as well as the way I chose to live my life, were probably not optimal in terms of facilitating a healthy awakening process.

The awakening process began to intensify for me in the fall of 1985 at the age of 28. I had just graduated from business school and was living in New Jersey. Suddenly I had a strong desire to return to church, and I felt a soothing, calming spiritual presence envelop me one day. This feeling remained with me for some time. Then in 1989 at my grandmother's funeral in Davenport, Iowa, I observed a stunning, radiant, otherworldly light piercing through the clouds when I was at her gravesite.

The ongoing awakening process stirred again in a stronger fashion in 1992 as I approached 35 years of age. Suddenly I was directed toward the life of Mahatma Gandhi and the ideals of truth and humility. I felt a strong desire to be honest in all my dealings and behavior. I thought in new and deeper ways while experiencing a flow of fresh insights and understandings in many different subject fields including the areas of business, politics, spirituality, and the meaning of life. The power of my mind seemed to have increased. I also became enthralled by the beauty of nature. Nature had come alive and was dancing with new vibrant colors and energy. I found myself constantly conversing in my journals with an Intelligent Presence that I called God and writing about the mystery of consciousness. One day I wrote that I would become involved with bringing a new consciousness to the world (I didn't really know what the term consciousness meant at the time and I held this message with some humor and much humility and skepticism). This was also around the time that a new talent developed as I began to write in poetic verse.

The strongest phase of the awakening began around 1997 as I was approaching 40 years of age. As previously discussed, I began to experience premonitory dreams and psychic and paranormal experiences as well as my mind seemed to have expanded and my vision and hearing changed. For the first time I physically felt the sensation of a strong luminous current of energy flowing throughout my body and into my head as well as experienced other physiological and psychological changes. I also found that the speed of my poetic verse writing, in terms of the number of verses I was writing per year increased greatly.

More Profound Experiences

As the years progressed, there were even more profound otherworldly experiences, pointing to even a deeper change in my consciousness. The following are some examples of these types of experiences.

In the year 2000, I found myself driving down Third Street one afternoon in San Rafael, CA. It was a beautiful sunny day. I stopped at a stoplight and looked out the window when suddenly the sky above was filled with what seemed like a fountain of continually expanding waves of joy interfused with a bright light. This lasted for perhaps a minute. It was a stunning experience. I had a very similar experience that summer as I gazed up at the blue sky while walking through the Marin County Fair with a dear friend. I continued to have these experiences in different places over the years. What was even more profound was that as time went on, I found my inner state of being was gradually becoming filled with a never ceasing and ever-increasing bubbling fountain of joy and bliss.

One day in 2004 as I walked outside the National Gallery of Art Museum in Washington, D.C, I looked up to the sky and suddenly there was no differentiation between myself, others and the rest of the world. Everything and everyone seemed to have merged together into this oneness and unity. At the same time, I felt the presence of this one great Intelligent Being that we were all enclosed in. I find myself struggling to find words to describe this experience. It came and went quickly but has remained permanently etched in my memory.

One night in 2014 I was waiting for a train on the platform at the Tysons Corner Metro Station. As I looked up in the night sky and off to the distance, suddenly, the whole sky was filled with a sparkling, vibrating, shimmering radiance, lightness and airiness. I believe I was seeing Consciousness or Life, in its native form. It's almost impossible to describe how wondrous it was. The scene held me completely in awe. It also filled me with a feeling of deep yearning as I intuitively knew that this is the world we really belong to.

Finally, in 2018 as I drove eastward from California through the vast open spaces of New Mexico, I suddenly found myself wonderstruck as I stared ahead at what I can only describe as a titanic consciousness, a bubbling fountain of joy, light and peace, that permeated the whole of the distant sky. Once again it was a fairly brief, but stunning experience, one that left me with feelings of great hope and inspiration.

Afterwards, as I continued to reflect on what I had just beheld, this analogy came to mind. Gopi Krishna also used similar analogies to describe the difference between normal human consciousness and the Divine Intelligence or Consciousness behind the universe. This titanic-like Consciousness could be likened to the full splendor of the radiant sun, and, by comparison, my normal human awareness was more like that of the feeble glow of a tiny firefly. It was also apparent that if I were to experience the full power and splendor of this Consciousness all at once, I would be fried, like a mosquito being torched by a bug zapper!

I perceive these experiences as different from the psychic and paranormal occurrences I described earlier in chapter 10. They were more powerful and all-encompassing and spoke to an upcoming change in the volume and depth of my own consciousness. I saw them as individual experiences of different characteristics of the Cosmic Conscious state of mind, which eventually blend together in a more permanent fashion (i.e., the Cosmic Conscious mind represents a permanent composite of all these types of experiences and probably many more that my limited awareness cannot yet comprehend).

When I reflect again on the events and experiences of my life, I realize that I have been encountering short tastes of this new consciousness (what I call early hints or whisperings) all along the way. These experiences were gradually preparing me for a more permanent change of consciousness that would occur later in my life. When I was in the ninth grade my family went on a spring vacation cruise that was sailing from New York City down to the Caribbean Islands. The night before the ship embarked, we stayed in a New York hotel. As were standing in the lobby waiting for my dad to check us in, I suddenly felt an intense loving connection with every person that walked past me. At the same time, I experienced tremendous sadness because I realized I would never see them again. This is my first remembered experience of feeling that everything and everyone is connected in love.

If this new consciousness had arrived all at once, I would have been completely overwhelmed. The Kundalini process needed to unfold gradually. I believe God was preparing me in small ways, bit by bit, for an eventual entrance into this new world of awareness.

All these experiences were pointing to my true path and purpose in life as well as my True Self. They were indications of a future destiny for the whole human race of amazing new experiences and perceptions. There was an inner universe, a deeper level of creation waiting to be explored, with gifts beyond compare.

As one begins to have experiences and receive communications from this higher dimension of consciousness, it takes time and effort to understand the new language and integrate these experiences into one's daily life. What do the experiences mean? What is this higher dimension trying to communicate? How do these things affect how I'm meant to be living my current life? In time, answers to such presently obscure and confounding questions such as, who are we, why are we here, where do we come from, and where are we going, all become clearer as one advances deeper into this next dimension of consciousness.

These experiences were gradually preparing me for the onset of a new state of consciousness filled with gradually increasing levels of joy, peace, beauty, radiance, sublimity, light, new knowledge and love. I will discuss these changes in my consciousness in more detail in the next chapter.

The process of the stronger awakening continues unabated today. On the physical side, I still experience the following: a luminous energy current flowing into my head; some form of secretions or essences flowing upward from my reproductive area also into my head (It is interesting to note that the Taoists and ancient Chinese in the practice of Qigong, wrote about the energy flowing up to the brain from the reproductive area); a melodious humming sound in my head and ears; and finally certain changes in my bodily functions including increased digestion and elimination processes. On the mental or psychological/psychic side, new inspirations and knowledge continue to flow into my awareness along with deeper vistas of this sublime world.

I believe working to personally, psychologically, and spiritually develop and heal myself since my early 20s, and to live my life as best as I could on spiritual and ethical principles, facilitated this strong awakening. This work has also helped the ongoing process to progress in a relatively healthy manner.

I was fortunate in that heredity endowed me with a strong physical body and mind. This not only allowed me to withstand the tremendous force and upheaval that accompanied the stronger awakening in 1997 but has also enabled me to handle the rigors of the ongoing process.

I'm not discounting the fact that the tremendous stress and pressure I experienced during my "dark night of the soul" period in 1996-1998 may have played some role in triggering the more powerful awakening.

Furthermore, it is believed that intense meditation and/or concentration are levers that can ignite a Kundalini awakening. I have meditated on and off since my late 20s and have always concentrated hard in my studies and work. These factors may have played a role too or perhaps it was a combination of all the aforementioned factors?

Finally, I believe it is the grace of God that ultimately determines when an awakening will occur. What I'm saying is why an awakening happens when it does, is still beyond our human understanding. More of the laws that govern creation and human evolution, as well as the processes that occur in our bodies, brains, and minds, will have to be discovered and sufficiently understood, before we begin to comprehend the mystery of Kundalini.

In poetic verse #30 (see complete verse included as #6 in Section II - Poetic Verses), "Silvery Radiance and Deep Peace", I wrote:

> "… All of a sudden, the door opens, and a new layer of creation is revealed, embedded in an existing layer; so simple, yet so profound, the key to the mystery. One can only enter on God's terms. A whole new set of laws governs this creation. Only God knows the time when the curtain is lifted. It is never lifted on our terms."

Humility and Surrender

Experience taught me that once the awakening occurred, I was totally dependent on the guidance of this Intelligence within to first stabilize me, and then to help the ongoing process proceed in a healthy manner. I found that deep humility and surrender to a Higher Power were absolutely critical in this regard. I define humility as being in right relationship with God, myself and others. For me this means asking continually for guidance from God throughout the day and trusting this guidance. I also must do the footwork that I'm asked to do. In terms of others, it means seeing myself in an equal and loving relationship, and living a life based on giving, serving, and receiving. For myself, it means loving myself and taking care of myself so that I can give to others in an appropriate way without losing myself.

I found myself praying constantly for greater humility. I joked with my friends that they should beware of what they pray for, because in my case, it seemed I would always be given difficult trials and tribulations. Perhaps I needed these to bring me to my knees to surrender my pride. After each challenging experience, it always seemed like I was left with a little less of my self-will and a little more of God's will operating inside of me.

Gopi Krishna shared that the Intelligence within us that directs the evolutionary process, is far superior to the intelligence of the product that it creates and directs (i.e., our brains, bodies and intellects/egos). Therefore, unlike the material world, one does not wrest control of this subtle world of Intelligence by force of arm or use of self-will or intellect. This is also why a complete surrendering to this greater Intelligence is necessary.

One must learn to approach the subtle intelligent forces of life with an attitude of great reverence and humility. This does not always come easy to our often-proud egos and intellects, which want to remain the rulers of our personal destiny. This is why it often takes significant trials and tribulations, intense suffering, and/or personal failures for our egos/intellects to relinquish control.

In verse #30, "Silvery Radiance and Deep Peace", I wrote:

"Where have you been hidden? I searched forever. Now the door to my heart swings open, and God reveals a new layer of creation; so beautifully simple, yet so elegant, so majestic, so full of grandeur.

Where have you been hidden? One does not enter by force, or by self-will, a complete yielding to God is necessary. We must be cleansed of all impurities, all selfish tendencies."

Dr. Bob and Bill W.

One of my favorite definitions of humility, as well as acceptance, comes from Dr. Bob, who was co-founder of the 12-step program of Alcoholics Anonymous (AA). Dr. Bob kept a plaque on his bedroom desk at his home in Akron, Ohio, which said the following:

"Humility - perpetual quietness of the heart. It is to have no trouble. It is never to be fretted or vexed, irritable or sore; to wonder at nothing that is done to me, to feel nothing done against me. It is to be at rest when nobody praises me, and when I am blamed or despised, it is to have a blessed home in myself where I can go in and shut the door and pray to my father [and Mother] in secret and be at peace, as in a deep sea of calmness, when all around and about is seeming trouble."

Interestingly enough, Bill W., the other co-founder of Alcoholics Anonymous, had simultaneously both a deep surrender experience related to his life and death struggle with alcohol, as well as what could be considered a Kundalini awakening experience. Robert Thomsen wrote the following stirring account of Bill W.'s experiences in his book <u>Bill W.</u>:

> "The cancer of alcohol had already killed his mind, his will, his spirit, and it was only a matter of time before it would kill his body. Yet at this moment, with the last vestige of pride, the last trace of obstinacy crushed out of him, still he wanted to live…He would do anything, anything, to be allowed to go on living.

> 'Oh God,' he cried, and it was the sound not of a man, but of a trapped and crippled animal. 'If there is a God, show me. Show me. Give me some sign.'

> **As he formed the words, in that very instant he was aware first of a light, a great white light that filled the room, then he suddenly seemed caught up in a kind of joy, an ecstasy such as he would never find words to describe. It was as though he were standing high on a mountaintop and a strong clear wind blew against him, around him, through him but it seemed a wind not of air, but of spirit - and as this happened, he had the feeling that he was stepping into another world, a new world of consciousness, and everywhere now there was a wondrous feeling of Presence which all his life he had been seeking. Nowhere had he ever felt so complete, so satisfied, so embraced."**

In fact, it's my understanding that Bill W.'s spiritual or Kundalini awakening experience was one of the impetuses that led him to eventually help co-found the worldwide 12-step program of AA.

As I read the description of Bill W.'s "surrender" experience, I could relate to his deep feelings of helplessness and need to surrender to God, because of my own life struggles and experiences. In addition, I found that the descriptions of his "white light" experience, his experience of an indescribable joy and ecstasy, his stepping into a new world of consciousness, and finally his feeling of a Presence everywhere, mirror aspects of some of my experiences as well as certain attributes of my own ongoing state of awareness today.

22 – New Consciousness: My Soul and Mind Awakened

So where do I find myself today with my Kundalini process and what is my present state of awareness?

The psychic, paranormal and visionary experiences have continued but occur less frequently and have gradually been subsumed by what I would describe as an alluring, mesmerizing, and sublime state of consciousness. I have also developed some new gifts and talents, as well as a more powerful, holistic, inspired and intuitive mind.

This is how I would describe my present state of consciousness. It is profoundly different than before my Kundalini awakening. I feel like I live in two worlds at the same time. One is the normal physical world that we all experience and inhabit, and just a hair's breadth away is the world of Consciousness and Intelligence. There is a fine line separating these two realities. Over time, the boundary between them is slowly melting away with the physical world beginning to exist or appear as an image in this world of Consciousness. I will try my best to describe this as well as share some passages from my verses to help place you in my consciousness. Here are some highlights.

The onset of this new consciousness over the years has been quite gradual. Today I live in a peaceful, balmy, joyful, inner state of being. It feels like I have awakened from a dream and landed in a soothing paradise of love, beauty, harmony, happiness, and light. I am slowly experiencing a new Heaven on Earth! Bubbling fountains of joy and cascading waterfalls of happiness fill my interior; while the enhanced world picture I now see is occasionally interpenetrated by melting waves of soft, beautiful rainbow-like colors. When I focus my attention inward, the intensity of this experience increases, and I am absorbed in a soft, radiant, and sparkling ocean of light and bubbling joy. This state of being is always present within me, but it seems to ebb and flow with sometimes greater or lesser intensity. It appears to be slowly growing stronger and steadier as the years progress. This indicates to me the Kundalini process is progressing in a healthy manner.

My soul feels liberated, and now mixes with this sublime ocean. Like the genie leaving the bottle, my consciousness seems to float out of my body, beyond the anchor of flesh, spreading outward in increasing waves of joy and happiness. When younger, I was sometimes claustrophobic. I remember one time being stuck in the middle of a crowd at a University of Wisconsin basketball game and I panicked. I felt like I was going to be suffocated. My biggest fear was to be buried alive and now I know why. My soul was buried in a tomb, the tomb of my body, waiting to one day be released by the power of Kundalini.

I feel a deep and more lasting peace within myself. In verse # 30, "Silvery Radiance and Deep Peace", I wrote:

> "We sit quietly. We are beyond the veil of tears. A deep silence enters our hearts. We have entered the silent chamber of God's heart. We now are held deep in the heart of God's love; never again will we doubt. Deeper and deeper we enter. We penetrate to the heart of eternity; all form passes away. All that is left is a deep silence, a deep peace, a sea of consciousness forever graces our hearts."

Now when I look out upon the world, it appears more transparent, soft, alluring, and embracing, somewhat like a cross between the appearance of a clear Jell-O substance and the mirror-like surface of a calm lake, in which you see reflections of objects. The outer world seems to be a projection of my own consciousness, with everything happening inside of my own awareness, instead of being composed of separate, material objects or events happening outside of it. Creation is reflected in the mirror of my own consciousness and the physical world has lost its dimension, substance, and separateness.

I relate this to watching a movie in the theater. You see moving images on the screen that seem to have dimension and separateness and substance but are really only a projection of film images through a light onto a screen.

In my case, it's as if I now see my Self as both my mind, which is the projector of my life and the universe, and also, simultaneously, as a physical being or actor in the play of life. These images are projected, through the vehicle of the brain, onto the screen of space or this living, Intelligent Consciousness. The brain being a receiver, recorder and transmitter of mind or consciousness rather than a generator of such. The difference is that now I see my real Self as my mind or this radiant, joyous consciousness, which has a permanent existence, as opposed to thinking I'm a frail, mortal body, which will eventually die. It is a stunning yet very difficult to describe transformation.

For years, I've heard a musical melody in my head. Lately it sounds like a gently flowing stream or the sweet hum of a swarm of bees. It's gradually becoming more pleasant; for a number of years after my initial Kundalini awakening, the sound was strident and harsh.

I have a strong knowing that we are all immortal; that our souls are eternal: that nothing can harm, disturb, or cause the death of this eternal reality. With my inner sight I perceive that this same eternal reality, or consciousness, that runs through me, is also running through you, other forms of life, and all of creation.

I also have a deep knowing that as we continue to evolve and heal, this eternal reality (this deeper level of consciousness, love, and connection to God), is slowly unfolding from within ourselves to heal the seemingly outer physical part of our past life experiences and present existence. Creation sits in an ocean of love, mercy, light, and intelligence, and becoming aware of this is one of the gifts of the next state of consciousness. I have a mild awareness now of this ocean and it is gradually getting stronger as the years progress.

In verse #26, "The Diamond Within", I spoke to this inner healing process and its ultimate goal when I wrote:

> "All of creation has been healed and returned to its rightful state. Every act, every energy, every part of existence has been healed by God's sweet love, gentle, caressing, peaceful, merciful, and tender.
>
> The outer garment of flesh has been stripped away to reveal the diamond within. The diamond within then unfolds to heal all of our existence; nothing is left untouched; nothing is left impure…
>
> All of history is healed. The temporal now becomes the eternal, forever transfigured in God's healing, glowing love."

I also see with my inner sight that this material level of reality we experience (i.e., the physical world) really serves as a container (in a sense a transport system), for our rebirth into this next state of consciousness. When one fully awakens to this new reality, then one realizes that he, she and the universe never dies, and that all are part of God.

It seems as if this deeper, more substantial and permanent me, is now observing my surface daily life pass by as if I'm watching myself in a movie or dream.

Here's another way to picture the relationship between normal reality and this next state of awareness. Gopi Krishna mentioned several examples of this type in his writings. It's as if all of physical existence, including human beings, are like the fish or sea life you see beneath the surface of the clear, calm ocean. You perceive them vividly, but they exist in this ocean of water. In a like manner, all of physical reality seems to exist as images on this titanic ocean of intelligence, which seems to be spread everywhere, and is conscious, living, and loving. It also seems far more real and permanent than normal physical reality. I realize my own awareness is a drop from this ocean of intelligence and seems to spread beyond the confines of my body and intermix with this ocean of intelligence and infinitude. When this happens, I become the universe, I become eternal.

I contrasted these different levels of reality - normal physical existence and this ocean of consciousness - in verse #26, "The Diamond Within", when I wrote:

"The phenomenal (physical) world retreats and becomes a mirror image of itself; within the heart of

our souls is a universe so expansive, so great, that
surface consciousness appears like the frosting on the
outside of a cake…

Now the individual material parts look like pearls
strung together on a necklace, held together by the
garland of existence, floating in a sea of love…

Within mortal man and woman is a gem so great, that
the best of the physical creation looks like the fleeting
shadow of a vanishing ghost. Now we are whole, now
we are eternal, now we know our true selves."

In our normal state of mind, we are not able to perceive this ocean of
consciousness, at least I couldn't. It's as if our minds are sealed in
watertight compartments. We see ourselves as separated from each
other, like desert islands floating in a vast ocean, and aren't aware that
we are all connected and part of this one conscious, living, loving,
eternal consciousness.

In verse #14 "Our True Home" (see complete verse included as #4 in
Section II - Poetic Verses), I referred to this deeper unity and level of
reality when I wrote:

"Now I know my true Self that exists in you and you in
me. We are no longer separate, separated by vales of
tears, but we are the perfume of cosmic holiness that
reaches out in Love, embraces all in Love, and creates
a space for all to unite."

It also becomes clear that our ego/intellect level of consciousness is inadequate to understand this greater reality. It's like an ant trying to explain the workings of the universe or a fish trying to gauge the size of the ocean. Gopi Krishna gave numerous examples of this form in his writings.

What also becomes starkly clear is that humanity is not free to do whatever it pleases in this world. In addition to physical laws, it becomes patently clear that there are also spiritual laws or laws of consciousness as well as evolutionary laws, that govern our thought, behavior and growth as human beings. It is imperative that we begin to more fully understand these laws and how-to-live in accordance with them. It is humanity's violations of these laws that have put it in trouble today. We don't realize that there is a greater goal for humankind, the Cosmic Conscious Mind, which requires different ways of thinking, behaving and living than we are doing currently.

In summary, I believe that with our arrival at the next destination in our evolutionary life, our view of creation will be flipped on its head. The material universe will lose its size and substance and our mind and being will become a titanic giant, a monarch, a king and queen, an eternal drop of glory in this infinite ocean of Consciousness.

We will no longer see ourselves as an inconsequential grain of sand in an unfathomably large material universe, that could be blown away by a gust of wind, like a speck of dust, and never be missed; but we will see the truth that we are a blazing eternal ray of a living, loving, conscious Sun which shines forever.

23 – Crucifixion and Resurrection

As I've shared in this story, my journey toward God and birthing of a new awareness have involved a fair amount of suffering. This was necessary to clear away my old self, to allow a new Self to slowly emerge. The birthing process generally involves significant labor pain and birthing a new consciousness and a deeper spiritual orientation in life are no exception, at least at this point in our evolutionary development.

I also discovered I didn't have to go into a monastery, forest, ashram, or live an ascetic life for this to happen. I have lived a fairly normal life, however with some important modifications as I described earlier in my story. In many ways, it felt like I had undergone a crucifixion, yet I always felt the presence of God's love nearby. And I understood this love was behind my crucifixion.

The "good news" is that my story does not end with a crucifixion. I have also experienced a resurrection. The changes that have occurred in my being have opened up a beautiful new world; one that I never knew or dreamed existed!

Resurrection

The joy and stunning nature of this resurrection is probably best poetically described in the following passages from verse # 44 entitled, "Cosmic Consciousness" (see complete verse included as #10 in Section II - Poetic Verses), in which I wrote:

> "I now see the truth. This is our future; this is who we really are. I have left the tabernacle of flesh to soar to

regions of empyrean joy and unspeakable glory. My soul is lifted up to Heaven! The trumpets sound, the celestial angels sing, God's loving embrace sweetens every pore of my body. I have become pure spirit, with some invisible link to flesh, roaming the celestial vault, drinking in the nectar of the gods, sailing with angels, floating on streams of light, emblazoned with hues of color, light as a feather. We have become the ocean, love's pure light… We are now sailing on celestial seas of glory, happy and free, liberty emblazoned in our heart; our eternal freedom, the touch of God, the sweet kiss of our ancestors, a dreamlike existence; oceans of bliss, the pure blue sky, deep blue waters, fresh breezes, swaying palm trees, daisies, the flowers of heaven; filled with light, streams of joy, blazing light, never ending delight. We float, we caress, we absorb, we dance. We have found heaven in our souls, here on earth while alive in flesh, **Earth's new Eden**."

This is the good news that awaits us all, whether in this life, or a future one to come.

Finally, in verse #37, "Resurrection/New Science and Religion" (see complete verse included as #7 in Section II - Poetic Verses), I wrote:

"We are not specks of matter, conceived by chance, brought to earth to live a flickering existence, soon to turn to dust, forever gone, with no meaning, no truth, no continuity. These are fables of old. This is the old science.

The new science of life recognizes our eternal being, the permanent nature of our souls. The world is forever born inside of us. We see new vistas of creation, for eternity.

This is the new science of which we are touching the frontier. It is both a science and religion. It is a universal religion embracing all of humankind. It heralds a new chapter in the life of humankind, in the history of the world. We come face to face with a great truth, the eternal nature of our beings, the discovery of new energies, new planes of creation, and the intelligent forces of life.

This is where the new science and religion begins. We are infants in our evolutionary development destined to become super men and women in the future, forever approaching the divine light, the source of our being. This is what keeps our hearts young and our hopes eternal, allowing us to withstand the rigors of life; our glorious future destiny, unfolding from the seeds of our souls, deep within our hearts."

These passages reflect the knowing that many of us hold dear in our hearts that this journey on Mother Earth does have enduring meaning, that we are not alone, and our existence does not end with the physical death of our body.

My story which began as a young child so excited about the future and the possibilities it offered, yet also filled with some anxiety and fear, now finds me arriving in a new world of light and delight,

with the glee and wonder of a small child, knowing a new treasure hunt has begun, one that goes on forever; as I am now exploring the mystery behind the Mystery of the universe - Consciousness.

24 - What I Have Come to Believe

In summary, looking through the lens of my own life experiences and accumulation of knowledge, and based on the teachings of Gopi Krishna and others, I have come to believe the following:

• The ultimate purpose of life is to know ourselves. It is to realize that we were created for a purpose, that our individual life has meaning, and that each of us has a duty to fulfill in life. It is also to realize that another channel of perception and source of knowledge, what could be called a sixth sense, is slowly blooming in the human race.

• The Cosmic Conscious state of mind is the evolutionary blueprint imprinted in our brains and minds, which human life is inexorably evolving toward.

• The power of the Super Intelligence that guides the race is slowly rising through the vehicle of humankind. As we become more evolved; as our minds, bodies, brains, and nervous systems become more developed, refined, purified, and attuned; we are better able to generate and assimilate a higher quantity and more potent form of this Intelligent Life Energy flowing inside of us. This process of increased Intelligent Life Energy flow is accompanied and supported by other physiological processes that simultaneously occur in the body and brain. The flow of this more powerful Intelligent Life Energy and vitalizing reproductive essences into our brain energizes and nourishes a newly activated area, and also leads to changes in the brain at a very subtle level. This results in an increase in the power and performance of our brains and minds and the opening up of a new channel of perception. This new channel of perception allows us to directly access a more powerful source of knowledge and also enables us to perceive more of what I believe is an infinite creation. Gopi Krishna wrote the following in his book <u>Kundalini - The Secret of Yoga</u>, referring to the currently underutilized Intelligent Life Energy potential that lies within humankind:

> "In his present way of life, man utilizes only a small part of the psychic force [Intelligent Life Energy] residing in his body."

• As the Kundalini hypothesis suggests, we will never be able to fully understand the goal of the next step of evolution through our intellect and five physical senses. This is one of the reasons why another channel of perception is slowly emerging in the human race through the mechanism of Kundalini and the evolution of our brain. Once we have reached a certain level of spiritual, material, and intellectual development, we often develop a consuming thirst to know ourselves at a deeper level, and to understand the purpose and meaning of life. The opening of this other channel of perception allows us to begin to solve the riddle of our own existence. Gopi Krishna also said in the book <u>The Way to Self-Knowledge</u>, in terms of our ability to know our souls:

> "This is beyond the normal brain and needs a rare organic change in it to bring the intangible plane of soul within its widened range."

• The material world we live in is a stern reality but seen from a higher dimension of consciousness, it appears dreamlike, almost like an illusion. Gopi Krishna wrote in <u>The Wonder of the Brain</u> about the possibilities inherent in Kundalini and our future evolution:

"...the normal human mind is a prison for the soul, and... nature has already provided the key [Kundalini] to open it to allow individuals to soar to freedom in regions of unspeakable glory and joy."

• I believe scientific research will in the not-too-distant future, substantiate the following critical concepts related to Kundalini:

There is a <u>Biological Evolutionary Mechanism</u> in human beings whose activity involves the whole human body. One of this mechanism's most important functions revolves around reversing the normal action of the human reproductive system. This results in it functioning more as an evolutionary mechanism. The powerful energy concentrated in the reproductive area, which is normally primarily used for sexual experience and procreation, can also be sublimated into a more refined essence, resulting in the creation of a more potent form of this Intelligent Life Energy, which then flows upward through the spinal canal into the brain. This enhanced Intelligent Life Energy in turn feeds a newly opened center in the brain and can lead to an increase in the performance of the brain and an expansion in consciousness. This possibility is built into the organic system of every human being.

The <u>Evolutionary Impulse</u> to evolve to a higher state of consciousness in human beings, results from this organic process in the body, this more potent Intelligent Life Energy flowing into and pressing on the brain, which results in a desire to experience this next state of awareness. The desire to practice religion, perform spiritual exercises, or live life based on spiritual or ethical principles, are offshoots of this Evolutionary Impulse. These practices facilitate the healthy activation of Kundalini and the resultant movement toward developing an expanded state of consciousness and derive from this inherent desire to grow into and experience this new state of being.

This evolutionary process, in which the enhanced Intelligent Life Energy presses on the brain and creates the desire for a higher state of consciousness, is very analogous to the reproductive process in terms of how sexual/reproductive energy presses on our sex organs and creates the urge for sexual experience and procreation. In the case of procreation, it may result in the birth of a new human baby. In the case of Kundalini, it may result in the birth of a new man or woman with an expanded consciousness.

There is a <u>Predetermined Objective</u> to this evolutionary process - the Cosmic Conscious mind.

In one of Gopi Krishna's discourses, he discussed how throughout history, at different times, and in different cultures and areas of the world, a common set of religious/spiritual practices, exercises, and disciplines developed, centered on the following four areas:

1. <u>Cultivation of certain virtues</u> such as self-restraint, truthfulness, purity of mind, benevolence, and the like,
2. <u>Concentration based mental practices</u> such as meditation and yoga,
3. <u>Self-purification practices,</u> both physical and mental,
4. <u>Devotional practices</u> including prayer and worship and constant thought of the Divine.

He said it is obvious that this systemization has a particular influence on the body and mind complex to create the state of awareness called Cosmic Consciousness. If this were not so, the various practices and disciplines would be so widely dissimilar to have nothing in common.

I believe this again points to the immense importance and necessity of the practice of healthy forms of religion and spirituality, as well as the importance of human development practices (all spiritual, ethical, psychological, mental, and physical disciplines), which promote healthy physical, mental, emotional, moral, and spiritual development. These practices are necessary to facilitate not only our overall healthy development as human beings, but also are requirements for the ongoing cleansing, reconstruction, and organic evolution of the human brain and achievement of higher states of consciousness. As such, these practices are really not a luxury to be practiced by a few people in their spare time but are actually a necessity to be practiced daily by almost all people today.

• The cultivation of deep humility and the ability to surrender to a Higher Power or God are critical elements on the path to reach this destination. To open the door to higher states of consciousness, our egos need to be pruned significantly so our Higher Self can emerge. We then become a more expanded expression of this Divine Intelligence. Our egos and intellects will desire to be in service to the Divine Intelligence within. It does not work the other way around.

• One way to reduce the power of our egos is to share with others our human vulnerabilities and divine qualities, including our fears, struggles, imperfections, failures, joys, successes, gifts, and love. This creates a merciful and inviting space to know and love one another, and to grow spiritually. The material world is temporal, the development of our souls is eternal. The story of our lives is the story of our unfolding spirituality. All our life experiences, both good and so called bad, ultimately serve the following purposes: 1) to grow our souls, the permanent nature of our beings, and to lead us to higher states of consciousness and eventually the Cosmic Conscious mind; and 2) to increase our awareness and understanding of the Divine Intelligence operating within us and creation, and to the knowledge that we are an extension of this Divine Intelligence.

• I believe it would benefit humanity greatly if we were to share stories like this on a broad scale, with this kind of human vulnerability. This form of sharing could be used as a springboard to touch the place deep within our hearts that knows the truth of our common humanity and divine heritage. This will lead to a deeper understanding of each other, help bring us into greater community, as well as galvanize us into more compassionate forms of action. Sharing ourselves and our stories is already happening in the 12-step programs of recovery, as well as in many other places. It is desperately needed in our political institutions and governments as well as in the relations between people, races, religions, sexes, and nations.

• Finally, no person has all the answers to the problems and challenges of life. The answers can best be gained in a loving and safe community where experiences are shared, and support is given. I believe it is time to embrace more deeply a spirituality of imperfection and humility. This is the seedbed out of which will help to flower the love that is the underlying constituent of us all.

25 – New Hope, Intelligent Evolution, and Children

I've previously discussed how there are many reasons for deep concern about the condition of the world today. And I also mentioned some of the areas where humanity has made great progress.

There are other hopeful developments. There seems to be an upsurge in the spiritual thirst and self-awareness of people, as well as an increase in the search for new ideals and healthier ways of living. For example, participation in yoga, wellness, mindfulness, and meditation classes, 12-step programs, and other types of personal development and spiritual programs, seem to be increasing rapidly. People are beginning to question our excessive use of technology, our fast-paced, frenetic lifestyles, and extreme focus on material pleasures. There is an increasing concern for the health of our bodies, the food we eat, the environment we live in, and the condition of the earth.

The advancement of technology, despite some of its negative consequences, has also played a positive role in society. It has helped people to become more efficient and productive in their work and lives. It has also helped create interesting and fun products and services that contribute to the enjoyment of life. Technological and material development together have improved our standard of living and have freed many people from the day-to-day drudgery of the fight for survival. This has helped give people time to enjoy themselves as well to develop their minds and bodies in a healthy way. It has also allowed people the extra time needed to explore the meaning and purpose of life.

The innovations of technology have also helped to shrink the size of the world. Inventions such as the telephone, modern airplane, Internet and social media (Facebook, Twitter, and YouTube, etc.) have connected people together like never before. The world in a sense has become one big neighborhood. Unfortunately, it has a long way to go before it becomes like *Mister Rogers' Neighborhood*, which was characterized by its quiet simplicity and gentleness. However, perhaps one day with the help of Kundalini, and the further healthy advancement of human consciousness and the ability to love each other, we will get there.

The peaceful collapse of the Soviet Union and the fall of the Berlin Wall in the late 1980s and early 1990s, as well as relatively recent pro-democracy revolutions in such countries as Egypt, Tunisia, Libya, Yemen, and Syria (collectively the "Arab Spring"), provide evidence that the time of the dictator and repressive state or authoritarian control, may be nearing their end. The Arab Spring revolutions in fact were helped along by the power to connect, communicate, organize, and raise awareness provided by Facebook, Twitter, and YouTube.

I remember being so moved as I watched on television as courageous protesters in different countries such as Egypt, Libya, and Syria, risked their lives to tell the story of the injustices that were happening in their countries during these revolutions. I felt a deep kinship with these people. Such peaceful movements and inspiring people are also highlighting for me the moral bankruptcy of the violent and regressive approaches employed by some revolutionary groups to foster change. No doubt there is the need for legitimate change in many countries, including in some of the behaviors of the Western world, but hateful thinking and extreme violence will never lead to lasting, peaceful change.

It seems like a bottom-up revolution is slowly spreading across the world. Ordinary people in more and more places are rising up and demanding and fighting for their basic human rights, including their need for greater equality, freedom, and opportunity. The good news is I believe such developments aren't random or temporary but will continue to gain momentum in the future. This is because they are reflective of the inherent need of individuals and the advancing human mind and brain for more freedom and equality at this stage of their development. I believe evolutionary laws are requiring change. However, one can expect that there will continue to be inevitable setbacks, such as recent events in Syria, Yemen, parts of Africa, and the rise and fall of ISIS, have shown. Evolution tends to proceed through fits and starts but the eventual progression is always upward to the Cosmic Conscious state.

Another important recent development has been the rise of the #MeToo movement, which is a movement against sexual harassment and sexual assault, particularly as it relates to women. The movement began in October 2017 as a hashtag on social media. It subsequently spread virally, in an attempt to demonstrate the widespread prevalence of sexual assault and harassment, especially in the workplace. The continued rise of the women's movement and, in general, the feminine in human society, is a critical development toward achieving a more equal, balanced, and just society.

Most recently in 2020, the United States has been experiencing civil unrest in many of its cities and is also seeing the rise of the Black Lives Matter movement (BLM) as a reaction to recent police shootings. BLM is an international human rights movement, originating in the black community, that campaigns against violence and systemic racism towards black people. It also calls for racial equality.

I believe the #MeToo and the BLM movements need to be understood in an evolution of consciousness context. They are not just random events happening at this time of history but are driven by evolution's underlying requirement that humanity eventually attain equality for all people. Speaking more directly, the continued rise of the women and BLM movements reflect evolution's need for humanity to achieve a more equal, balanced, just, and harmonious society. This unity and type of society is necessary for humanity to continue in a healthy fashion toward the evolutionary goal of achieving higher states of consciousness and a society based on equality, love and service. To be ultimately successful in creating lasting positive change, such movements need to be non-violent, peaceful, and driven by love. In Trudy S. Settel's book, The Book of Gandhi Wisdom, is the following Gandhi quote:

"Non-violence is the eternal law;
violence is only the law of expediency."

There is other hopeful news: there is an avalanche of interest in the study of human consciousness and increasing research by scientists in the study of the human brain. Many people, especially our youth, are in search of a new, healthier paradigm to live and work by, and new life affirming stories to embrace. They are also looking for more individually empowering and egalitarian institutional structures in which to live, grow, worship, and work: ones that are more in alignment with the continually advancing human consciousness. The youth of the world today also seem to have far less inherent tendencies toward racism, sexism, classism, etc., as well as a reduced thirst for materialism and consumerism, than prior generations.

Purpose of Life?

People are searching for new ideas that have the power to cause a global revolution in thinking. I believe one of the most important problems in the world today is that there is no universal agreement as to what constitutes the main purpose of life. To offer a few examples: Is the purpose of life to:

1) Achieve the maximum in material wealth, comfort, and leisure, during our short stay here on earth?
2) Live a simple life and enjoy good health, peace and serenity, adequate food and shelter, in loving support and connection with others?
3) Help create opportunities for each person to fulfill their God-given abilities and potential and help each other achieve health and prosperity?
4) Achieve equality of wealth and circumstances for all people as soon as possible, regardless of abilities and efforts?
5) Live a righteous life so one may end up in heaven after they die, or achieve nirvana while still alive?
6) Convert, fight, or even kill those who don't share a similar belief system or cultural, religious, or national background?

One can see how such lack of agreement on such a critical issue can lead to a myriad of problems including conflict, dissension, disunity, and even war. We have seen such problems occur throughout history, especially as it relates to different religious beliefs or lack thereof, and the propriety and utility of conflicting political, social and economic systems such as democracy, socialism, communism and capitalism. We are even seeing similar problems played out on the world stage right now. This is especially dangerous today given the existence of nuclear and other weapons of mass destruction.

It is time for us to become aware of our spiritual connection, and the subtle intelligent cosmic medium that connects us all. Kundalini can help do this.

Kundalini - Unifying Concept

Kundalini is potentially a world unifying concept because if it is accepted that we all are destined for a higher state of consciousness through the workings of Kundalini and the continued evolution of our brain, then we are all moving toward a common goal and purpose in life.

Toward this end, the following is an excerpt from a Gopi Krishna talk given in 1979, the content of which I believe is just as applicable to today's world situation:

"... how can you bring peace into a tormented and fragmented world? Fragmented thinking, fragmented social orders, fragmented political systems and fragmented faith. It is only a new gesture from Heaven and a new discovery that can cover all the fields - politics, science, society, religion, faith, scientific discoveries, technology ... that can bring order in this chaos and open up a new horizon for mankind. Kundalini provides the only alternative. It establishes that there is a divine mechanism in the human body, which can be verified: that the brain is already designed by Nature for a certain performance and that all our political and social systems will have to conform to it.

This very fact, that the brain of man needs this type of a social or a political order, will eliminate the differences in the political ideologies of the earth. How can you have a different political system when science shows that the human brain needs this kind of an order or a system? Similarly, it can prove that higher consciousness is the goal of man, thus bringing all the faiths together because it will show that all the prophets had the same power awake in them."

Gopi Krishna also said in his book <u>Three Perspectives on Kundalini:</u>

"Earth-wide dissemination of knowledge of the Glory dwelling in every human being is the only way to bring about the unification of all humankind. It will make known the common Goal prescribed by nature for the life of man. The solemn task in front of us is to provide empirical evidence for the basic reality of Illumination [i.e., Cosmic Consciousness]."

<u>Inner Astronauts and New Leaders</u>

Once the incredible possibilities inherent in Kundalini, and spiritual development in general, become more widely known, it will give people new goals and horizons to aim for in life.

I believe many people, particularly our young people, will come to embrace the challenge of this incredible journey within themselves. The journey into inner space toward the Cosmic Conscious state of mind is as challenging, difficult, and adventurous as any journey into outer space. People who embark on this journey will be the new "inner" astronauts. As people begin to understand what this search for the inner gold, or a new healthier and meaningful "El Dorado" represents, we will have a new spiritual gold rush. A new breed of triathletes of the body, mind, and spirit will emerge!

This in turn will produce a new group of leaders, exhibiting both an intellectual depth, and a balanced blend of soul qualities. Such qualities will include a greater measure of wisdom, integrity, balance, empathy, and humility, as well as an increased ability to listen to and learn from others.

They will embrace different, more life affirming values, and be in service of higher ideals. Their leadership abilities will help to unite people and bring out each person's best. These leaders will be in touch with their inner wisdom and emanate a calm, open, reassuring presence. They will provide for the weary and thirsting world a soothing balm and refreshing drink.

I believe they will be the new leaders that will lead the effort to invent innovative solutions to some of the serious problems facing humankind. They will help to shift the current outlook in the world from one of negativism and fear, to one of increasing optimism and hope.

Gopi Krishna said the following in The Wonder of the Brain in regard to the immediate need for a new type of leader:

> "The impassable frontiers now reached by science, the disaffection with the prevailing political orders of the earth and the shortcomings of current faiths, coupled with the widening perspectives of leading scientists, the fast awakening political consciousness in the masses everywhere and the growing urge for self-awareness in

the rising generations, will soon make the existence of a wiser and more perspicacious rank of leading men and women, perceptive of the super-sensory world [higher or Cosmic Consciousness], imperative for the race to instruct and guide her in the knowledge of both the Kingdoms - the one we live in and the other to come."

I also believe knowledge of Kundalini will give older people hope and a new way of thinking about aging. Currently far too many seniors are growing old in great pain and discomfort, the fire and hope of their youth and prime years extinguished. Many are facing a lingering death with great fear and despair. It will become increasingly recognized that it is not meant to be this way. For many people as they age, their bodies can remain healthy and their minds can continue to grow and stay active, if throughout their lives, they have practiced healthy mental, spiritual, and physical disciplines, and engaged in right ways of living and eating. More and more people can look forward to a vigorous and creative old age, living fully, enjoying greater longevity and good health, while sharing wisdom and life's experiences.

Has Titanic Struck the Iceberg?

Western civilization is at a crossroad today. And like the Titanic, it has hit the iceberg and in certain vital areas is heading in a downward direction. This downward slide is reversible, however. I believe our collective egos and intellects are inflated and unbalanced due to our excessive tilt toward the material side of life. This has been caused by many things including our recent successes and advancements in material comforts, technology, and science; our lack of understanding of the real purpose of life and the requirements of spiritual and evolutionary laws to live life in a healthy, balanced way; as well as the disenchantment of many people with traditional organized religion, which previously provided healthy spiritual nourishment. As a result, we've lost touch with what is required for healthy evolution and the ongoing development of the evolving human mind and brain. We've lost our "way", we've gotten off the "path", and unknowingly have put the health of the human brain at risk. This in turn has set us up for a "fall" and the "sinking of its majesty, the titanic ego".

In some ways this may be seen as an unavoidable stage of our evolutionary development. We are like teenagers in terms of our development as a collective race. We have become "teenage gods", intoxicated by our recent material successes, technological breakthroughs and conquests of nature.

In the movie *Contact*, Ellie Arroway (Jodie Foster) was asked if she met up with aliens in her space travel, what question would she ask them? She shared she would ask how they survived their period of technological adolescence and not destroy themselves. She clearly was worried that the earth and its people were in a similar risky position to where we may be today.

I believe the possibility of a demonstrable scientific and spiritual discovery such as the Kundalini theory of evolution is one important answer to her question. It has the potential to reverse the current negative direction of civilization and is one very bright light in an otherwise darkening night. There are other bright lights.

Light of 12-Steps

Previously I mentioned that the 12-step programs have become universal healing and spiritual recovery programs. I have a personal conviction that the confirmation and acceptance of the Kundalini hypothesis will eventually lead to a massive expansion of the 12-step programs of recovery into the mainstream of societies, particularly in the West.

I view the 12-step programs as universally important at this time in history because of the widespread negative effects that excessive materialism and consumerism are having on humanity's continuing evolution. I also see them as critically important due to their ability to help us stay in harmony with the requirements of the evolutionary processes occurring within us.

I believe more people will realize that they can benefit from participation in the 12-step programs, and that they are not just for people dealing with addictions and their effects. I also believe new 12-step programs will continue to develop for people which are focused solely on spiritual growth and unfoldment. Finally, I think the 12-steps will eventually evolve into programs to help people have a healthy Kundalini awakening and to achieve higher consciousness in a safe way. This further expansion of these programs will be facilitated by the following:

- Their existing worldwide organizational structure ensures a consistency of approach and application of guiding principles wherever one attends a meeting in the world,
- Their ability to help purify our minds and bodies of unhealthy toxins and thought patterns, as well as to help cleanse and reform our brains,
- Their ability to help us change and heal from many different forms of addictive and other unhealthy behaviors,
- Their ability to help lessen our egos/self-wills and facilitate a deeper surrender to this Higher Intelligence working in and through us,

- Their ability to help us stay more in harmony with the physical, spiritual and evolutionary laws governing our behavior, thinking, and existence; and

- Their ability to help us lead a more sane, healthy, and balanced life in this fast moving, rapidly changing, unstable, and exciting world we currently live in.

I also believe that the confirmation and acceptance of the Kundalini hypothesis will further accelerate the expansion of already fast growing spiritual and personal development practices such as yoga, mindfulness, and meditation. Certain elements of such practices will in turn be integrated into complementary programs such as the 12-steps. In fact, this is already happening.

Gopi Krishna believed that in the future, all the different forms of spiritual practices and disciplines would slowly be knit into a regular spiritual science, much like what happened with the standardization of the treatment practices of medical science over time.

Spiritual Science and Intelligent Evolution

I also see in the distant future the driving force of materialism, which currently dominates the thinking and behavior of most of humankind, as well as the concept and practice of religion; will gradually be subsumed by the more universal concepts of a **"Spiritual Science"**, and **"Intelligent Evolution"** toward a higher state of consciousness.

The concepts of a Spiritual Science and Intelligent Evolution would be characterized by the mass of people practicing spiritual/mental/physical disciplines. This would include living their lives in conformance with evolutionary, physical and spiritual laws, as well as universally accepted moral and ethical principles (dictated by the requirements of the evolving human mind, body, and brain).

Guided by the Higher Intelligence that exists within all of us, a person's goal would be to live a simpler, more natural, balanced, loving, and service-oriented work and daily life, and to reach a higher state of consciousness. Work will eventually become primarily a platform for human development, material sustainability, and the development of our souls, as opposed to a vehicle for human material survival and expansion.

Higher states of consciousness present new goals, ideals, and values for people to strive for and live by. People will understand that all we truly need for true peace and happiness in life is adequate food and shelter, good health, a peaceful existence, moderate entertainment, leisure, adventure, and intellectual stimulation, as well as the loving support of others. As our collective awareness grows, we will increasingly realize that lasting happiness and peace of mind come from qualities found inside of ourselves, such as our character, attitudes, values, morals and ethics; as well as the quality of our relationship with ourselves, other people and a Higher Power.

As the 12-step programs of recovery continue to expand, I believe some combination and type of their main principles, steps, traditions, concepts of service, and organizing forms, will eventually serve as important pillars underlying new, more egalitarian systems, organizations and institutions, including future governments.

I believe the way the 12-step programs function, with their minimal structure and lack of hierarchy and formal control (obedience to the unenforceable); their belief in the equality of all people; their emphasis on service instead of governance (there are no leaders, only trusted servants); their rotation of service positions; their focus on common welfare and unity, and the ultimate authority of a loving God (not tied to any one religion and defined by each individual in a spiritual sense as a power greater than oneself); as well as the fact that they are truly run by the people; are in alignment with the advancing spiritual, emotional, and mental needs of people and the evolving human mind and brain.

These developments will eventually lead to the melting away of the need for the separation of church and state in our governmental structures. A society based on love, community support, and service will rise. This will further facilitate the liberation of our souls and the attainment of higher states of consciousness. Finally, all these things together would pave the way for the unification of the human race and lead us from the current age we are in - the age of progress, anxiety and division - to the "New Age" of sustainability, peace, and unity.

To quote Gandhi one more time from Trudy S. Settel's book The Book of Gandhi Wisdom:

> "I would not like to live in this world if it is not to be one world."

Gopi Krishna said in the book The Present Crisis:

> "The race cannot survive during the nuclear age unless there occurs a complete change in our social and political structures, and spirituality, pruned of all superstition and falsehood, becomes the guiding star of our life."

Children – Hope for the Future

Earlier, I described how I had adopted the cafe at the local Barnes and Noble bookstore as my second office and work community. As I worked, I couldn't help but notice the little children that often came prancing and careening through the store with their mothers. I loved to watch their expressive faces and spontaneous actions and emotions. You could see in their eyes that the world of Barnes and Noble was a wondrous, new, and exciting place. The littlest things fascinated them. They darted here and there, pointing and grabbing at things, screaming in defiance, or erupting in unbridled joy as they ran to take a thrilling ride down the escalator. You could see inquisitive looks on their faces as they strained to understand events and objects around them. They were spontaneous, authentic, open to new experiences, and free spirits.

I think in certain ways they set a good example for how we must approach the wondrous new and exciting world of higher consciousness. We must be like little children again: open-minded, inquiring, willing, and real.

An experience I had while at the bookstore continues to remain etched deep in my memory. One day I watched as an orchestra group comprised of fifth and sixth graders from a local school performed their songs. There were boys and girls of all colors, playing and blending together in beautiful harmony. I was mesmerized by their inspiring performance, youthful age, and seeming innocence. I thought to myself that this auditory and visual feast was a perfect model of God's plan for humanity where the human mosaic will, like this youthful orchestra, be knit together in a "blended harmony", all working in community to help one another find the "True Sun" or "True Reality" that exists within each of us. This will one day allow all of us to enjoy the immense pleasures and gifts of both the inner (spiritual) and outer (material) worlds.

Human Race in Disarray

Currently, however, the human race is in disarray and far from this model of harmony. In many ways, it seems to be afflicted by a potentially deadly form of "spiritual and physical cancer". Somewhat analogous to aberrant acting and fast multiplying cancer cells, which eventually kill healthy cells and put the survival of the whole living organism at risk, human beings also are fast multiplying, moving in different directions, often self-seeking and chasing unhealthy goals, and sometimes acting aberrantly and violently. And the sum of these actions and behaviors have put the health and survival of the whole human race at risk.

Previously I described some of the serious warning signs, threats, and "cancer-like" problems facing the human race today. I explained how I believe these are symptoms of a much greater problem or root cause: our ignorance of the real goal of human evolution, the best methods to achieve it, the type of environment we need to live in, and how to make wise choices in the living of our lives so we can advance evolution in a healthy manner.

One of my best friend's father-in-law was a doctor who died in his fifties due to lung cancer. He was an athlete and didn't smoke. Before he died, he told my friend that he didn't believe we would solve the mystery of cancer until we understood why we are here. I've thought about this a great deal and believe there is a deep truth to his statement.

I also think his statement could apply to some of the other massive and seemingly intractable problems humanity is currently facing including an exploding world population, hunger, war, terrorism, a widening gulf between the haves and have nots, increasing mental illness rates, and environmental and pollution problems, to name a few.

Confirmation and acceptance of Kundalini as the evolutionary mechanism will lead to a deeper understanding of and eventual improved conformance with the evolutionary, spiritual and physical laws governing the human race. In addition, it will help make clear the need for increased personal self-mastery and ethical and moral behavior, as well as greater humility, surrender, reverence, childlike wonder, and love when approaching the world of higher consciousness. The positive impact of these developments will help to gradually diminish the spiritual and physical cancers currently afflicting the race, help to knit it into the harmonious mosaic it is predestined to achieve, help answer the ultimate question of why we are here, and eventually lead to a paradise on Earth.

26 – A New Science, New Declaration of Independence and Peaceful Revolution

When I lived near Washington, D.C. I often visited the Jefferson Memorial. I was fascinated by Thomas Jefferson's brilliant mind. Jefferson talked about the importance of light and liberty, with light being thought of as knowledge, and knowledge coming from the human intellect/reason. He talked about the human mind's need for freedom of thought and expression, and how it had been held in bondage (he used the term vassalage) by kings, priests, and nobles for many ages before the American Revolution.

Jefferson was also a man of science. He was very much in tune with material realities, growth, and progress. He was behind the Louisiana Purchase, the Lewis and Clark Expedition, and the westward expansion of the United States.

The American Revolution led to a representative democratic form of government. It's interesting to reflect upon how the laws and institutions that subsequently developed, and the religious and personal freedom, and the industrial, scientific, and technological progress that followed in their wake, helped to create conditions that eventually liberated the minds of most Americans. Over time our minds flourished as did the growth of our society. At the same time, however, certain groups of people (many Black Americans, American Indians, and members of other minority groups and communities) were not treated justly and afforded equal opportunities to develop their minds and abilities. It's imperative that we continue to extend our efforts to help everyone who feels they have been left out or believe they have not had a fair chance to reach their full potential.

I feel we are making progress as a society but there is much more that needs to be done. Rather than pointing the finger at others, I know I must continue to work on reforming myself and to lend a helping hand to my neighbors, as well as to search for the good in all people, regardless of race, gender, social class, religion, etc. Once we understand that these kinds of behaviors are a biological and spiritual requirement for our evolution to a happier and healthier state of mind, I believe the urgency to develop these characteristics will accelerate. As we progress in our development, the sins and pains of the past will heal and eventually melt away in importance as we become a more just and equal society and together embrace a bright and promising future.

As I shared previously, I loved to visit the monuments, museums and historical sites in Washington, D. C. I admired and was inspired by the courage, genius, and spirituality that was behind the founding of America. The founders of this country were a collection of amazing geniuses and visionaries who also had human flaws. The conditions that have developed since the founding of the country have allowed me to find deeper and deeper levels of freedom and fulfillment in my own life, and in my continuing walk toward the ultimate peace and freedom in God and higher states of consciousness. It has taught me that freedom and my own liberation are in my own hands and God's. It has also taught me I need the help of others.

Today, however, it is interesting to note that some of the same ideas, underlying structures, and ways of living that brought many people freedom, may now be creating our bondage. This is due to the continuing evolution of the human mind, and as it grows, its need for more progressive systems, laws, and institutions, greater equality, as well as more spiritual and healthier ways of living. The tyranny of our unbalanced but powerful human intellects may be holding back the development of this higher faculty of mind that is gradually emerging in humankind.

Limits to Material Growth

Western civilization is running up against the limits of its rapid scientific, technological, and material progress. There are cracks or fissures developing in the underpinnings of our society. The terrible problems we are facing are telling us that it is time once again to change our ways of thinking and living. Future generations will look back at our civilization and shake their heads at its excessive preoccupation with physical reality, surface differences, material growth and war. It is time to move beyond the narrow grooves of our intellectual thought and the limited confines of material science.

The human mind is evolving a new channel of perception and out of this developing higher sense will emerge nascent and luminous knowledge to help guide the race, as well as new goals and ideals for human society to strive for and live by. This will eventually lead to the discovery of subtle energies in the universe and the Intelligent Forces behind life. It will also lead to the ascendance of a new type of science; a science that will one day, according to Gopi Krishna, far exceed in importance and magnitude the material science of today. We will slowly begin to recognize that we see and understand only the tip of creation through our five physical senses and intellect.

New Peaceful Worldwide Revolution

It is time for a new "declaration of independence" and a new revolution. This revolution will be peaceful and inclusive of all people worldwide.

Humanity is desperately in need of a new idea, discovery, or concept of life that has the potential to reduce the possibility of increasing human catastrophes: from warfare, terrorism, bloody revolutions, social discord, natural disasters, and environmental degradation. Reconciling science and religion as well unifying the various religious faiths and forms of government will be a high priority.

People are hungering for this new discovery that can bring hope to humankind. It seems too good to be true that such a possibility is out there and can be empirically tested and verified by science, as well as individuals in the laboratory of their own life experiences. However, the Kundalini hypothesis, with its astounding ramifications, is just such an idea!

I believe the verification of Kundalini as the evolutionary mechanism, will create the beginning of this revolution. It would result in a monumental positive shift in humankind's thinking, lead to an embrace of a healthier paradigm to live by, and pave the way to a new spiritual science, a science of the soul. It will also expedite positive changes in our institutions and systems, and eventually create a healthier environment to live in. All of these developments would be conducive to the emergence of this new channel of perception and source of knowledge in human beings.

We believe Kundalini theory offers staggering hope and possibilities to the human race at this time. It has the potential to light the flame for revolutionary positive change in the world.

To this point, in poetic verse #47, "Happy Days" (see complete verse included as #11 in Section II - Poetic Verses), the verse ends with the following:

"Evolution is at a point where people are now ready to see that consciousness is the All. This mechanism of Kundalini is a potential in the human body, waiting to be understood and embraced by the mass of people.

Humanity has evolved to a point where it is ready to see the Light, its brain is evolving, and new forms of life and creation are coming into view. We must embrace this new Light or face extinction. Death will lose its sovereign nature when this new Light is embraced.

Humanity on a mass scale has evolved to the point where this knowledge must be disseminated quickly. This knowledge will free humankind from the prison house of its senses that it has erected due to its over-reliance on its materialistic philosophies, old sciences, and old religions.

A new science and religion of life is waiting to be embraced. Eternal life will come into view, the fear of death will lose its grip, our life spans will be expanded, the dominance of the old materialistic science will die away, subsumed by this new philosophy of life, where new forms of energy and life, new layers of creation stand revealed. It is all within us, within our brains.

A thirsting humanity waits for this knowledge to be revealed. The story needs to be told, simple and to the point, universal in its nature, everlasting in its hope, embracing recovery, letting go of pride and prejudice, power and prestige.

The mass of humanity will lead, proud science will follow, recalcitrant religion will slowly accept; fear of war will lessen, violence will subside, terrorism will die away, disease and famine will slowly evaporate, and a new curtain on history will be raised, and a new paradise, a new heaven, a new Eden, will slowly descend upon the earth."

27 – Galileo and A New View of Humanity

We have come a long way since the time of Copernicus and Galileo when their scientific discoveries back in the 16th and 17th centuries revealed that the earth revolved around the sun, rather than the sun around the earth. This effectively relocated the center of the universe from the earth to the sun. This was in the face of fierce resistance from Roman Catholic religious authorities who believed that such concepts were not in accordance with the teachings of the Bible.

Since that time, the relocation of the universe's center has gone much further. Now most scientists do not think there is a center in what they believe is a universe that is expanding in every direction from every point of space.

Some scientists estimate the current size of the universe at 156 billion light-years wide! The nearest star to the earth is approximately 4 light years away or roughly 25.6 trillion miles. That means it would take light traveling at the speed of 186,000 miles per second roughly four years to reach the star! Now compare 4 light years with 156 billion light-years and you begin to get a sense of the unfathomable size of the universe we live in.

The earth, and therefore a human being's position on it, have gone from being seen as the center of the physical universe before Galileo's and Copernicus's time; to a position where human beings can be seen essentially as the size of microbes, on an earth which is the size of a pebble, in a large ocean which extends for thousands of miles. Human beings appear to be totally insignificant in a universe that is so large, that it is probably impossible for our minds to frame an accurate image of it.

And yet the story thankfully does not end here! The Cosmic Order is even more mysterious than we thought. As our brains continue to evolve, and a new channel of perception continues to slowly develop in the human race, a new picture of the universe begins to emerge.

We will come to understand that the universe, which we experience as something separate and outside of ourselves, is in reality not outside and separate, but is projected out from the inside of our minds. We don't live in the universe; rather it lives in us! We will come to know that one infinite, everlasting, living, loving, conscious Intelligence underlies and sustains us and the universe, and our souls are but an eternal drop from this stupendous Consciousness.

Just as the Roman Catholic religion initially resisted the new discoveries of Galileo and Copernicus, material science has for some time resisted any new vision and understanding of humanity, human consciousness, the universe, and the workings of the human brain. In recent times the hard attitude of science has begun to soften, spurred along by amongst other things, the impact of Einstein's theory of relativity, the implications of quantum physics, increasing acceptance of the reality of psychic and paranormal experiences, as well as recent findings in brain and consciousness research.

Ultimately, we will have to prove this new vision and understanding of ourselves and the universe in the laboratory of our own experiences and minds. For this to happen, we must continue to learn how to cooperate with the evolutionary processes operating within us, and with this higher sense that is slowly emerging in the human race. We resist or remain ignorant at our own peril, and our own loss and suffering.

The "good news" is that I believe the center of the universe will slowly be relocated once again, this time in a spiritual sense to the Eternal Sun, which shines within us all. We truly will have come a long way since the days before Galileo and Copernicus.

The joy of this realization of who we really are is expressed in the beginning paragraphs of poetic verse #37, entitled "Resurrection/ New Science and Religion", when I wrote:

> "There is joy in my heart, from the deep recesses of my soul wells up a joy and happiness beyond belief. I have touched eternity. Eternity has kissed my soul. Drenched with love, my soul touches all parts of the universe. Matter dissipates and all that remains is love.
>
> My heart speaks a great truth. God's immense love for humanity lights up the universe. The sky opens up, the material world dissolves; all that remains is my soul. I have touched a new dimension of being. I have been torn from my anchor in the material world. All that remains is consciousness."

Finally, the melting away of the physical universe in the highest states of consciousness, and the transition from the tiny "I" to the cosmic "We", is also expressed in poetic verse #46, "Unity and Infinity", where I wrote:

> "Infinity opens up and swallows the temporal universe. There is no beginning or end, no start or finish, no alpha and omega. There is just one everlasting ocean of infinity; a sea of energy glistening with life: eternal,

formless, timeless, effervescent, sparkling. The temporal universe has melted away, like the early morning dew when heated by the rising effulgent sun; like a wispy cloud, vaporized by a titanic sun. A bright light is spread everywhere.

I sit in stunned silence. I have come home. This is really who I am. The tiny I has become the cosmic we. We are everlasting rays, from a boundless sun, that shines for eternity. The curtain is pulled back, God steps forward, evaporating all thoughts of I, bringing in a colossal we. A bright light that will shine forever."

This is the "New Age", this is the "Good News", this is the "New Resurrection," the awareness of which is just beginning to dawn in the minds of the human race today.

28 – Dinosaurs and A New Positive Asteroid

When you walk into the Hall of Mammals at the Smithsonian National Museum of Natural History, you were greeted by a sign that says:

> "Welcome to the Mammal Family Reunion! Come, meet your relatives."

Not far away, another sign reads:

> "Evolution is the biological process responsible for the magnificent diversity of life on Earth. Over time evolution creates new species."

At the back of the Hall of Mammals is Evolution Theater, where a short film on the evolutionary history of mammals continuously plays. Over the years I watched this film countless times. The film states that we humans did not evolve from chimpanzees, but rather from one of the world's first mammals, a small four-inch mammal named Morganucodon (called "Morgie" for short). Morgie looks somewhat like a cross between a rat and a prairie dog.

The film describes how mammals arrived on the earth over 200 million years ago, almost at the same time as the dinosaurs. From 200 million years ago to about 66 million years ago, some of the dinosaurs grew larger and scarier, while mammals remained small. During this time period, the mammals did not evolve much because they were not free to come to the surface to grow and flourish. They had to remain underground to stay safe from the more powerful and threatening dinosaurs. Morgie would have to stealthily come to the surface at night to grab a dragonfly or two for dinner, while the dinosaurs were sleeping.

The film explains that the dinosaurs had a bad day 66 million years ago, when most scientists believe a large asteroid hit the earth. The resulting dust and smoke that enveloped the planet created wild climate fluctuations, and many animal species were not able to survive this catastrophe. It is estimated that 70% of the animals existing on the earth at the time were wiped out, including the dinosaurs. However, it is hypothesized that mammals, because they were small, warm blooded, and lived underground, were able to ride out the climate changes and survive.

With the disappearance of the dinosaurs, the mammals were then free to come to the surface and thrive. Their evolutionary progress accelerated greatly from that time forward. Over the next 66 million years they evolved into larger, more diverse, and more complex species on land and sea, and eventually into us, human beings.

The film states that if you condensed the whole 200-million-year history of mammals down to 60 minutes, Morgie lasted for approximately three minutes, and Morgie's relatives lasted for another forty minutes. Then the asteroid hit and eradicated the dinosaurs, and from that time forward, the evolution of mammals took off. The film says that human beings have only arrived in the last second of this hour and therefore have truly just arrived on earth. The film concludes by saying:

> "If we have evolved this far from mammals like Morgie, what new mammals will Morgie find at the next reunion?"

This film struck me on many different levels as I identified with the mammals, which had to hide underground to stay safe from the more powerful dinosaurs. So many-times over the last twenty-five years, while trying to stay true to my ideals and spiritual path, I also felt like I've had to hide "underground". I too, metaphorically speaking, would slip out at night to grab a morsel or two of food to survive. During most of this time period, the 12-step programs, in particular, provided a safe haven for me to survive and grow.

Present Day Dinosaurs and Dangers

The powerful dinosaurs and the survival of the fittest environment that existed at that time reminds me in some ways of the environment that exists in parts of our society today. This is evidenced by our powerful but often unbalanced and overly proud human intellects; our modern-day power and materialistic driven society; our large-scale and sometimes suffocating hierarchical systems and structures; as well as our sometimes power intoxicated, and prestige driven institutional and organizational leaders.

During my growing up and early adult years, I was able to watch my father rise up the ladder and eventually help run Oscar Mayer and Co. The Company cared about the welfare of its employees and took its responsibility to the community very seriously. Its paternalistic culture seemed to operate like a big family. It also adhered to a meaningful code of ethics, was long term oriented, and was not overly dominated by a drive for profits or power.

As my own business career progressed over the years, I observed that large businesses and corporations seemed to become more impersonal, power and money driven, and efficiency oriented.

The decade of the 1980s, in particular, were characterized by large corporate mergers and acquisitions and leveraged buyouts. Oftentimes it seemed that a few people benefited at the expense of the many. Some of this activity was necessary and helpful, yet more of it seemed excessive and damaging, especially long term. As some of the dinosaurs became larger and more powerful over time, business corporations were also becoming this way. In fact, many of our institutions, including the government, were becoming larger and more powerful.

Today with the technological revolution, some of this institutional and hierarchical power is lessening, as more individuals experience greater freedom and empowerment in their work and lives.

However, institutional power has also increased considerably in the information technology sector. Giants such as Google, Amazon, Facebook, Apple, Microsoft and Twitter control sizable resources and exert great power and influence over communications, information flow and the sale and distribution of goods. More people are becoming aware of this reality and some see it as a threat to fair competition and freedom of expression.

The growth in the use of technology has also led to increased automation resulting in significant gains in business and institutional productivity and efficiency. The negative side is that many workers have not developed the skills to use the new technology and have been left out in the cold employment wise. This has particularly affected smaller towns.

In a larger context, the use of technology seems to have become the overriding driving force in people's daily lives today, an end in itself.

I talked earlier in Chapter 25 of the many benefits that have flowed to us from such technology use. However, there has also been many negative consequences. Some studies show that the excessive use of technology can lead to physical, mental, and emotional health problems, as well as stunted social development, poor interpersonal communication skills, and addictive behaviors. The good news is I believe these problems will lessen as humanity begins to understand the true evolutionary goal of human life, which will lead to a more sober and balanced use of technology. **Technology will eventually then be seen in its right position as a means to an end, not an end in itself, and as a key contributor to our material and spiritual liberation.**

I believe that our advancing human consciousness has begun to outgrow the current paradigm of power and materialism, and these top-heavy hierarchical systems, and sometimes head heavy leaders. Some of the problems we are experiencing today seem to be designed to shake us loose from the excessive strictures that this paradigm, and these structures and leaders, have placed on our ability to grow in a healthy manner; and to live a satisfying and gracious life.

I have often wondered whether it will be necessary that some other type of large "asteroid" hits the earth today to help clear it of these present-day dinosaurs, and shake us free from a way of living that seems to be slowly killing some of us?

Are the troubles that modern civilization is currently experiencing, including the 2020/2021 COVID-19 pandemic, part of the onslaught of even larger "asteroids" hitting the earth? Will an exploding nuclear bomb, biological/chemical catastrophe, excessive population growth, greater natural or climate disasters, or larger and more deadly pandemics, be the next large asteroids to devastate the earth?

Positive Asteroid

Alternatively, I have also wondered if there could be a so-called "positive" event that plays the role of change for the next large asteroid? Does it always need to be a stick that forces us to change, or could we change from the lure of a carrot this time? Or perhaps it could be a mixture of a carrot and stick?

I believe that the confirmation of Kundalini as the evolutionary mechanism in human beings can indeed play the change role of a massive "positive" asteroid. Amongst other things, I believe verification and acceptance of Kundalini would help to shift our orientation and values from an excessive preoccupation with material goals and the pursuit of power and prestige, to a greater spiritual, service oriented, and moral focus in life. It would also help mitigate the negative impact on our way of living from the actions of our powerful, but often excessively proud and unbalanced egos/intellects. This would serve to create a more balanced human mind and personality as well as society.

In order for human beings and society to continue to grow and evolve in a healthy manner, I think it is critical that we deepen our connection to the Higher Intelligence that exists inside all of us. Recognition of Kundalini as the evolutionary mechanism would accelerate such a development.

Years ago, I wrote:

"Let's share this great story of Kundalini and our wondrous stories of love and humanness. Let's share with people the news of this atomic-like source of love within our bodies and the divine potential of human beings. Let's voluntarily do the suffering, cleansing, and purging called for. Let's share arrows of love, rather than bombs of hate. Let's not force Nature to have to humble down our narrow human ego and intellect, and a straying humanity from its ordained path, through outer bombs of destruction and other calamities."

The evolutionary progress of mammals is believed to have accelerated once the dinosaurs disappeared from the earth. I believe this is one major factor that paved the way for the faster emergence of human beings and their ability to reason and think, and to create the world we live in today. In a similar fashion, once the pernicious influence of the present-day dinosaurs is lessened, this higher sense and illuminated mind, will be free to emerge more quickly. This will allow human beings, civilization, and life to once again experience another rapid advance in healthy evolution and progress, and create a new, more magnificent earth.

Modern civilization's excessive striving for material goods, technology, power, and wealth needs to be curbed and replaced with new values and ideals that allow a simpler, moral, egalitarian, slower paced, and humane way of life to emerge and flourish on this earth. This will lead to a life characterized by giving, rather than taking; by serving, rather than exploiting; by sharing love, rather than hate. I believe this will lead to innumerable positive changes in human life, including less environmental and climate damage, more prudent natural resource use, greater equality between people, as well as the facilitation of a non-violent, love and compassion driven, natural redistribution of wealth from the wealthy to the needy. Our evolving human brains, as well as the mass of humanity, would applaud such a development.

29 – Our Brain and Mind – Keys to A Stunning Future

In September of 2000, I wrote verse #13, "Storm Clouds/Brilliant Light". This was one year before the horrific events of 9/11 in the United States: I said the following:

> "The time has come for great change. The world is at a crossroad. Major trial and tribulation ahead for the world followed by great peace and light."

Verification and acceptance of Kundalini as the evolutionary mechanism has the potential to not only lessen the world's current trial and tribulation, but also to speed up the arrival of greater peace and light.

Let me refer again to the film on the evolutionary history of mammals and the idea that humans have just arrived on this earth. Perhaps it would be helpful for us to ponder more deeply the idea that humanity is just beginning its evolutionary ascent, rather nearing the pinnacle of its progress. In verse #42 "Our Brain and Mind - Keys to a Stunning Future" (see complete verse included as #9 in Section II - Poetic Verses), I wrote:

> "We are just beginning our journey. We are like Stone Age creatures when it comes to the spiritual world. We are due to soar beyond the temporal world to regions of Cosmic Light.

Soon the universe will be our playground.... The brain is the key to life. As our brains evolve, our view of creation changes."

The film concluded by asking:

"If we have evolved this far from mammals like Morgie, what new mammals will Morgie find at the next reunion?"

Gopi Krishna provided a stunning answer to this question. It speaks to humanity's further evolution as a mammal, and, in particular, the further evolution of our mind and brain. He discussed the emergence of a new species on earth, a new human species! It is a possibility that I imagine most people, including the makers of this film, probably have not envisioned.

Gopi Krishna spoke of the glorious future that awaits humanity. He said that despite the current wayward direction of our present civilization, a "New World" or "Heaven on Earth", is predestined to happen. He shared the following magnificent vision of humanity's future, in the book <u>Higher Consciousness and Kundalini</u>.

"Imagined in the context of the potentialities present in Kundalini the vision of the future is so alluring, so full of beauty and majesty, so replete with astounding achievements and possibilities for the race, that it is not possible to draw even a distant image of it...

The earth is to become an abode of a graceful, highly intelligent cosmic conscious race. Wafted to another dimension of mind, as the result of organic changes in the brain, it will be equally cognizant of both the worlds - the outer and the inner or the material and the spiritual.

It will be brought in touch with another level of creation, other intelligences and states of being pervading the universe, a universe now completely shut out from our sight because of the limited capacity of our brains.

It is not some aliens from other planets but we who will be the future enlightened denizens of the earth, just as we have been of the savage past. The life of our distant progeny will be so full of charm and beauty, harmony and music, love and romance, adventure and exploit in space (both inner and outer), wonders and marvels, that no imaginative thinker has so far been able to frame a picture of it.

They will have such an extended span of life, long-lasting youth and vigor, freedom from illness, want and oppression, that this will be the Kingdom of God, Paradise, or Nirvana, prophesied by the great seers and prophets of the past. It is to be gained, not in a hypothetical heaven, but here on earth, in the organic frame of man. It is the sublime state of beatitude that is promised in every holy scripture of mankind.

In this vision of the future, even the ideas of "Resurrection", "Liberation", and "Salvation" will find fulfillment in a dramatic way. What we now experience or know of as clairvoyance, astral projection, telepathy, premonition, or prophesy, are but faint glimpses of a future enormously extended state of consciousness.

In rapport with the ocean of Cosmic Intelligence, man will be able to trace the whole drama of life on earth, and even on other orbs, and know himself for what he really is - a drop in the everlasting ocean of being. He will be eternally serene and unaffected by the costumes he wore and the scenes in which he acted in all the aeonic dramas since life started on this planet.

Therefore, whether he awakens to his majesty now or in his still-distant future progeny, the enlightened individual will realize himself as the Sun that had merely lit up the stage. He will see the scenario and the action of the dramas that he thought he had played - whether as a sub-human or a civilized human being - but will himself remain untouched and unchanged, to come out of the happy or unpleasant episodes as a sleeper wakens from a dream."

In 1961, visionary leader and 35th U.S. President John F. Kennedy threw out the challenge to the United States to land a man on the moon and return him safely to earth within the decade. It was successfully accomplished eight years later on July 20, 1969 when Neil Armstrong became the first human to walk on the moon. Who can forget his immortal words?

"That's one small step for [a] man, one giant leap for mankind."

This was a revolutionary accomplishment for humankind as it was the first time a human being had stepped foot on a new world, a surface other than the earth.

Just as we stepped onto a new world when we walked on the moon, we are once again on the brink of taking a greater step into a whole new world, a fascinating inner universe of our minds; a universe, which in extent and magnitude, as well as mystery and intrigue, dwarfs the physical universe that currently absorbs almost all of our attention. Just as 95% of the world's oceans remain unexplored, so too does this incredible inner universe, in which we will find treasures beyond our imagination. New answers to our present-day problems as well as new hopes, possibilities, and life lie concealed within this unseen, unbounded universe.

I believe that the theory of Kundalini could be proven within ten years, if the people of the world would unite their efforts behind a worldwide research project. Think of what profound hope and excitement such a project would bring to the human race, especially during the trying and uncertain times the human race is currently experiencing.

In my mind and heart, I believe Kundalini theory represents a bridge from an uncertain present to a bright future.

As a young boy, I was so excited and inspired by the landing of a human on the moon in 1969. After the recent passing of the 50th anniversary of that historic day in 2019, this same now middle-aged man, feels that same sense of excitement and hope once again with this revolutionary Kundalini theory of human evolution. What new worlds may appear and improvements in human life that may occur are not even imaginable at this time.

I can't think of a more hopeful note on which to end my story. Thank you for reading my story!

Section II - Poetic Verses
Introduction

I composed 48 poetic verses over a period of almost 18 years from November 1991 to February of 2009. It was a period characterized by major life and work changes, many difficult personal challenges, and terrible financial upheaval. It was also a period that brought rapid personal growth and deeply meaningful spiritual development. I found myself constantly needing to let go of my old reality to allow a new reality to enter.

The verses arose spontaneously from within. They always provided comfort and hope. I usually felt an inner prompting to write early in the morning. Oftentimes, I would be writing in my journal when the words naturally flowed into verse. Other times I would "hear" the still small voice within say "Scott, it is time to write". Whenever I wrote, I remained clear minded and alert, yet at the same time my conscious thinking was relaxed as the writing flowed effortlessly through me. In the beginning, I was blown away by this. I knew something unusual was happening within my being. Before this time, I did not have the ability to write in verse or even compose a single line of poetry. Now it felt as if I were taking dictation from an Intelligence that far surpassed my normal mind.

The fact that none of the verse writing was planned in advance was further evidence to me that the entire 18-year process of writing was being directed by this Inner Intelligence. It was as if there were two minds within me now. It became clear this Intelligence had a goal and purpose that I didn't fully understand, until I was able to read all of the verses in sequence and deeply reflect upon their meaning.

It was many years before I culled the verses out of my handwritten journals and typed them into the computer. I was really surprised by their profound and hopeful spiritual content, as well as the story they told of my journey toward God and the dramatic changes in my own consciousness and understanding of God.

Summary of Verses

The following is a selection of eleven verses which summarize key milestones of my journey to a new state of consciousness as well as describe in sometimes metaphorical language, different facets of my voyage and this new dimension of mind.

The journey of the verses began in a state of fear and uncertainty in 1991 and ended with me in a place of joy, peace, beauty and love in 2009. I believe the process of Kundalini, the guidance and workings of God, and a great deal of challenging spiritual and personal development work were responsible for this profound transformation over time.

#1 in 1991, verse #1 "Contact":

I was seated in the top bubble section of a 747-plane flying from Washington, D.C. to San Francisco, when suddenly, I "heard" in my interior a voice calling itself Jesus. It stated there was a great divide I needed to cross and that my life would become challenging. And he shared that Paradise could be found on the other side of this divide. This was the first time that I felt God, or some form of Higher Intelligence or higher faculty of mind, was contacting me, and that I was to take dictation in the form of poetic verse. From then on it became apparent that this Intelligence was indeed within and wanted to be listened to, followed, and had a message for me to deliver through a series of ongoing verses.

#2 in 1996, verse #3 "A Dark and Light Night":

I was experiencing some extremely challenging life events. I wrote that I was terrified of facing the darkness that seemed to be enveloping me. This was my 'Dark Night of the Soul' period. Most times I tried to ignore the darkness and hoped it would disappear. Other times I simply ran from it. I knew however that I must eventually face the darkness and these profound life challenges. My acceptance would be life transforming. It was time to mourn and let go of the past so new life could enter. I found that when I embraced the pain and emptied myself, this action created a new blank canvas. And new images of a more profound and balanced life would cast forth their meaning here. This period of darkness was the beginning of an acceleration in my rebirth and in the development of a new consciousness, a new way to see and be in the world.

#3 in 1999, verse #7 "New Millennium - God is Revealed":

This Higher Intelligence shared what it is, including what truth and love are. I learned how everything in creation is meant to be in relationship. We were born upon this earth for a purpose, and that purpose is learning to love; that love underlies all; that all the trials and tribulations of this world are nothing in comparison to the vast sea of God's love. I was shown that I would see God's face and realize it is my face, mysteriously connected, bathed in love, with all, for all, never forsaking anyone or anything.

#4 in 2000, verse #14 "Our True Home":

Here I described my first experience with a new state of consciousness, where my experience of the physical world began to merge with the experience of an eternal consciousness. I learned my deepest calling was to merge with this eternal consciousness, and to become one with creation. I would know my True Self existed in you and you in me, and that we were not separate. And I realized we are all held in the arms of Love and that this new state of mind is ordained for us all.

#5 in 2001, verse #19 "A Message of Hope":

I spoke of being at a crossroad in my life. I'd been stripped of much of what was meaningful to me. I had little money left, lots of debt, and was scared. Despite all this I was at peace and confident that God was leading me to a better place. I wrote it is paradoxical that as I let go of some of the things that are meaningful to me, in return I received more freedom, a deeper trust in God, and a better future. Being born again from our normal consciousness into an enlightened awareness of our true heritage is a deep and painful experience. It feels like a dark journey as, like a snake continually shedding its outer skin, we shed layer after layer of our outmoded beliefs and behaviors. The light never goes out however, it is always present enveloping the darkness. I step forward, not looking back, as I know my future will capture all of my lost pasts. It is a path that winds down a never-ending road into a magical kingdom of life, light, peace, and love.

#6 in 2002, verse #30 "Silvery Radiance and Deep Peace":

Here I described the experience of this new radiant consciousness and the joy, peace, beauty, and love that lies deep within each of us. I wrote that we must journey inside of ourselves to find this gem; hidden in creation are new layers of creation, beyond the probe of our physical senses; hidden in form is formlessness. This understanding becomes evident as we develop a new consciousness. We are like ants floating on a boundless, formless ocean. Creation is infinite and for eternity we probe its mystery.

#7 in 2004, verse #37 "Resurrection/New Science and Religion":

I shared that the goal in life is to transcend the limits of our five physical senses where a whole new view of creation opens up. The lens of our mind is widened, and a hidden window into the soul opens. Our vision is expanded, and we see with new eyes, the eyes of our souls. We are not specks of matter, conceived by chance, brought to earth to live a flickering existence, soon to turn to dust, forever gone with no meaning, truth, or continuity. These are fables of the old scientific perspective. The new science of life recognizes our eternal being, the permanent nature of our souls, and that our consciousness lights up the world. The world is forever born inside of us. We behold nascent vistas of creation, for eternity; we see that this wondrous state of being is the light shone throughout history by the lives of our prophets, mystics and saints, the past specimens of future evolved man and woman. This luminous consciousness represents a universal religion that embraces all; that recognizes all as my brother and sister, all as my friend, all as my kin, all as myself, the family of Life.

#8 in 2004, verse #38 "Our Future":

I described the dimensionless nature of the universe in this next state of consciousness. We all are the same essence of an eternal presence that lights up the world for eternity. When I look out upon the world, all appears as one and is part of my soul. It was inspiring and hopeful to learn that we do not die, that we only change form for eternity, and that the future is bright and can be trusted.

#9 in 2005, verse #42 "Our Brain and Mind - Keys to a Stunning Future":

I shared how our brains hold the key to our existence and as our brains evolve, our view of creation will change. Within our brains sit new universes, new empyrean regions of light, and the answer to the riddle of life. Humankind is now facing a crisis of enormous proportions and is stuck in old ways of living and old grooves of thinking. Research into Kundalini will provide the key to unlocking the mystery of Life. A new universe of thought and life will open up once this key is discovered.

#10 in 2006, verse #44 "Cosmic Consciousness" and #11 in 2008, verse #47 "Happy Days":

I described the blossoming of a new state of awareness, as well as revealed different facets of the glory of the soul and our eventual arrival at an inner state of joy, peace, beauty, and love. This is the new Eden or Heaven on Earth that one day awaits us all. In "Happy Days" I described Kundalini in greater detail and its enormous implications for humankind. These are particularly stunning verses and are two of my favorites.

Please enjoy the beauty, splendor, and hopefulness of these verses! My fervent wish is that their truth and wisdom touch your deepest essence and remembrances, and help to heal and transform your body, mind, heart, and soul. I also hope they grace you with a new vision of who you really are, an eternal extension of, as well as co-creator with, an everlasting loving Intelligence that underlies and sustains the universe and all of Life.

Appendix of Poetic Verses

1. #1 - Contact - Nov. 30, 1991
2. #3 - A Dark and Light Night - Dec. 27, 1996
3. #7 - New Millennium - God is Revealed - Dec. 30, 1999
4. #14 - Our True Home - Oct. 28, 2000
5. #19 - A Message of Hope - Jan. 29, 2001
6. #30 - Silvery Radiance and Deep Peace - June 14, 2002
7. #37 - Resurrection/New Science and Religion - Aug. 6, 2004
8. #38 - Our Future - Aug. 30, 2004
9. #42 - Our Brain & Mind - Keys to a Stunning Future - Dec. 14, 2005
10. #44 - Cosmic Consciousness - Feb. 11, 2006
11. #47 - Happy Days - Feb. 17, 2008

1) #1 - Contact - November 30, 1991

(Scott) I am flying from Washington Dulles to San Francisco. Sitting in the top bubble on a 747 plane. I feel very nervous today, anxious. I am scared of crashing or dying. I have a doomed feeling. What happens if I die? I'm afraid there is a void, there is nothing. Spiritual void is what I am afraid of. I am afraid there is no God.

(Jesus) Do you believe there is a God?

(Scott) Yes.

(Jesus) Do you believe out of fear?

(Scott) No, I believe that there is ultimate sense in the universe. That this world is an incubator for growth, and that life goes on forever.

(Jesus) Why are you terrified?

(Scott) There is this primal fear in me. I was scared of the darkness. I was so afraid that if left alone, I would die. When I fly on an airplane, I get this terrified feeling inside. It is very painful. It feels like acid is running through my system. I pray to the Lord for deliverance. Take this burden Lord. How do I increase my faith?

(Jesus) By listening to me.

(Scott) I have tried.

(Jesus) Have faith, and never give up. You will become stronger, more confident in yourself.

(Scott) Why does the turbulence scare me?

(Jesus) It signifies storms, trouble in your soul.

(Scott) Lord, I pray for direction to control this trouble in my soul. I pray for faith. Lord, how do I conquer my fear of death?

(Jesus) By living life, going all out, love, enjoy, share love, share meaning, share feelings, help people grow, expand, be positive, build people up, let go. Then you won't be afraid of death. You can handle anything that comes your way. Have faith in God, unceasing faith.

(Scott) I have tried, it only seems to get marginally better, the terror remains. I can't seem to overcome these periods of ups and downs.

(Jesus) Accept it, don't fight it, it is part of you. It is what fuels your growth. It fuels you to higher spiritual planes.

(Scott) It is so tough, so painful.

(Jesus) How do you think I felt on the cross? Terrified, I was terrified that God would not be there, but he was, she was there. Have unceasing faith; you are called to do much. It will take a great reservoir of strength to handle. I do not give out more than one is able to handle. You may think so at times, but I don't.

(Scott) Am I just trying to soothe myself by believing this?

(Jesus) One must go deep within to find the faith. You are on the right track. You can handle anything. Go slower at times, be easy on yourself, you will slowly gain the faith and strength. Ultimately, peace will come to you. You are in a very early growth stage.

Deep down inside that terror you feel is the motivation for growth. It will fuel you, use it to your advantage; embrace it, see it as your friend, my peace I guarantee you. You have much to accomplish, have faith in this. I am proud of you. I am with you always; this I guarantee you. I have been talking to you, trying to get through. I will keep knocking. Don't be afraid. When you are afraid, call me. I will be there to comfort you.

The terror you feel is similar to the terror I felt on the cross. Will God be there? Is he always there? That is where faith comes in. I have risen. It has been fulfilled. Relax, you are going to live a long and fruitful life and you deserve to. I felt terrified on the cross.

(Scott) What did you do?

(Jesus) I endured it and found heaven on the other side. I can share this with you. It is a tough divide to cross.

The terror you feel is separation from me. It is the terror that you are meant to endure to bring you close to God. It is the terror of separation from God that we all endure. It is the firing pit. The suffering you endure now is nothing compared with the glory you will find in the world to come. Have faith in me.

(Scott) How did you endure the terror?

(Jesus) I was very much afraid, alone, left to my internal will. I found paradise on the other side. The suffering, although it feels great to you, is very minimal, compared with the contrast on the other side. I implore you to go forward from here with a spirit of courage, of living life to its' fullest.

(Scott) Lord, how do I increase my faith?

(Jesus) By knowing me, following me, believing in me, and loving me.

(Scott) How do I do that?

(Jesus) By reading scriptures and practicing fundamental spiritual growth. I say don't be afraid of death, live life, grow, reach out to people. It will become apparent what to do.

(Scott) Lord, I am much calmer now.

(Jesus) When you are afraid, listen to the depths, which is where God is. Don't be afraid to go into the depths.

(Scott) I am so terrified at times that I will lose control to evil, that I will be overcome.

(Jesus) Don't worry, I am in control, have ultimate faith in me. I am with you. I will be with you until the end of time. The victory was won on the cross. I know you are terrified at times, so was I. I had faith as a mustard seed, as do you now. Your faith will slowly grow. Change is good. You are growing up, no longer the terrified child. I have spoken to you directly.

You have to go into the valley, before you climb the hills. Your mettle has to be tested under fire, where it will be honed and strengthened.

You can do anything you choose. Live life to its fullest, have a spirit of courage, and not of fear. Reach out with love for your parents and friends, and everyday people you meet, expecting nothing in return. Love is the ultimate perfection; it is on the other side. The other side is the next growth phase.

(Scott) Lord, what is on the other side?

(Jesus) Paradise: love, unity, one, perfection, peace, and spirituality.

(Scott) Why is it necessary to stay on this side?

(Jesus) To prepare for the other side.

(Scott) Are all these ups and downs necessary?

(Jesus) Yes, they facilitate change, they create humility; they stop personal inflation.

(Scott) Am I on the right path?

(Jesus) Very much so, I am so proud of your strength, your courage. Keep meditating, go within, you will become calm; self-confidence will flourish. I will be with you forever.

2) #3 - A Dark and Light Night - December 27, 1996

Oh, how I have tried to flee from you. Yet you were always there.
I know I needed to go through this, yet I have been terrified of you.
You always followed patiently, respectfully, yet at a distance.

Now I can no longer flee. I will look you in the eye and accept you
into my Soul. You, whom I have been so afraid of; Now our eyes meet,
our hands clasp, our body's embrace, our souls accept.

I now realize you are not the enemy; you are my friend.
When we embrace pain and empty ourselves, a new canvas is created.
A blank canvas awaits new images to cast forth their meaning upon.

You allow life to be recreated, not reproduced or recycled.
New forms of life can arise out of the ashes.
New meanings, new ideas to be embraced.
It is so terrifying to say goodbye to the old.
But unless I do, there is no room for the new.

I have treated you as death. Yet you bring new life.
In the deep moist soil of nothingness, a little seed is planted.
A new deeper self is poised to emerge.
A new Self conceived in Divine Love, ready to radiate Divine Love.

So now we meet. Our souls embrace. I feel the nothingness, emptiness.
Your pain greets me, leaves its mark. I now understand it moves on; I
do not die; I die to old ways!

I accept you are not the enemy. You are the reverse side of the face of
God. I now see that wholeness embraces both lightness and darkness.

Out of both, lives are transformed. I mourn the past to let new life begin. This is how creation proceeds. I let go. I learn to accept.

3) #7 - New Millennium - God is Revealed - December 30, 1999

The New Millennium approaches. I have seen the light; it is brilliant, it is pure; it is full of life and energy; it is infinite and infinitesimal; it is nothing, it is all; it is close, it is far; it is contained in a single point, it is everywhere. It is love, humility, charity, and meekness.

We were brought to this earth for a purpose. That purpose is love. Love underlies all. There is no other purpose, other gifts pale beyond comparison to this.

I am all. I am in all. I am peace. I am truth. I am one. When you follow the truth, you are set free. Following the truth is not easy. It takes discipline, sustained practice.

I am as real as the ground. I am the ground. I am the tree of life. I am all-knowing but I am humble. Through me all is transformed. Nothing is feared. I am like a sweet melody, soothing to the soul.

I am eternal, never changing, always with you. Through me, all things have their substance. I am sweet music. I will never forsake anyone. I am the jewel of creation. When you touch me, you touch the infinite; I give rest to hearts.

Now you see me dimly, soon you will see me face to face. Then you will say to yourself, I have seen the truth, it sets me free.

I am unchained, I am unbounded. I am conceived in divine love. This suffering is but a mere pittance compared to the glory that is being revealed.

I am filled with love and joy because I have come home. Home is what I imagined it would be. It is like a crystal palace into which no germs can penetrate. It is a divine mansion, radiant, pulsating with love.

There are no errors here, no mistakes. Everything is grounded in love, connection, and humility. When you see God, you will know that he has always been with you. When you see God, you will know that she has never left you. When you see God, you will be welcomed home.

You will say where have you been and then realize that you were never far. Our ears strain to hear the music, the sweet music of heaven. Now it is faint, soon it will penetrate to the very essence of our being. We will realize that we are made of music.

Soon we will be home, drinking in the divine love, knowing we were never alone. Our minds and hearts will be at peace. We will be at one with our divine past, present, and future, and realize it is all coalesced into one imperceptible whole, pulsating with love, the microcosm and the macrocosm, the finite and the infinite.

All is so mysterious but soon a great truth will be revealed. Right now, the mystery is beyond our comprehension but soon the veil will be lifted, and the mystery forever enshrouded to protect the creation will be revealed.

The creation is clothed in mystery to protect our humanity and divinity. The world is not an isolated place. This creation is not meaningless. Life was meant for love.

All the trials and tribulations of this world are nothing in comparison to the vast sea of God's love. Soon you will see me, my divine face, and realize it is your face, mysteriously connected, bathed in love, in all, with all, for all, never forsaking anyone or anything.

4) #14 - Our True Home - October 28, 2000

I feel like I am at another turning point in my life,
Where the temporal is merging into the eternal.
I no longer have to grasp, to doubt, to cling to uncertainty.

I know of God's deep Love for us,
A Love that transcends our human failings.
A Love that awaits us with arms outstretched,
To greet us, to forgive us, and to embrace us in its infiniteness.

I have come home to a Place that is beyond all temporality,
A Place of eternal beauty and rest.
A Place where the human and divine merge in a
Timelessness that creates a space of merciful Love.

A Love that never forgets; never holds on.
An all encompassing Love that holds all of our
Failings lightly. I have come home to a place
Beyond space and time, where my identity merges
With the eternal substance and Love called God.

Now I no longer exist; personalities disappear and merge
Into the cosmic space that holds all in Love.
This is my true inheritance; my deepest calling is to merge
With God to become one with creation.

Now I know my true Self that exists in you and you in me.
We are no longer separate, separated by vales of tears,
But we are the perfume of cosmic holiness that reaches out in Love,
Embraces all in Love and creates a space for all to unite.

This is the mystery, the eternal mystery we are all reaching toward.
A mystery enshrouded in cosmic and divine Love. A Love
That always forgives, never condemns, and always awaits us.
It is our true home.

Our spirits are restless until we find our true home.
Forever searching until we reunite with the divine one.
A one that encompasses all that is merciful, compassionate,
Kind, loving, gentle, humble and everlasting.
This is our true home. What we are all inexorably heading toward.

When we reach home, we will realize we never left.
We will see all is familiar; all is embraced by God's Love.
No one is left a stranger; all return from that distant land
To reclaim and hold their true heritage.

5) #19 - A Message of Hope - January 29, 2001

In my life, I'm at a crossroad. I've been stripped of much of what has been meaningful to me. I have little money, lots of debt, and I'm scared. Yet paradoxically, I also feel free.

This is the treasure I have received. It is so paradoxical, I give up involuntarily/voluntarily what is meaningful to me, and in return I receive my freedom, my deep trust in God, and the natural, nurturing, and nourishing unfolding of the future.

I stand in peace, in the cloud of unknowing, not knowing where the future will lead, but I stand with a trust knowing that it will lead to a meaningful place. Like being carried on the wings of an angel, I know God is guiding me to my next destination. I also now know it is a God full of love, beauty, kindness, gentleness, tenderness, compassion, and humility.

I now have seen, felt, tasted, heard, and touched God deep in my heart. It is not the God of my inherited beliefs. It is a God way beyond my wildest dreams. It is a God slowly but surely leading me to the Promised Land, the land of milk and honey.

It is not a God that wishes us to suffer. We suffer temporarily, as we are born into a new existence. We are being led deep into the heart of God. It feels like a dark journey as, like a snake shedding its outer skin, we shed layer after layer of our outmoded beliefs and behaviors.

It is a God of deep love who wants great things for her children. It is a God that never denies, always accepts, and fervently desires our true peace and happiness. Being born again from a dark primitive

316

consciousness into an enlightened awareness of our true heritage is a deep and painful experience. The light never goes out however, it is always present enveloping the darkness.

Soon we will be brought fully into the light of God. Then we will know our true home, our true sanctuary, as we reside deep in the heart of God. Forevermore we will put aside our fears. We will know the truth, a truth that resides in eternity, an eternity that holds all of our pasts, presents, and futures. It is our true essence, our eternal being.

Soon all will be bathed in love and light. I say goodbye temporarily in the present to welcome a future that will be bright beyond my conception. It is a future born out of a deep trust and love for God.

I step forward, not looking back, as I know my future will capture all of my lost pasts. It is a path that winds down a never-ending road into a magical kingdom of life, light, peace, and love.

There is magic in the air, the stars will forever be lit up. The angels will be dancing, as I soar into eternity with my feet on the ground.

There is magic in the air, a true magic awaits me. I've given up much to receive all. I see the world now through different eyes. My sight is no longer murky. I see a deep blue ocean of being, beyond my wildest dreams.

Where can this path be leading me? To a land way beyond my dreams. I now see that what I let go of is returned forevermore in a form and peace that will forever astound me.

It is dazzling, radiant, streaming, shimmering, glistening, glittering, blazing, streaming with light, dancing with joy, and says, this is your past, your present, and your future. This is your God.

6) #30 - Silvery Radiance and Deep Peace - June 14, 2002

Throughout all of eternity we sit, God's great grace descends upon us. We will never be the same again, our vision has been altered, our life changed. We see through to eternity, time fades away. A grand era of peace is ushered in.

A soul cries out for help. Where is God, where has God been? Seemingly lost forever. Then in a twinkling of an eye, all is changed. God is found. God has always been present. God never fades away.

Our eyes stretch forever. God's grace descends upon the earth. A deep peace enters our hearts. Smooth flowing waters. We are never lost again.

We see the faces of our grandmothers and grandfathers. The face of God is present. The sweet fragrance of eternity fills our hearts. An era of immense peace has begun. We have come home, to eternity, beyond space and time, our new home for eternity, a deep peace within.

Our hearts are changed, graced forever. We float in a sea of tranquility. The heavens open up, immense peace and love, eternal beauty and rest, all doubt banished forever. We see with new eyes. Deep peace, plush, velvety, the sweet ointment of God's love.

For eternity we rest. Our hearts are filled with love. God's voice calls, I have never left you, all must be as it is. In a twinkling of an eye, the old passes away and the new enters.

We sit frozen in eternity: changeless, formless, beyond description, beyond words. Forever calm, the turbulent waters cease. All is held softly in God's love, caressed, soothed, celebrated, forever changed.

We sit quietly. We are beyond the vale of tears. A deep silence enters our hearts. We have entered the silent chamber of God's heart. We now are held deep in the heart of God's love; never again will we doubt. Deeper and deeper we enter. We penetrate to the heart of eternity; all form passes away. All that is left is a deep silence, a deep peace, a sea of consciousness forever graces our hearts.

We float in a sea of peace. We penetrate deep into the heart of the mystery. All time passes away, all that is left is eternity. God speaks softly, reminds us of our inheritance, our deepest calling, the eternal truth. We awaken from the dream and we realize our true home. We see the truth deeply. Reality is not as it appears. True reality exists in the heart of God.

Deep into the mystery we penetrate; so soothing, so peaceful, nothing looks the same. A silvery radiance, a sparkling sea of consciousness; we have entered a new world, a new existence, our true inheritance; sparkling, glittering, majestic; a sea of throbbing, living, vibrant consciousness.

Form disappears into eternity. The face of God switches appearances. We float in this sea of consciousness, graced beyond words. All is new, nothing looks like the same; a sweet melody, encased in God's love. The deep longings of our heart are filled in this sea of love. Cleansed of all impurities, we see a new world.

We have entered a new world, beyond the vale of tears. The curtain is pulled back, the veil is lifted, a whole new view of creation presents itself. Where have you been hidden, beyond our reach? Now you reveal yourself, new layers of creation open up.

Hidden in creation are new layers of creation, beyond the probe of our senses. Hidden in form is formlessness. All of a sudden, the door opens, and a new layer of creation is revealed, embedded in an existing layer; so simple, yet so profound, the key to the mystery. One can only enter on God's terms. A whole new set of laws governs this creation. Only God knows the time when the curtain is lifted. It is never lifted on our terms.

Deeper and deeper layers of creation are revealed. Creation is infinite. We forever move closer to the eternal truth. We are like ants floating on this boundless, formless ocean, this sea of eternity.

Deep into the heart of the mystery we enter. God has opened up another chamber of her heart. Oh my God, a blazing new discovery! Deep into the silvery radiance we penetrate, a creation we never dreamed existed.

We enter new worlds, deep into the heart of God. We have been granted entrance. It is an honor beyond comparison. God only opens this door when one is truly ready. It's like receiving a pass into a new magical kingdom.

Where have you been hidden? I searched forever. Now the door to my heart swings open, and God reveals a new layer of creation; so beautifully simple, yet so elegant, so majestic, so full of grandeur.

Where have you been hidden? One does not enter by force, or by self-will, a complete yielding to God is necessary. We must be cleansed of all impurities, all selfish tendencies.

We float in a sea of eternity. We enter into the grace of God. We step deeper into the mystery. We have become a silvery radiance. The mystery revealed, yet new layers of mystery open up.

For eternity we probe the mystery. We leave the surface of existence and a formless, boundless, infinite creation is revealed. Mortal life sits on a sea of infinite eternal life.

Beyond the probe of our senses, the veil is lifted. Now we see, a new layer of creation is revealed, a new layer of existence; so simple, so incredible, so profound; all done with God's infinite grace. God has opened the door to his greatest prize, eternal life.

7) #37 - Resurrection/New Science and Religion - August 6, 2004

There is joy in my heart, from the deep recesses of my soul wells up a joy and happiness beyond belief. I have touched eternity. Eternity has kissed my soul. Drenched with love, my soul touches all parts of the universe. Matter dissipates and all that remains is love.

My heart speaks a great truth. God's immense love for humanity lights up the universe. The sky opens up, the material world dissolves; all that remains is my soul. I have touched a new dimension of being. I have been torn from my anchor in the material world. All that remains is consciousness.

I am no longer anchored in my body. I float effortlessly, roaming the skies, touching all parts of the universe. I have become the universe. I am without dimension. I touch the sky, I roam the stars, I glow, I reach for the firmaments, I am happy beyond compare.

I have seen the reality of my soul. I've been released from the bondage of flesh. I climb the stairway to heaven. I kiss the stars. I roam the amphitheater of my mind, the cathedral of my heart. My soul stretches forever, lighting up the sky, effervescent, glowing.

My mind has transcended the limits of my body. I am no longer confined in time and space. I am eternal, formless, I stretch to infinity. All of me encompasses you. I sing with joy, dance with glee, I am the ether of the universe.

My heart glows, my soul expands, I stretch beyond the confines of my body. I am no longer a prisoner of my flesh. My soul roams free, stretching out to eternity. Like a feather, I float effortlessly. The moon glows, the sun shines, distant planets become my friend. They are no longer distant, or separate; they are part of me, part of my eternal soul, part of yours. We kiss, we embrace, our souls dance. We have touched heaven, here on earth. Heaven is part of our souls.

The goal in life is to transcend the limits of our senses where a whole new view of creation opens up. The lens of our mind is widened, a new window into our soul opened, our view expanded, we see with new eyes, the eyes of our souls. We are no longer a puny mortal, encased in flesh, but are a jewel, shining for eternity.

The universe is in us. We stretch beyond the last limits of the universe. We have reached a wonderland, a fairyland of infinite proportions. It is our natural home. It is who we are.

We are the sky, we are the moon, we are the planets. Our minds roam free, the world is not outside of us, it is born from within. We evolve forever, reaching new heights of glory.

We have been resurrected. We have left the tomb of our body. The Mary's cry and they say goodbye. However, we are not gone, we are transformed to the farthest reaches of heaven, here on earth. The stone is pulled back, our spirits roam free. This is the purpose of human life, to leave the tomb of the body, to touch the ether, to roam the skies.

We leave the cross, our shadowy forms leaving the tether of our body. We are resurrected to new life. We assume our eternal form. We are a shining energy, a light unto the world. We are dazzling, radiant, white as snow, pure, formless, eternal, sparkling, brilliant, gleaming, streaming, effervescent.

This is the good news, the glorious message which prophets, mystics, and saints of yore brought to humankind. Our consciousness lights up the world. It heralds a new religion, a universal religion that embraces all; that recognizes all as my brother and sister, all as my friend, all as my kin, all as myself.

This is the mystery of our life. It is the mystery of our souls. It is the mystery of our eternal being. It is the light shone throughout history by the lives of our prophets, mystics and saints, the past specimens of future evolved man and woman.

We are not specks of matter, conceived by chance, brought to earth to live a flickering existence, soon to turn to dust, forever gone, with no meaning, no truth, no continuity. These are fables of old. This is the old science.

The new science of life recognizes our eternal being, the permanent nature of our souls. The world is forever born inside of us. We see new vistas of creation, for eternity.

This is the new science of which we are touching the frontier. It is both a science and religion. It is a universal religion embracing all of humankind. It heralds a new chapter in the life of humankind, in the history of the world. We come face to face with a great truth, the eternal nature of our beings, the discovery of new energies, new planes of creation, and the intelligent forces of life.

This is where the new science and religion begins. We are infants in our evolutionary development destined to become super men and women in the future, forever approaching the divine light, the source of our being. This is what keeps our hearts young and our hopes eternal, allowing us to withstand the rigors of life; our glorious future destiny, unfolding from the seeds of our souls, deep within our hearts.

8) #38 - Our Future - August 30, 2004

So now it is time to write, once again I have been summoned. A window in my soul has opened up. I become the mouthpiece of an intelligence that far surpasses my normal understanding.

I look out upon the world. All looks as one. There are no distinctions. All is part of my soul. Everything is transparent, all fused into one.

I have become a sacred vessel of God. I am transported beyond time and space. I sit quietly. I enter God's heart, a silent chamber of infinite peace. Heaven plays a melody upon the harp of my eternal existence.

I have become a receptacle for God's love. We are infinite, filled with light, dancing with delight, never alone, always creating, new forms, new ways of life, for eternity.

I sit amazed, what has become of me. No longer the same. I am infinite, stretched out to the sky and beyond, love's enchanting melody forever playing in my heart. We are a medley of different notes played by an infinite God.

I am the moon, I am the star, I am the dark, I am the light. I am all, I am in all, I am nothing, I am everything. I am formless, changeless, directionless, yet I exist, forever.

My eyes open up, new vistas come into sight. I explore the universe, floating here and there, effortlessly, like a feather, carried away by the wind. I dance, I float, I sing, I wait; I wait for eternity to sing its tune through the vessel of my body.

I am an instrument of God, never to be forsaken, never to be abandoned. I sing with delight. I never knew this was I, or you. It is all of us, our eternal heritage, our priceless prize.

I look out upon you and realize you are me. When you hurt, I hurt. When you grieve, I grieve. When you are lost, I am lost. Soon no distinction is made. We are the same essence of an eternal presence that lights up the world, for eternity.

My heart is filled with love and hope. All things are transitory. Soon I will change my cosmic form, I will wear a new costume in the eternal game of life.

Closer and closer to God we move, for eternity. We reach new and brighter shades of light, new dazzling displays of creativity, new levels of grandeur. We are jewels of creation transformed.

God has come to tell us that we never die; we only change form, for eternity. The future is bright. It can be trusted. We are all vessels of light, heirs to our eternal birthright, infinite peace and joy.

9) #42 - Our Brain and Mind - Keys to a Stunning Future - December 14, 2005

I sit on the beach. I look out upon a vast ocean. A stunning new light enters my life.

I see beyond form to an eternal brightness. I have entered a new land, a grand new beginning.

My heart is filled with love and light. I feel a warmness permeate my body. I am free: beyond pain and death, beyond light and darkness, beyond all temporality.

Matter glistens with a light so bright. I have entered heaven here on earth.

I float out to the moon and stars. I reach beyond the universe; there is no longer me, only we. I jump with delight, a stunning new sight, an indescribable beauty.

All of this is contained within the tiny seed of our hearts. Here sits a grand new universe, a parallel universe of infinite delight. It is our future birthright.

Our brains hold the key to our existence. Within our brains sit new universes, new empyrean regions of light, the answer to the riddle of life.

We only need to be purified to see the light. New layers of consciousness, new treasures, new wonders, to discover for eternity.

We are just beginning our journey. We are like Stone Age creatures when it comes to the spiritual world. We are due to soar beyond the temporal world to regions of Cosmic Light.

Soon the universe will be our playground. There are an infinite number of universes to explore. The brain is the key to life. As our brains evolve, our view of creation changes.

Space exploration will be done in and through our brains. The blueprint of our future sits encrypted in our brains, deep within our souls. It is a glorious, stunning future.

Humankind is facing a crisis of enormous proportions. It is stuck in old ways of living, old grooves of thinking. Research into Kundalini provides the key to unlocking the mystery of life. A whole new universe of thought and life will open up once this key is discovered.

When our physical form dies, our souls live on. They are transported to new vehicles, new vessels of life. Our individual souls travel through new universes, visit new planes of creation, for eternity.

We never lose touch with our past. Nothing is lost, nothing is forgotten. All ties are continued.

10) #44 - Cosmic Consciousness - February 11, 2006

I step out onto the beach; a warm tropical breeze greets my face. The ocean is a pure blue color. It is a breezy, beautiful, balmy, summer day. I can see forever. What a wonder world awaits us. The palm trees sway, my heart expands, my joy never ending, home sweet home.

I sink my feet into the warm sandy beach. I have touched the everlasting fount of joy. This is paradise! I am free! The chains have been removed. I live in a fantasy world: fountains of joy, unending bliss, beautiful colors, rapturous vistas; the divine within.

The sweet gusher of success, the never-ending triumph of love. God's grace, nature's bounty, warms our heart, lets us know we are destined for great things. God's grace, nature's charm will make our hearts sing with a joy and happiness that never diminishes, that continues to mount as we rise up the scale of evolution.

It is a celestial voyage of everlasting glory. I climb onto the ship, cast off to the unknown, sail through uncharted waters, endure dark trials, bounce on wavy seas, navigate through dark chasms. All of a sudden, when all hope is seemingly lost, I see a bright light. I sail toward the light; darkness begins to fade, the shadows disappear, greater light begins to shine. My heart lifts, my soul awakens, my flesh is stripped.

The glorious dawn has arrived! The curtain is lifted. God's face shines through. It is now a brilliant light, a soothing medley of colors, a beauty impossible to describe. A lightness in the air, fountains of joy, pools of bliss. My soul expands, it becomes the Light.

The future is so bright. I have touched heaven here on earth. We clean away the mud and impurities and find our everlasting glory. Our souls fill the universe. God's grace descends into our hearts. We have arrived at the celestial port! A long voyage, a frightful night; in darkness we sat, in lightness we rise; ever thankful to God that we have embraced the Living Light, the only sure way to heaven, while here on earth.

I now see the truth. This is our future; this is who we really are. I have left the tabernacle of flesh to soar to regions of empyrean joy and unspeakable glory. My soul is lifted up to Heaven! The trumpets sound, the celestial angels sing, God's loving embrace sweetens every pore of my body. I have become pure spirit, with some invisible link to flesh, roaming the celestial vault, drinking in the nectar of gods, sailing with angels, floating on streams of light, emblazoned with hues of color, light as a feather.

We have become the ocean, love's pure light. Our hearts dance, our souls smile. We are now sailing on celestial seas of glory, happy and free, liberty emblazoned in our heart; our eternal freedom, the touch of God, the sweet kiss of our ancestors, a dreamlike existence; oceans of bliss, the pure blue sky, deep blue waters, fresh breezes, swaying palm trees, daisies, the flowers of heaven; filled with might, streams of joy, blazing light, never ending delight. We float, we caress, we absorb, we dance. We have found heaven in our souls, here on earth, while alive in flesh. **Earth's new Eden.**

11) #47 - Happy Days - February 17, 2008

"Happy Days" House - 565 Cahuenga Blvd., Hollywood, CA.

I walk up the stairs, onto the porch; I open the door, my heart bursts with joy. I have come home, to my true home, to my true mansion of God. I step inside. I have entered paradise. I am happy beyond compare.

I walk through the house; my heart skips a beat. The sea voyage has ended, my ship has come into port. I step out upon the other shore. The moon glistens, stars radiate, planets shine. All of this is enshrined in my heart.

I am back in familiar surroundings: my birthplace, my true self, my true home. Bathed in humility, I see the Lord, a resplendent glory. I touch everlasting life, kiss its soul. I float through the house, going from room to room. All is so familiar, like I never left. I greet ancestors, share memories with loved ones; sweetness imprinted in my heart, my heart filled with purity and joy.

I am a new person, yet this is really who I am. Mother smiles, Grandma hugs, Grandpa embraces, Aunt Jean greets, Sarah licks, Noel beams, Uncle Bob laughs, Rolph says job well done, Charlotte gushes, the silvery moon glows nearby. I have arrived home.

Happy Days are here again. My heart glows with an appreciation that goes back to the beginning of time. The material world evaporates, replaced by a shining radiance, an overflowing happiness, a gaiety beyond compare.

Into the silvery moon I travel, my heart radiating deeper layers of love, a peace beyond compare; God nearby, welcoming me home, telling me I never left.

Into the silvery moon I travel, my heart aglow with new wonders, my face beaming with light, my body shuddering with joy, my soul dancing with delight.

I leave my body and rush up to the stars. I jump from star to star, Walt Disney's magic inscribed in my heart. I descend into Niagara Falls, dancing with the sprays of joy, floating on waterfalls, heaven filling my heart.

I soar up to the stars at lightning speed, my heart bursting with joy, my mind ablaze with glory, I burst into the universe; I open the door upon a silvery, lustrous, magical, gleaming, glistening, fairyland of my heart.

I am the universe. All is my soul. The soils of culture and evolution have been cleansed, my primitive past purified. My self expands, my heart reaches out and touches all that exists. I jump from planet to planet, I dance with the stars, flow with galaxies, laugh with the solar system.

I rush out past the stars, past the galaxies, past the edge of the universe. I am light as a feather, traveling everywhere all at once, leaving terror behind, embracing joy, melting with love, extending everywhere in space. Every pore of my body filled with joy, dancing with glee. I am a whole new person.

My soul bursts its seams. I rush out into the universe, past the moon, past the stars, past the galaxies. I jump black holes, ski on galactic nebulae, spin on quasars, race past white dwarfs, dance with red giants. I touch the ether of the universe. I am the universe. The universe has burst its seams, the ghost has melted, form has disappeared, true reality appears.

Into the silvery moon I head. I fly past blazing suns, I rush past radiating stars, I windsurf on streaking comets, I soar into empyrean regions of joy.

I am face to face with a whole new consciousness, a whole new view of the universe, a whole new view of myself. Oh, my goodness, this is really who I am. It is really who you are. It is really who we are. What joy, laughter, harmony, and peace. What beauty, love, lightness, and happiness. What hope, possibility, good news, and radiance.

Now I travel up to the furthest reaches of heaven. I have reached rarified air, left behind gross matter, embraced subtle worlds; new worlds open up, vibrating with light and love, laughter and joy, beauty and radiance. A whole new view of creation! As far from this present reality as lightness is from darkness, as beauty is from ugliness, as laughter is from despair. A world of infinite beauty and peace.

I sit on the edge of the moon, reach out to the stars; I realize they are my soul mates; christened with heaven's touch, heaven's beauty, heaven's radiance, heaven's glory, love's laughter, nature's freshness.

I sit on the silvery moon, travel out to new worlds, the richness in my heart ablaze with new glories, new wonders, new dreams, new possibilities. I leave behind the old, find revealed in the new, new forms of creation, new layers of creation, new life forms, new energies, new friends.

My narrow mind has burst the seams of its tight enclosure. It soars out into the universe, expands, and becomes the All. In this I see new worlds, new universes, parallel universes of infinite delight. I am infinite, everlasting, omnipresent, bursting with wonder, dancing with delight.

My old view of creation is blown up, blown away; replaced with cosmic sight, ever expanding, never ending; rapturous sights, new worlds to view for eternity.

I streak out to heaven, leaving the flat earth behind. Traveling on celestial seas of new glory, I blaze new trails, climb new heights, soar to empyrean regions of joy, ascend the stairway to heaven, float on ethereal orbs, bounce from heaven to heaven, strut with majestic glory; filled with endless humility, stargazing to heaven, flowing on rivers of love, dancing with streams of joy, wafted to new planes of glory.

I sail out to heaven, my celestial sails ablaze with glory, streaking with light, overflowing with joy; new heavens, new majestic sights of creation, now hidden from sight, suddenly brought into view. I burst my seams, I reach out to heaven; celestial angels carry me on their wings, with herculean might and strength. New visions greet my sight.

I am a purified, blazing sea of glory, dancing on oceans of light, leaving worry behind, forever laughing at death. The old creation dies away, my old view of God evaporates. I become the blazing sun, I now melt in God; the I leaves me, the we greet me.

I sail out into the universe, am a man greeting new worlds, embracing a new God; my view expanded, my heart extended, my soul enchanted, my mind entranced, my body enraptured; filled with new joy, bursting its seams, creating new worlds at a dizzying pace, filled with laughter, dancing with delight, radiating joy, never the same, always new, always fresh, always creating, always alive, never bored, one with God, one with you, one with creation.

Alive with new possibilities, seeing the universe as my friend, I burst into heaven with my feet on the ground. I yell out to everyone, never give up, heaven's delight is never far, we all have this possibility within. We just have to change our view of evolution and creation to see that we are evolving toward the light, with right spiritual and bodily practices, right thinking, open minds, leaving prejudices and old dogmas behind.

We need to open our mind to a new view of creation, realize that we were created for everlasting glory, that our bodies contain a wondrous secret, a marvelous form of evolution within, a powerful energy waiting to bring new light to humankind; a mechanism in the human body, a new organ, a new potential waiting to bring in new life.

It is time to change our narrow view of God to see that we have God within; that God is reaching out to touch us with new light, new wonders, new possibilities, new hopes for eternity. We just have to realize that this potential is within. It is a potential of our bodies, of our minds.

There is a potent energy within us, bursting again on the scene at this stage of evolution and history, to introduce us to new wonders, and a new view of creation. It is a revelation from God, the eternal source of all that is.

It is a wonder energy in our body that needs to be nurtured and embraced; so that our bodies can change, our nervous systems evolve, our brains expand, to bring in a new picture of heaven, a new form of life, a new form of religion, a new science; now not separate, but all connected.

There is a potential in the human body. It is a radiant form of intelligent energy, a different form of creation that is beyond our sensory probe. This powerhouse of energy is waiting to transform our bodies, minds, nervous systems, organs, brains, and ways of thinking, so that we know that we are beams of light from an eternal sun, always resplendent, always shining, always existing, never dying.

Evolution is at the point, our minds and bodies are ready, to embrace this new theory of life. It is time to leave behind the old narrow theories so that new life can be created, and terrible disasters averted.

Evolution is at a point where people are now ready to see that Consciousness is the All. This mechanism of Kundalini is a potential in the human body, waiting to be understood and embraced by the mass of people.

Humanity has evolved to a point where it is ready to see the Light, its brain is evolving, and new forms of life and creation are coming into view. We must embrace this new Light or face extinction. Death will lose its sovereign nature when this new Light is embraced.

Humanity on a mass scale has evolved to the point where this knowledge must be disseminated quickly. This knowledge will free humankind from the prison house of its senses that it has erected due to its over-reliance on its materialistic philosophies, old sciences, and old religions.

A new science and religion of life is waiting to be embraced. Eternal life will come into view, the fear of death will lose its grip, our life spans will be expanded, the dominance of the old materialistic science will die away, subsumed by this new philosophy of life, where new forms of energy and life, new layers of creation, stand revealed. It is all within us, within our brains.

A thirsting humanity waits for this knowledge to be revealed. The story needs to be told, simple and to the point, universal in its nature, everlasting in its hope, embracing recovery, letting go of pride and prejudice, power and prestige.

The mass of humanity will lead, proud science will follow, recalcitrant religion will slowly accept; fear of war will lessen, violence will subside, terrorism will die away, disease and famine will slowly evaporate, and a new curtain on history will be raised, and a new paradise, a new heaven, a new Eden, will slowly descend upon the earth.

Section III - Inspired Prose

Introduction

In the summer of 2018, my inner guidance communicated to me the following inspired prose. It was over nine years since I had written my last poetic verse. It occurred at the culmination of a profoundly meaningful phase of my spiritual and life journey. It describes the important pillars underlying the journey to the Cosmic Conscious state of mind, the ongoing evolution of our mind and brain, the purpose of our existence, as well as our relationship to God and our never-ending journey toward the Infinite. It also speaks about the meaning of creation, the infinite number of creations that exist, and how all the different creations eventually unite in one titanic jigsaw puzzle of Love. It is a staggering piece of writing to comprehend. I believe these inspirations reveal a deep truth, are incredibly hopeful in nature, and I would only ask that you open your mind and heart to these possibilities.

Creation, Life, Love
and Our Future Path

1) The first thing I realized is that this dimension of consciousness, what we call normal human awareness and physical existence is, in essence, a transport system to another dimension of consciousness, beyond our five physical senses, called Cosmic Consciousness. It is the next step of human evolution.

This creation is a play of love invented by an unimaginable loving intelligence. We are the actors in the play. Achieving a oneness with creation and God, realizing our eternal nature, and experiencing a permanent Love beyond our physical senses is the goal of this next state of evolution. We need each other's help to reach this next level of reality. Kundalini and the resulting evolution of our bodies, brains, and minds expedites this process, but at this stage of our development, Kundalini is still a fairly rare occurrence and often fraught with peril and danger.

2) We need to create an environment that allows for the healthy development of Life, Kundalini and the unfolding of our Cosmic Conscious sense. Sound physical, mental, spiritual/religious practices, moral and ethical ways of living, a clean and life sustaining environment, supported by our cultivating eternal values like love, kindness, compassion, truth, honesty, and service to others, become imperative.

We need to help each other to love, create, and unify rather than hate, compete and divide. It all starts with our selves. We must become "Inner Activists" and do the work to change and purify ourselves and

343

become who we are meant to be. When we create peace and harmony within ourselves, this allows us to bring peace and harmony to the world. As we change and purify ourselves, this can have a ripple effect and lead to positive change in others and the world.

3) In this next level of reality (Consciousness), the whole truly is greater than the sum of the parts. There, when we work together, everyone wins and there are no losers. It is not like in the physical level of reality, which is often a zero-sum game, where one wins while another loses.

Although there is much hate, pain, disease, loss, death and destruction in the world today, and it is probably difficult to imagine how this can be a play of love; as Lois W., co-founder of the Al-Anon 12-step program said in her memoir Lois Remembers:

> "Gazing at the sky on a bright starlit night, we are overwhelmed with wonder at the seemingly limitless universe. Our finite minds cannot envision its extent and complexity, much less the possibility of other universes beyond. Likewise, our finite minds sometimes question why a loving God seems to permit apparently God-loving and virtuous people to suffer the tragedies that occasionally befall them.
>
> But our hearts do not need logic. They can love and forgive and accept that which our minds cannot comprehend. Hearts understand in a way that mind cannot."

The healing and love that takes center stage as our inner being of love unfolds eventually transcends all the pain, loss, and destruction that has taken place in physical reality.

This is the "atonement", or the "to one movement."

4) In the material, or physical sense level of reality, it appears as if we and all life forms, including planets, suns, galaxies, the universe, etc., all eventually die. It's a living and dying universe. The world looks separate, divided, and full of material elements. We are separated from each other and all of life.

In the next level of reality, consciousness takes center stage, the world loses its dimension and separateness. Everything is connected and seen as one whole. The same eternal consciousness is recognized to be flowing through all of us. It becomes a Mind and motion universe rather than a material universe of separate objects and people - an eternally living, giving and re-giving, service oriented, mutually balanced, two-way universe. Death disappears. Love reigns. Our consciousness evolves forever as we now understand we are an extension of this one Universal Mind or Intelligence which is eternally living.

The more one purifies oneself and develops the attributes of what we often call God, the more loving, merciful, light, beautiful, intelligent and conscious our consciousness can become. The material world sits in an ocean of love, beauty, mercy, light, intelligence and life which for the most part we cannot perceive until we reach this next level of consciousness. This requires as Gopi Krishna said, the further organic evolution of our brain and body and the development of this new faculty of mind. The process of Kundalini is the force and mechanism to effect this change.

5) The creator is eternally creating a creation, forever painting an evolving, more harmonious picture. We are one eternal unit, forever creating, always painting our one unit of creation.

As we evolve in a healthy way and begin to develop the Cosmic Conscious sense, we become a much greater co-creator with this eternal Intelligence. We can choose between painting our unique contribution to the picture automatically, with little freedom of choice, with our instinct, or "Blind Eye" as our animal ancestors did. Or we can use the limited intelligence of our physical senses, ego, and intellectual minds, or "Limited Eye", as most people are doing now. Or we can become more like Picasso or Michelangelo, and paint with our Cosmic Sense or our "Super Eye". We can then create, directly in concert with the creator, a forever evolving, more lovely, beautiful, harmonious, joyful and peaceful universe, a truly symphonic creation of music of the spheres!

We will have evolved from Instinct Animal to Intellectual Human and now Illuminated (Cosmic Conscious) Super Man and Woman.

6) Our lives are like a Playlist. But instead of having 50 songs, we have an infinite number of lives on our individual Playlist. Each interval of life, like the quiet and silence between each new song on the Playlist, is separated by a period of rest before the next act of the play or our new life begins. Walter and Lao Russell, founders of the University of Science and Philosophy, wrote about how when our physical bodies die, much like nature which cyclically regenerates itself, our eternal minds build our new bodies, and we begin anew. We

carry forward the essence of who we are to the next life, but don't remember the details. There is no death. There is no good or bad, simply experiences that help us to grow our souls. Since it is a Mind universe in reality, we always will keep growing and advancing our consciousness/souls to the day our material body dies. However far we advance our consciousness in this life, this is where we will begin our next life.

7) As we begin to explore consciousness, we explore the Intelligence behind the universe, that we name as God. We forever approach this Love and Light, like a spiral, drawing nearer, slowly understanding more, for eternity. We act in different theaters and planes of creation forever. We never lose touch with our past. Nothing is lost, nothing is forgotten. All ties are continued.

In verse #29, "The Sweet Nectar of Eternity", I wrote:

"Our Souls are imprinted with the blueprint of eternity, forever unfolding as we approach the source of all, the sweet flowing waters of the land of milk and honey. New vistas will open up forever! Time will lose its essence. Layers and layers of existence unfold before our eyes, deeper layers of beauty and love."

8) There are an infinite number of creations, each creation has a happy ending, each creation is a piece of the puzzle, all creations unite together in Love. To begin to get a minute glimpse of this truth, our minds have to evolve a new super channel of perception or this Cosmic Sense - Cosmic Consciousness.

Author Biography

Scott Hiegel runs an entrepreneurial consulting business called Solquest. He has a BBA from the University of Wisconsin and an MBA from UCLA. He is a former CPA, CFA, Vice President of Corporate Finance, entrepreneur, and investment banker. He enjoys writing and speaking about his experiences with Kundalini, and his lifelong roller coaster and, at times, perilous search for inner peace, the Divine, Love, and higher consciousness. Through speaking, outreach, film, poetry, and other creative expression, his goal is to entertain and inform people about the gifts and profound importance of Gopi Krishna's work, Kundalini, higher states of consciousness, as well as key aspects of Walter and Lao Russell's natural science and work. His interests include visiting museums and historical sites, traveling, listening to holiday music and oldies, and watching movies. He enjoys sports, hiking, and attending 12-step meetings. He loves reading books about spirituality and inspiring people who have helped make the world a better place.

For speaking requests, please contact him at <u>shiegel@verizon.net</u>. For information on Kundalini theory, source books and other materials by Gopi Krishna, please visit the Institute for Consciousness Research (ICR) at <u>www.icrcanada.org</u>. He highly recommends reading <u>Living with Kundalini: The Autobiography of Gopi Krishna</u> as well as Michael Bradford's book <u>Consciousness: The New Paradigm</u>. Michael's book may be found on Amazon.